Struggling
with
(Non)violence

Julie Marie Todd

Struggling with (Non)violence

Copyright © 2020 by Julie Marie Todd

Cover Design and Image of "Five of Wands"
Copyright © 2020 by Mekhi Mendoza

in medias res

In Medias Res, LLC
1009 Quincy Street
Onalaska, WI 54650

ISBN: 978-0-9911005-8-3

Library of Congress Control Number: 2020914921

Todd, Julie Marie 1968–
Struggling with (Non)violence / Julie Marie Todd
1. RELIGION / Christian Theology / Nonviolence
2. RELIGION / Religion, Politics & State
3. SOCIAL SCIENCE / Violence in Society

This book is an update of a dissertation presented to the faculty of the University of Denver and the Iliff School of Theology Joint Ph.D. program, *Evaluating Violence and (Non)violence: A Critical, Practical Theology of Social Change* (2012).

The original dissertation is available at https://digitalcommons.du.edu/etd/652/.

The interviews are available for further scholarly research by contacting the publisher or author.

Interviewees

Rita "Bo" Brown (B♀)
Ward Churchill
John Dear
Vincent Harding
Dolores Huerta
Derrick Jensen
Kathy Kelly
Alice Lynd
Staughton Lynd
Katherine Power
Sarah Schulman
Akinyele Umoja

Table of Contents

LOVING-THE-ENEMY   85

TACTICS   125

Acknowledgments

This volume is a book version of my doctoral dissertation for the University of Denver/Iliff School of Theology Joint Ph.D. program in 2012. I published it with the title *Evaluating Violence and (Non)violence: A Critical, Practical Theology of Social Change*.

The original acknowledgments are still true.

I express my deep gratitude first of all to the twelve persons I interviewed for this dissertation. Taken together, they understand more about the violence in and of the United States than I can reasonably communicate so as to do justice to their experience and knowledge. These twelve persons have studied, experienced and articulated for and with their communities more about suffering and death, resistance and transformation than is almost fathomable. I both honor and lament what they know. I was humbled by their acceptance of my invitation to interview them and continue to live in awe of what I learned from them. They will forever inspire me as a scholar, activist, and human being.

I thank my dissertation committee chairperson, Dr. Katherine Turpin, for her unending encouragement that this was an important project, and so to improve the quality of my writing and the clarity of my thinking.

With undying affection and respect, I thank my student colleagues in the DU/Iliff Joint Ph.D. program, without whose camaraderie and support this program would have meant little.

I offer my gratitude and love to the community at Nada Carmelite Hermitage in Crestone, Colorado, who provided me solitude and refuge during which the bulk of this project came together.

To my parents, Mary and Jim Todd, thank you for your unconditional love for me and whatever I seek to do in this world.

I also acknowledge Wesley White, the publisher and primary editor of this book project. Since I completed the dissertation in 2012, he has consistently encouraged me to publish it. Without his persistent nudges and detailed attention to its editing and formatting, this book would not be in the world in this form. In addition, I thank Brenda Smith White whose never-failing personal encouragement and attention to word choice make what I wrote so much better.

Thank you to Mekhi Mendoza for the original cover art. I love the image that he offered in response to the themes of the book I described to him. Here's what he wrote about the meaning of his original drawing:

> The Five of Wands in tarot is the fifth card of the wands, the fire element of the Minor Arcana. It is associated with the planet Saturn, and the dates between July 21 and August 1, which is when this statement is currently being written. My own rendition of the Five of Wands shows a seemingly chaotic arrangement of 5 intersecting wooden sticks within a circle, all of which are in flames. The energy of this card is challenging. There is strife as each of us strives for our individual and collective desires to be tended to. Pressure is building and is seeking release due to inner and outer conflict. A revolution is on the horizon. What would happen if we collectively strive for each other's liberation?

I dedicate this particular volume to my mentor and one of the interviewees for this study, Dr. Vincent Harding. My eternal gratitude to you, Dr. Harding. I know your power and guidance continue on in this earthly realm. May your spirit of struggle rest in peace and your soul live on in all of its power in those of us you have touched.

Preface

One of the biggest blessings of being in Denver at the Iliff School of Theology for my Ph.D. was getting to know and be mentored by Dr. Vincent Harding. Dr. Harding was the Emeritus Professor of Religion and Social Transformation, President of the Veterans of Hope Project, and was himself the quintessential veteran of hope. He and his wife, Rosemarie Freeney Harding, were central figures in the Black Freedom struggle in the American South in the 1950s and 1960s. He was a deep listener, most pointed questioner, and profound respondent in conversation. His deliberate pace of thought and cadence in speech would literally stop this anxious querent of spirit and struggle in my tracks.

I visited Dr. Harding in his book-filled, first-floor office in the Veterans of Hope office in Schlessman Hall. He would sit in the same wing-back chair. He always inquired about my parents. We would discuss this or that life, school, or world topic. Then he would proceed with, "So, sister Julie, what would you like to talk about today?" After that I would carry on about whatever philosophical or personal issue I was having. He listened intently with his eyes on me and occasionally asked questions for clarification. When I finished, he would raise his two hands from his lap, palms together, rest them against his lips and chin, close his eyes, breathe through his nose, pause for a while, then begin to speak his thoughts. His responses always attended to the deep layer of meaning underneath the apparent surface of my presenting ideas and questions. He provided concrete insights, guidance, and resources. He was always connecting me with people he thought might help me.

When it came time to focus on the work of my dissertation, I knew I wanted to write about (non)violence. I didn't know how to approach the topic. Dr. Harding told me that writing a dissertation was like being married to a person. You had better truly love your topic because you were going to spend a lot of time with it and, at times, dislike it intensely. If you were not committed to it completely, you would never see it through. So he asked me, "What would you do if you could simply do what you love?" I said, "Interview people about violence and (non)violence – people who have really been in the middle of struggle and have thought through these things because they have lived it." He told me to make a list of dream people I would want to talk to if I could. He told me that he could put me in touch with some people that he would recommend, which included Dolores Huerta and Alice and Staughton Lynd. And that was the beginning. I interviewed twelve amazing individuals who have committed their lives to the pursuit of justice and the liberation of human communities.

The worst part of this project was to put those conversations in an academic form. But my dissertation advisor, Dr. Katherine Turpin, encouraged me to make the writing my own. Nonetheless, it was an academic project that had to meet certain expectations. This book is my light rewrite of that project, eight years after I completed the dissertation. My purpose in rewriting is to make what I already wrote accessible in a book form, removing unnecessary jargon, footnotes, and methodological and theoretical description.

OVERVIEW

I just don't want one person killed. I don't believe in that any more. I don't want to kill anybody, no matter how noble the cause is. I don't see it. I don't see that as bringing peace. I don't understand it any more. So, it's all bad…. I'm against all violence at all levels.[1]

I believe very strongly in nonviolence. I really believe that it does have a very strong spiritual force. Because I've seen it…. When I talk about the strength of it, it's also a communication. It spreads from the person to the perpetrators.[2]

I thought [nonviolence] was a good idea. I don't have a problem with that. Whatever works! It's all tools. By any means necessary. Sometimes you need a hoe; sometimes you need a shovel. Sometimes you need a mule. A plough. It depends on the ground.[3]

You want to do a million people protest? You did that at the onset of the Iraq war. Biggest protest they say, ever. At the very onset of a war, did you notice some kind of effect on the war? I didn't. I drew a lesson from that. And this is my point. If you believe in it, try it. If it works, great. But when it doesn't work, now what? Well, now, that's a different question for you, having your moral objections when there's people who are literally being turned into hamburger.[4]

These four quotations represent a "spectrum of belief" about the justifiability and effectiveness of social change strategies from principled nonviolence to "by any means necessary."[5] These words come from four of twelve persons I interviewed for my dissertation, all of whom represent different histories and emphases along this spectrum. Some believe that only nonviolent practices of social change are appropriate, effective, and justifiable means to greater economic and political justice. They reject violent tactics as a means of social change. Others believe that circumstances of suffering and oppression are so extreme, so intractable and accepted by the population at large, that a commitment to nonviolent means alone will never mount a strong enough challenge to structures of injustice. Therefore all means, violent and nonviolent, must be potentially considered and employed. The main topic for this book is to consider the contours of these varying perspectives along this spectrum. Also examined are how these perspectives relate to the social location of individuals and communities and the religious/ethical resources in which they are grounded, deliberated, and decided.

These questions are of central importance to my own life and work. I am a white, middle-class, Christian, cis-gender woman, and U.S. citizen. I was raised in a United Methodist pastor's household during the era of anti-Vietnam war protests and the racial integration of schools through busing. I was born and bred into an activism in which nonviolent protest was assumed. I understood that nonviolence flowed naturally from biblical-prophetic, theological mandates for peace and justice rooted in the call of Jesus Christ, as found in the Bible. I assumed that the best form of social change was nonviolent social change, or, at the very least, the most suitable place to discover authentic forms of spirituality and religious practices that propel public faith.

Influential scholars in my doctoral studies encouraged my investigation of this topic by calling me to interrogate nonviolent theological proposals and religious practices from the perspectives of marginalized and oppressed communities. Through their influence, I began to suspect, despite what I understood to be the faithful successes of religiously motivated nonviolence in social change, that some theological commitments and practices of nonviolence might also be present in the maintenance of systems of injustice. This suspicion made me very uncomfortable. This project challenged me to continue to sit with this discomfort.

Other circumstances during my doctoral research also caused me to wrestle with alternative perspectives. Activist struggles with marginalized communities exposed me in greater depth to experiences of violence in society and social change movements. I witnessed the impact of the daily, brutal impact of all levels of violence upon undocumented day laborers. I began to understand both the motivating and debilitating effect of the consequences of state and interpersonal violence on organizing oppressed communities. In a nonviolent protest, I experienced the impact of police brutality in my own body, which shook the foundations of my privileged, white, Christian, citizen identity. While continuing to live my life in highly privileged communities, these glimpses into the realities of violence caused me to move in and perceive my world differently and uncomfortably, particularly regarding my assumptions about the role of nonviolence in social change.

My first foray into a critique of Christian nonviolence was an investigation of Matthew 5:38–48, Jesus' commandment from the Sermon on the Mount to love the enemy, not resist an evildoer, and turn the other cheek. Walter Wink's exegesis of this text results in an ethic of nonviolence that was extremely influential on me.[6] Liberal Protestant peace and justice circles often refer to Wink. Yet no scholarly exegeses on this particular biblical passage appeared from marginalized perspectives. At the same time, I was reading *Stony the Road We Trod: African Americans and Biblical Interpretation* for a class. The author related a story about a grandmother's outright rejection of Paul's letters because they endorsed submission and slavery.[7] Was there a similar dynamic going on here? Might some marginalized communities reject Matthew 5:38–42 because it has historically oppressed others by using Jesus' words to demand passivity in the face of violence? I realized that to talk about nonviolence from the point of view of marginalized communities meant, first, to move away from a dominant interpretation of the text. This move surfaced one point immediately: the daily reality of the vast majority of exploited people in the world is that of violence, not nonviolence. To begin an analysis from a position of nonviolence may be to miss the reality of the oppressed.

If I have come to grasp one thing with clarity through writing this book, it is this very point: ignoring the complexity of what constitutes violence is where the nonviolent thought and praxis represented by white, liberal Christians in the United States has fallen short. We have failed to include a comprehensive analysis of concrete situations of structural violence and oppression within which nonviolence has historically operated. Any practice or theology of nonviolence must begin with a critical examination of the location of violence. This examination should make us extremely uncomfortable. Speaking about Jesus' words in the Sermon on the Mount, Paul Ricoeur, a French academic, wrote that nonviolence "…introduces vertically into this history an extremely difficult demand."

> The first condition which an authentic doctrine of nonviolence must satisfy is to have passed through the world of violence in all its density.… It is first necessary to have measured the length, the breadth, and the depth of violence – its expansion throughout the length of history, the spread of its psychological, social, cultural, and spiritual ramifications, its deep roots in the plurality of consciousness itself. The recognition of violence must be extended to the point at which it displays its tragic grandeur, appearing as the very motor of history itself – the crisis, the critical moment and the judgment – which suddenly changes the configuration of history. Only at the price of this veracity does the question arise as to whether or not reflection reveals something left over, something greater than history, whether or not consciousness has any real basis for making claims against history and for recognizing itself as belonging to another order than the violence which forges history.[8]

In a seminal 1969 essay stimulating the field of peace research, Johan Galtung suggested that if the definition of peace is the absence of violence, then any viable discussion of peace "hinges on making a definition of 'violence.'"[9] Similarly, in this book, I attempt to understand nonviolence for social change in the context of the depth and breadth of violence. In our interview, Dolores Huerta echoed the common lament, "One of the things I say is we don't have a good word for nonviolence. You know, it's two negatives: 'non' and 'violence.'" Huerta makes a familiar point: in our efforts to speak about eradicating violence, our primary option to describe an alternative to violence emphasizes its centrality.

While Huerta regrets this limitation of the English language, with this book, I decided to start writing the term (non)violence with parentheses because I believe it is critical to identify the pervasive violence to which (non)violence is a response. My purpose in parenthetically marking off the prefix "non" from the word violence indicates that it is impossible to entirely negate the reality of violence with appeals to (non)violence either as a principle or as a strategy. We need to overcome an overly false dichotomizing of violence and (non)violence in historical analysis, as incompatible tactics, or as separate dimensions of social change. This parenthetical formulation is a form of accountability as it recognizes that even the most thorough-going efforts at individual and collective (non)violence are still implicated in violence.[10]

In the purest sense, there is no such thing as (non)violence. Feminist ethicist Beverly Wildung Harrison makes this point, critiquing an era of scholarship when white, male, progressive, U.S. academics in Christian theology failed to develop a critical awareness of how social location affected their theological and moral ethics, including a generalized opposition to the use of revolutionary violence advocated by some theorists within the early traditions of liberation theology. She wrote,

> The presumption in favor of nonviolence must not be confused with the actual existence of nonviolence in our world. To discuss moral principles of nonviolence as if nonviolence existed is a fallacy of moral reasoning that renders a discussion untruthful from the outset.[11]

Harrison recognized that these debates over the nature of violence and (non)violence were not new to Christian communities. The World

Council of Churches argued and documented many of these issues, particularly during the emergence of Latin American and Black liberation theologies from world-wide revolutionary situations in the 1970s. Yet these rigorous and heated conversations have had little influence on white, liberal, Christian theology in the United States, which continues to privilege (non)violence alone despite the experience and knowledge of an earlier generation of activists and scholars living in and representing oppressed communities. Entering into similar discussions today reveals little to no knowledge of these earlier discussions. Why haven't these controversies and insights been more thoroughly integrated into primarily mainstream, white, progressive, religious, peace and justice circles in the U.S.? Part of my answer is that the (non)violence of my own community is more spoken of than practiced, more individual than collective. It is a (non)violence that is *not*, by most standards, a challenge to the status quo. It is a (non)violence advocated by those of us who are part of the dominant power structure. As such, we are generally unwilling to sacrifice the many privileges our dominant identities bestow, but which radical social transformation demands.

Beverly Harrison provocatively suggests there is no such thing as (non)violence. It is not my intention to argue against (non)violence. Certainly (non)violence in practice not only exists but has arguably been a powerful force of positive, progressive, social change in modern historical memory. Some argue that the problem is not white, Christian (non)violence but white, Christian violence. The particular suspicion I bring is that the white, liberal Christian discourse and practice of (non)violence has to some extent served to obscure the operation of political and economic power and violence. Keeping these processes hidden maintains the violence and privilege of those in power, thereby undermining fundamental social transformation. Therefore, both the practice and the outcome of (non)violence constitute a kind of comfort zone where we demand change, but rarely have to reckon with the profound consequences of the change we seek, should we achieve it. I have desired to discover the ways in which my suspicion was both true and false, as well as any ways it is true or false. From my perspective as a white, middle-class, Christian woman in the U.S. whose own commitment to (non)violence was shaped by this social location, in practice Christian (non)violence has been neither sufficiently self-critical nor sufficiently revolutionary.

I am primarily writing to my own people – white, middle-to-upper-middle-class, U.S. Christians – invested in progressive or revolutionary social change. If white, Christian scholars and activists desire to continue to work for social transformation through (non)violent means, we must deepen and broaden historical, theological, and strategic analysis across different contexts and analyze the location of our own point of view. In our contemporary context, we have failed to address critical questions of our complicity in violence, failed to address power, and failed to define for ourselves the contours of violence and (non)violence.

Ward Churchill provided me with the term, "the comfort zone," in relation to (non)violence.[12] I believe (non)violence, if it truly is going to address violence and create fundamental social change, must include multiple practices that take us out of our comfort zone. Part of getting out of the comfort zone means confronting histories of violence and critiques of (non)violence. Without getting out of this comfort zone, we may as well consign our practice of (non)violence to practical irrelevance. If we wish to argue *against* there being "no such thing as (non)violence" in this country, then we had better be prepared to argue what constitutes a sufficiently transformational (non)violence and demonstrate that "such a thing" exists in our practice. This book seeks to give people who claim social justice as a goal the critical skills to think about their practices and to challenge them to greater commitment outside of their comfort zones.

The Interviews

Questions and discussions about violence and (non)violence cannot be properly understood outside of a given historical context. Interviews with activists ground the ideas and practice of organized violent and (non)violent social change methods in the concrete experience of practitioners in social struggle. I focused this project on the thought and praxis within recent and contemporary historic social change movements in the United States. I hoped the interviewees would provide insight for analysis about social transformation at a critical time in which the United States continues to reveal itself as "the greatest purveyor of violence in the world today."[13] There are a number of tensions with such a choice. The United States is not the center of radical or revolutionary movements in the world. It could be argued that the most interesting contexts for thinking about radical social change are found outside of the United States. But this would ignore our history of radicalism.

The twelve persons interviewed[14] represented, as broadly as possible, some of the most forceful movements for social change in the twentieth century: Civil Rights and Black Power, Indigenous Sovereignty, Women's and Gay Liberation, Worker Justice, Immigration, Earth Justice, anti-War, and anti-Globalization. Each one of these movements has held within it the tensions between the use of organized violence and (non)violence to achieve the movement's various liberation aims. As both activists and scholars, the individuals demonstrated significant investment in reflecting on the efficacy of various means and ends for social change. I chose these persons because of their apparent commitments in their activism and scholarship to one or the other "side" of a so-called violence–(non)violence spectrum. However, none of these persons fall neatly into one place on this spectrum. While their perspectives become apparent, I resist pigeonholing their positions. By engaging various perspectives on (non)violence – asking persons with a variety of commitments and diverse backgrounds in an open-ended, open-minded way – a more nuanced and accurate picture of organized violence and (non)violence emerges. Through this process, I do not intend to present a definitive position but to illumine the confusions, the contradictions, and the limitations of violence and (non)violence within the context of contemporary U.S. social change.

I intended that the interviewees' identities would differ from one another as much as possible: where they live, their religious perspectives, race, gender, sexual orientation, and socio-economic class status. Although all of them were born and reside in the United States, they hold different views of their citizenship status. The advantage of interviewing such a diverse group of individuals, versus focusing on one movement, one racial/ethnic group, or religious perspective, is that it provides the kind of rich, complex, and grounded information that upsets neat answers to questions of violence and (non)violence. Structures of oppression and privilege in social change cannot be adequately understood through only one lens of identity, such as race or class.[15] Additionally, my own Christian, liberationist commitment recognizes that movements for social change generally do not originate from the center of societies' dominant cultures. I made every effort to include persons in the interview group who did not identify as white nor Christian with the assumption that their knowledge is critical to future movements for progressive social change.

I wanted to inspire myself and be challenged to deeper levels of awareness and action by speaking with revolutionary elders. All of them have confronted questions about the realities and uses of violence and (non)violence in social change. We talked about how they believe social change happens and the means by which they understand it is necessary to respond to end suffering and injustice. I asked them about their social locations and how their own and others' race, nationality, socio-economic class status influenced the ways in which they understand violence and (non)violence in social change. I talked with them about what it means to be an ally across differences in social location in the pursuit of social transformation and also what it means to be in solidarity with persons and movements that differ over the means to achieve social change, violent or (non)violent. I inquired about their religious faith, non-religious, spiritual, and intellectual commitments and how they saw different aspects of identity impacting or not impacting perspectives on violence and (non)violence.

As well known as these persons are within certain circles of social struggle, most of these scholars and activists are not widely known in liberal-to-progressive Christian circles. Very little has been written about most of them. Many of them are prolific writers, and all of them have been featured in biographies, documentaries, and histories of their respective social movements. Many of these resources are footnoted in the text and found in the bibliography.

This book is intended to contribute to a transformative, social change practice of theological reflection for persons and communities committed to (non)violence. Through interviews evaluating Christian (non)violence and violence, I look at how engagement with differences of social location, experience, and opinion among seasoned activists and scholars might affect Christian praxis for social transformation. Without a serious engagement with differences of all kinds, Christian theology and practice has little chance to remain relevant in our contemporary context. This is particularly true for Christian practice in the realm of broad-based, broadly conceived social change efforts in which Christians must consider their role in a world where "the world" is quite tired of Christian impositions.

Chapter Outline

In Chapter One, I set out to define the broader context of violence within which violent and (non)violent actions for social change take place. I begin to develop a method of analysis of violence and (non)violence for social change that is critical for understanding what follows. I use Johan Galtung's theory of violence to frame the interviewees' responses to my questions about the means, violent and (non)violent, of social change. Interviewees' perspectives draw out and complicate Galtung's notions of *direct, structural,* and *cultural violence* as the context in which actions for social change take place. These categories help us broaden the common understanding of violence. Interviewee information sharpens the need to critically identify the cultural bases for the mystification of violence, particularly within the United States: the mythologic historical U.S. narrative and traditional Christian theology.

The mystification of these broader understandings of violence then takes on a certain reasoning that the interviewees' experience illuminated:

   1) the *denial* of the violent history of the United States' dominant culture,

2) the *reversal* and projection of this violence onto the victims of violence by portraying them as the perpetrators of violence, and

3) the construction of a sense of *entitlement* gained by the material and psychological advantages of this violence by members of the dominant culture.

In the first chapter, I describe the terms *social location* and *dominant culture* and how identities and communities condition an understanding of what violence is and how different groups respond to various uses of violence within society. Social location influences views on who the perpetrators of violence are. The justifiability or unjustifiability of the use of violence is based on the dominant historical U.S. narrative and cultural determinants. Individual and community self-defense will serve as an example of how the trajectory of rationalizing violence in dominant culture – denial, reversal, entitlement – works.

Chapter Two covers the relationship of the Christian tradition to the three forms of violence – direct, structural, and cultural. From the interviewee's data, we consider the ways Christianity has been implicated in various forms of violence within the creation and maintenance of dominant U.S. culture. I will look at Christianity as a "deep structure" of Western consciousness and ask if it is possible to assert the Christian tradition, in light of its theoretical underpinnings and historical role, is a source or norm for violence and oppression. Understanding the rationalization of violence in dominant culture through denial, reversal, and entitlement helps us to see if and how (non)violence, in thought and in practice, contributes to the reasoning and mystification of violence in the United States. Also considered is the counter-cultural role of Christian (non)violence as a principle and strategy of resistance to oppression and a vehicle of social change. Consideration will be given to how Christian (non)violence may undermine the dominant practice of rationalizing certain kinds of violence: how it exposes denial, potentially reverses the reversal of violent perpetration, and functions to dismantle entitlement.

If Christian (non)violent activists take their own words, beliefs, and actions seriously, then they must examine the actual impact of their discourse and tactics. My analysis of the interviews led me to identify two normative categories within the tradition of Christian (non)violence – "loving the enemy" and that social change actions must be "faithful, not effective." Chapters Three and Four will use these themes to investigate the ways white, liberal, Christian (non)violence – as practice and theological discourse – obscure the operation of power and undermine the potential for a structural transformation of violence.

Chapter Three takes up the theme "Loving-the-Enemy" within the Christian theological discourse of (non)violence. Christian scriptural references, particularly loving the enemy, are repeatedly cited in Christian demands for (non)violence. Interviewees' perspectives illuminate what it means – concretely – to deal with adversaries in the context of social struggle, who or what the enemy is, and what loving the enemy looks like in socially-located, historic practice. The interviews highlight tensions and contradictions between a reverence for all of life and the realities of violence towards those who "don't matter," both human and other-than-human. These points of view complicate what it might mean in practical terms to love the individuals and structures responsible for various levels of violence. Reflections by interviewees pose questions of how an abstract, human-centered, Christian, moral demand to love, embedded in a Christian history of violence, squares with the maintenance of structures and practices of violence and the entitlements that violence justifies. "Loving-the-enemy" may manifest as an ideological discourse that obscures and perpetuates violence in various forms.

Yet both interviewee perspectives and the tradition of Christian (non)violence also indicate the power of two essential insights of loving the enemy, and therefore its potential transformational power:

1) the interconnectedness of all life, and

2) a vision of a world without violence.

Since the purpose of this project is to construct both a better theology and practice for transformation, I begin to construct a more robust idea of what a meaningful concept of loving the enemy might be and might mean for social change.

Chapter Four engages the claim within Christian (non)violence that Christian agents of social change are to be "faithful, not effective." As Chapter Three also describes, (non)violence is named as the most faithful, moral, Christian response to injustice, regardless of whether or not (non)violent practices effectively reduce structural violence and make real and lasting social change. The interviewees' experiences in social struggle challenge this claim and reveal the need for effectiveness. My analysis of the interviews identified a constellation of four actual, collective practices of effective social change tactics and strategies in history:

- *consciousness-raising,*
- *organizing for people power,*
- *building alternative communities,* and
- *disruptive, collective action.*

The interviews underscore the conflict between the need for social change tactics and strategies to be effective and the reality that the transformation which social change agents seek is often not realized in the course of one generation or lifetime.

Interviewees also emphasize that all effective social change in any historic moment has required remarkable levels of sacrifice. The willingness or unwillingness to make sacrifices, to go outside of our comfort zones, for effective social transformation is often conditioned by social location and the fear of loss of privilege and entitlements. Therefore, the notion "faithful, not effective" may serve to conceal individual and collective fear to make the material and psychological sacrifices required for an effective and profound transformation of the structures of violence. On the other hand, Christian interviewees appeal to certain aspects of the Christian tradition of (non)violence as a unique source for effective social change: the language and examples of Christian sacrifice in scripture and history, a language, tradition, and practice of consciousness-raising and community-building. Christian history and practice include alternative communities that actually and potentially resist the dominant U.S. political and economic order. In light of a need and a desire for effectiveness, and in the face of profound structural and cultural resistance in dominant U.S. society, we consider what a critical Christian practice of effective tactics might include.

Chapter Five is about solidarity. All interviewees recognized that transformation of the structures of violence will only be accomplished collaboratively across various kinds of differences: differences of identity, power, belief, and practice about the legitimate means of change – violent and (non)violent. As allies in social struggle from the dominant culture bring their patterns of dominance into movements, alliances among groups have been fraught with problems of power associated with their differences. Social justice movements have reproduced the very forms of violence, power, and privilege they say they oppose. In this chapter, I consider the various answers that the interviewees gave in response to the meaning and practice of solidarity, historically and currently. They identified multiple practices of solidarity that embody dismantling the inequalities of structural and cultural violence.

A liberationist commitment privileges the knowledge of the oppressed and recognizes that historically long-term social change has rarely, if ever, originated in the centers of dominant identities and culture. Interviewees reaffirmed this radical-liberationist commitment to solidarity and the self-determination of the liberation struggle of the victims of violence. Conflicting interviewee perspectives questioned if it is possible and desirable to think through to a more comprehensive position on solidarity based on genuine mutually-shared struggle. Interviewees affirmed that it is challenging to make collective contributions to social transformation as privileged allies in a social struggle that do not amount to the reproduction of the values and practices of the socio-political, economic order of white, heterosexual, bourgeois, Christian dominant culture. But it is possible through practices that the interviewees named.

In light of this evaluation of violence and (non)violence for social change, Chapter Six presents a critical, contextual, and theological model for thinking about and acting for social transformation outside of our comfort zones. This model will attempt to construct a role for

Christian (non)violence, including the role of social location, as a potentially liberatory practice of social struggle. The model itself will invite criticism by revisiting the questions, limits, and problems of setting and interpreting diverse experiences of social struggle within a normative, dominant, and historically violent U.S. Christian theological frame.

– 1 –

WHAT IS VIOLENCE?

To understand violence and (non)violence for social change, we must first come to grips with the nature and scope of violence.

The interviewees described various forms of violence at length. All of them recognized different kinds and levels of violence, mentioning the following forms in their discussions:

- warfare and training for warfare
- violence of poverty
- imposition of religious and cultural norms in Christian missions
- dehumanization
- nuclear proliferation
- consumerism
- indifference to suffering and death
- verbal abuse
- domestic abuse
- physical retaliation
- colonialism
- state-police repression
- individual and community self-defense
- property destruction
- murder and the death penalty
- rape
- racism and racial violence
- queer-bashing

- hate crimes against gender non-conforming persons
- patriarchy and misogyny
- armed struggle
- rebellion and riots
- domination of the earth by humans
- exploitive working conditions and
- diseases of industrialization
    - genocide
    - incarceration
    - toxic waste
    - unjust legal systems
    - commodification of the other-than-human natural community.

Given this wide range of understandings of violence, we face three challenges:

1) To make sense of how one thing named violence takes so many forms;

2) To understand what we regard as justifiable or unjustifiable forms of violence and why; and

3) To consider how views on the use of violence are based upon one's social location in the dominant culture.

Understanding (Non)violence in the Context of Violence

Interviewees indicated that *they were always discussing violence, because the entire context for social movements and social struggle is violence.* Dear's initial response to this line of questioning was, "I've been in that conversation every single day of my life. I mean, if you are involved in nonviolence, it means you are dealing with violence. And if you are not dealing with violence, then it's not nonviolence." Only Schulman responded that in her experience within the context of ACT-UP New York, there was never a discussion about the use of violent tactics.

The main thrust of Kelly's interview was to understand violence primarily as the consumptive lifestyle of the United States and her community's call to (non)violently resist the structural violence of warfare required to literally fuel that consumption.

> There has to be some serious grappling with the inherent violence in being part of the haves and the privileged people in this world. You know, the privilege of being able to flip on the electricity and consume like there's no tomorrow. Or having access to transportation modes that are so safe compared to other people. Having access to food without having to pull it out of the ground or engaging in back-breaking labor and having ample amounts of it. And all of it, this is a privilege that I think has been protected with just an obscene and a menacing level of violence…. the war against the poor I think is constantly being waged, decade after decade in this country. And one of the reasons that impoverished people in this country don't get a fair share of the pie is because so much of the wealth and productivity goes to make even more obvious and often brutal and lethal warfare against people in other countries, ostensibly to protect an American way of life, which is an unattractive way of life in the first place.

Dear connected the development of nuclear weapons and warfare abroad with poverty and individual violent behaviors in his home state of New Mexico, the poorest state in the country. "Number one in nuclear weapons, number one in military spending, and number one in drunk driving, domestic violence, suicide, worst education system in the country." He described how the thousands of very impoverished parishioners he served had no money, no jobs, and no health care: "You get sick; you die…. You get cancer; you're dead." While Dear was ministering to thousands of poor people, he was also demonstrating against the war, "Even though they hated it, and against nuclear weapons even though they hated that." From Dear's perspective, "The money going to Los Alamos belongs to the poor people of New Mexico, and the United States, and the world. Los Alamos is destroying the land and the water of these poor people – from the Indigenous people to everybody."

By directly invoking the experiences of social struggle, the interviews revealed there are conditions of violence structured into society that can and must be identified. Conditions of suffering, poverty, injustice, exploitation, and death evoke transformation through social conflict and are the experiences out of which social movements are born and formed. Whatever the principles and practices of these movements are, whether violent or (non)violent, their participants are responding to pre-existing conditions of what is called "structural violence."

Direct Violence, Structural Violence

The reason for the existence of various forms of injustice is that some persons have political and economic power that bring material and psychological advantages, while others do not. Privileged status requires injustice and the suffering of others to gain and maintain that advantage. Dear points out not only that a majority of persons in New Mexico are poor, but the vast majority of persons in New Mexico are poor and deprived of state resources *because of* those who profit enormously from the wealth of the military-industrial complex. The people of Iraq suffer under military occupation *so that* multinational companies and political elites may profit and *so that* U.S. citizens may continue to lead the material lives to which we have become accustomed. At issue here is how these structures of violence and the everyday operations attendant with the structures come to be seen as normal and natural for some people and experienced as violence by others.

The common, everyday understanding of the word violence is not typically understood as related to the larger forces of violence the interviewees described. Liberation theologian Robert McAfee Brown writes that "our immediate response to the word violence is to think of it as describing an overt, physical act of destruction..."[16] As opposed to this forceful, observable behavior, the interviewees primarily identified violence with structural violence, a term often credited to and described by Johan Galtung. Galtung's theory of violence includes direct violence, the observable and overt violence described by McAfee, a form of bodily incapacitation as the result of direct, physical force, and the range of deprivations such bodily harm causes. Yet there are also severe need deprivations that are the result of poverty, hunger, racial discrimination, and so on that cannot easily be traced back to individual persons as agents of violence. Whether or not there is or appears to be a subject (person) who acts violently is critical to comprehending structural violence. "There may not be any person who directly harms another person in the structure. The violence shows up as unequal power and consequently as unequal life chances."[17] The fundamental characteristic of structural violence is inequality. Inequality is neither merely random nor strictly a matter of choice, but structured into society itself. Galtung urges making a distinction between direct (personal) violence and structural violence. This is a basic point of comprehension in peace studies, as "there is no reason to assume that structural violence amounts to less suffering than personal violence."[18] In fact, structural violence often leads to a kind of wretchedness of survival in many parts of this country and world, a depth of deprivation that persons in privileged social positions can barely conceive.

None of the interviewees reduced the causes of all forms of direct, interpersonal violence to structures. Yet every one of them stated or implied a relationship between structures of violence and acts of individual and group violence, whether for political or non-political purposes. This connection of different violences was true of the maximum-security prisoners with whom Alice and Staughton Lynd worked. Many of these men committed extreme acts of personal, direct violence against other human beings. The Lynds described these men, almost all men of color, had, without exception, been subjected to extreme deprivations and dehumanization of both direct and structural violence in their young lives. Galtung emphasizes that structural violence cannot be simplified as the root of all personal, direct violence. For our purposes, however, it is critical to grasp the "cross-breeding" of personal and structural violence, the scope of the genuinely harmful consequences of structural violence, and to understand more fully who the subject/ actors in structural violence are. For most of the interviewees, engaging in action for social change happened when the connection between the overt forms of direct, physical violence they witnessed or experienced and the systems they identified as primarily engendering this violence became clear. While the interviewees all took seriously individual acts of direct, interpersonal violence, this was not the focus for any of them.

Institutions, Structural Violence, and Accountability

When discussing violence, Dear and the Lynds referred to the writing of Archbishop Oscar Romero of El Salvador as a source for grasping various kinds and levels of violence. Romero echoed the analysis of the Roman Catholic Latin American bishops' gathering in Medellín, Colombia, in 1968. These bishops and founders of Latin American liberation theology were central to introducing the notion of institutional violence to Christian audiences as they grappled with the centuries-old violence of their continent.

> The violence we are talking about is the violence that a minority of privileged people has waged against the vast majority of deprived people. It is the violence of hunger, helplessness, and underdevelopment. It is the violence of persecution, oppression, and neglect. It is the violence of organized prostitution, of illegal but flourishing slavery, and of social, economic, and intellectual discrimination... We call this "violence" because it is not the inevitable consequence of technically unsolvable problems, but the unjust result of a situation that is maintained deliberately... rooted mainly in the political, economic, and social systems that prevail... based on the profit motive as the sole standard for measuring economic progress.[19]

The bishops describe structural violence as deliberate. Yet this structural understanding is not understood to be violence by dominant classes in society because they rarely feel it. Nor do most members of the dominant culture perceive themselves as implicated in these structures of violence or benefiting from them. This "commonsense" understanding and use of the term violence as only coercive, physical action functions to marginalize and obscure competing accounts of how violence maintains the privileges of the members of the dominant culture.[20]

The terms institutional violence and structural violence are often interchangeable. Using "institutional" instead of "structural" may help identify specific institutions of violence. Then those who operate, benefit from, and, therefore, are implicated and responsible for the consequences of their behavior can be identified. I will continue to use the term structural violence throughout this book, hoping that the reader will continue to keep in mind that concrete institutions of power and the actors within them are at the heart of structural violence.

The activist orientation of the interviewees demonstrated that researching, discovering, naming, and analyzing the agents of structural violence within institutions is a key to accountability and structural transformation when we are considering (non)violent social actions. As organizers, Huerta, Schulman, and the Lynds all described concrete processes by which local and national institutional agents of structural violence came to be known and targeted in their advocacy and movement work that specific social changes might come about. Huerta described organizing in central California to get water sewers for poor farm workers by identifying the processes and agents of power on the water board and replacing them locally one by one. Schulman talked about research and tactics involved in holding pharmaceutical companies and the U.S. government accountable to provide needle exchanges and housing for homeless people with AIDS and to make needed HIV/AIDS drug treatments available. Jensen identified certain cases where Union Carbide CEO Warren Anderson and Tony Hayward of British Petroleum were responsible for the destruction of human and other-than-human life within the corporate structures of economic and environmental violence. It is easy to identify the U.S. government as responsible for war and the occupations of Iraq and Afghanistan, but making this general claim does not change the conditions and precedents of war-making. Identifying the concrete actors is crucial.

The matter of accountability is critical as a broader definition of violence unfolds. A more expansive comprehension of violence illuminates how conceptions and practices of violence and (non)violence interrelate. The extensive, all-pervasive nature of structural violence implicates not only executive power-holders that are responsible for the institutions and enterprises that perpetrate violence; everyone is implicated in this violence.

"Where You Stand Determines What You See": Social Location and Structural Violence[21]

To understand the pervasive implications of structural violence, it is necessary to understand oppression and privilege in the United States. How we determine who is privileged and who is oppressed relates to what is often referred to as "social location." Social location denotes various markers of social identity which have been constructed under historical circumstances. Race, class, gender identity, nationality, ethnicity, sexual orientation, physical/cognitive dis/ability, religion, and citizenship status are the most common identifiers of social location. In the United States each of these categories of identity offers material advantages to members of one group while disadvantaging others. More often than not, persons with institutional power in this society come from favored categories, the combination of which constitutes them into a dominant, cultural identity in the United States. This constellation of favored groups is what is meant by "dominant culture." Furthermore, to be a white, heterosexual, middle-class, able-bodied, Christian, U.S. citizen of European descent becomes a norm for what it means to be human. The not-white, not-heterosexual, not-Christian, poor, female or genderqueer, non-citizen person gets demarcated as not normal, less than human, or "other."

We must understand but not oversimplify this analysis. Within any one person, social group, or movement, there are multiple privileged and marginalized identities that intersect to create a complex mix of identity that manifests in socially complex relations.

For example, Schulman asks what "white" means:

> Does "white" mean working-class Italians, new immigrants from Eastern Europe, low-income artists, low-income students, low-income homosexuals, who are out of the closet and don't want to be harassed? Or does it mean whites who are speculators, or who come to work in the financial industry to

profit from globalization, or who live on income other than what they earn?[22]

Identity categories are not easily kept discrete. The employees at the nuclear development complex that Dear protests at Los Alamos, New Mexico, are most likely a mix of many identifiers of social location: men and women, white people and Mexican-American/Indigenous, upper-class and working-class, gay men and straight women, Christian and non-religious persons. While some working-class people benefit from jobs in these industries, the point is that those who are in power and who profit at extreme levels in these industries consistently represent persons from the dominant categories of identity, the dominant culture: white, male, Christian, and so on. These systems of oppression and privilege exist to maintain the continued political and economic power of these groups. To reiterate, structural violence – the conditions of oppression and injustice, whether poverty or racism or sexism – exists because some persons have power that others do not as a result of the identity groups to which they belong. Persons from primarily privileged social locations are socialized to believe that this is not the case. On the contrary, the U.S. dominant narrative leads most citizens to believe that all persons are created equal and have equal opportunities to participate in the pursuit of life, liberty, and happiness.

The interviewees came to personally understand and demystify these larger forces, narratives, and operations of dominant culture through different routes. Some were not members of dominant cultural identity groups; they were not white, not Christian, not heterosexual and they grew up poor. For many of them, the experience and deprivations of direct and structural violence in their early years were real. Their social location influenced what they could see and understand about violence. Umoja grew up in Compton, California, but his earliest memories are from the time his family lived in Oklahoma, which was still racially segregated into the late 1950s. B♀ described growing up working poor in rural southwest Oregon. She explained that the main difference between the rich and poor classes is the ability of the rich to insulate themselves from certain kinds of structural violence, though not always direct violence. For example, though growing up in a relatively economically and racially privileged family, Jensen writes openly about the vicious domestic abuse perpetrated on his family by his father.[23]

Others' eyes were opened to the structures of violence because of a change in their geographic location. Kelly described how her consciousness of the daily operations of power and violence began to change after college when she moved from an affluent area of Chicago into one of its poorest neighborhoods in the late 1970s. This shift in location provided Kelly with two points that profoundly influenced her radicalization and the beginning of her long career in activism.

> The first was to better understand the violence of impoverishment and then to understand my own personal collaboration with that violence by paying taxes.... Secondly, to embody this notion of "where you stand determines what you see" – if you are standing with people, alongside of people who are in the crosshairs of the bombs or of the snipers or of the potential explosions, you have a different perspective than the persons who are either comfortably not even engaged, even though they might be paying for the whole thing, or part of the country that's launched the war, or if you are ready to shoot or launch the explosives, whatever the weapons are, or the economic weapons.

Kelly identifies that "where you stand" – your identity as it relates to dominant structures of power – determines what you consider to be violence. A dominant cultural, social location most often prevents understanding the realities of structural violence as well as protects privileged individuals and groups from the most harmful effects of all forms of violence. As she pointed out, "the privilege of being able to flip on the electricity and consume like there's no tomorrow" in this country is "protected with just an obscene and a menacing level of violence," from the war on terrorism to the war on drugs. Kelly writes,

> Many of us westerners can live well and continue "having it all" if we only agree to avert our gaze, to look the other way, to politely not notice that in order to maintain our overly

consumptive lifestyles, our political leaders tolerate child sacrifice.[24]

Those of us who use electricity and consume products in this country collaborate with the direct violence by which our material culture exists. We are implicated in the violence because we allow our tax dollars to pay for the system that perpetrates war. Therefore we are responsible, if not accountable, for the direct and structural violence that characterizes our life as a society. Broader understandings of violence complicate and expand the implications for personal responsibility. There are important distinctions between perpetrating violence and benefiting from it, whether directly or indirectly. War is only one example. Members of the dominant culture participate in structures of violence in multiple ways. To grasp the complexity of the actors involved in structural violence we must understand how these structures came to be and why these structures of violence are so unclear to members of this culture.

Cultural Violence

Twenty years after defining structural violence, Galtung marked cultural violence out from structural violence. He defines it as "the symbolic sphere of our existence… that can be used to justify or legitimize direct or structural violence."[25] Whereas Galtung describes structural violence as an uneven process, cultural violence is characterized by its permanence, a "deep substratum" from which direct and structural violence flow.[26] According to Galtung, cultural violence can be categorized into six domains – religion and ideology, language and art, and empirical and formal science (logic, mathematics).[27] Galtung's definition of cultural violence is somewhat imprecise. Still, it describes a process by which cultural ideals, thought processes, habits of speech, and practices become norms by which non-normative individuals and groups become marginalized, violated, and exploited in numerous ways – *how* they become the victims of structural violence.

From the interviewees' perspectives, there were two primary sources for the universalization of U.S. dominant cultural norms:

1) the marking out of marginalized and oppressed others through a mythic historical narrative, and
2) the consequent mystification and justification of structural violence through Christian theology.

The second will be taken up in the next chapter.

Structural and Cultural Violence: How We Came to "Where We Stand" in the United States

The dominant historical narrative of the United States is a primary form of cultural violence by which the direct and structural forms of violence are defined, legitimated, and obscured. The popular U.S. historical narrative universalizes the experience of white, male, Christian historical actors in their quest for freedom, equality, and liberty and establishes it as the norm for what U.S. history "is." The normative history reinforces the position of elites through a positive, moral interpretation of the events of history. This interpretation obscures and, in effect, erases from dominant narratives the actual violence and subjugation necessary for white, male, land-owning Christians to come into and maintain power.

Churchill and Harding's scholarly works help us to understand how interrelated structures and institutions of economic and racial privilege and oppression came about in United States history and how these relate to conceptions of violence. Harding details some of the precise historical mechanisms by which those who immigrated to North America from Europe came to understand themselves as white in relation to the developing economic system of servitude and slavery for the Black descendants of Africans.[28] At the time of the arrival of the first slave ship in Jamestown, Virginia, the category of "slave" was not clear. In the earliest years of the southern colonies, not all Africans were limited to the status of slaves.[29] What was at first a fluid society of racial identity, status, and servitude became increasingly codified over the next few centuries as the United States established itself as a nation-state.

The high demand in Europe for certain goods such as tobacco and rice made it apparent how profitable such crops could be with the use of slave labor. Throughout the 1600s and 1700s, states such as Virginia introduced laws to establish categories for life-long slavery and perpetuating slavery to the children of slaves, followed by other laws constraining Black behavior. Those later laws included prohibiting black-white intermarriage and property ownership by Africans, denying Blacks basic political rights, outlawing the assembly and education of Africans, banning the ownership of weapons and forbidding Africans to raise their hands against whites in self-defense, making African religious ritual practices illegal, and proscribing the use of African languages.[30]

The laws served a two-fold purpose:

1) to establish economic, political, and cultural domination and definition of Black captives from Africa, and

2) to build a new – fundamentally false – solidarity between the upper and lower economic classes of the white population based on race and racism.

The growing legal structure of the early colonies created antagonism between these newly historicized races of people.

By defining the black workers as permanent slaves held out of the mainstream of human development; by defining Christian whiteness as automatically privileged; by developing a situation in which the economic welfare of every white seemed to rest on enslaved black labor – by all these means and more, the dominant classes of the colonies consciously worked to create a white laboring force isolated from and antagonistic to black concerns…. The dangers of black-white solidarity at the bottom of society were decreased as poorer whites were legally and socially defined in a distinctly favorable status relative to Africans, and as Africans were forced to become the slaves…. From the outset, then, European laws for African people meant black subjugation and repression, arbitrary advantages for whites, and racist distinctions among laboring forces. Always behind the laws were the whips, the scaffolds, and the guns, buttressed in turn by the ever deepening layers of fear and mistrust.[31]

The power that whites sought over Blacks was to hold Blacks and their children as prisoner-laborers for their entire lives. Harding writes,

> Even more profoundly, it was the power to define them in North American terms according to Euro-American social, political, and economic needs. Whites in this way attempted to deny millennia of African history, pressing the tragic ironies of European names, faiths, and categories on the black present.[32]

Note the levels and kinds of violence Harding described. There is the direct violence of slavery and law enforcement: the "whips, scaffolds, and guns" which enforced slave labor and disciplinary punishment. From within the structure of laws and the legal system itself, a deeper layer of violence emerges. The construction and codification of racial categories and the prohibitions on Africans and their descendants literally create the economic and political advantages which accrued to white, Christian men and which oppressed others. This process forms the basis of structural violence, the effects of which continue today. The very history and existence of U.S. institutions of law and commerce that we now take for granted depend on inequalities that are structured deeply into society. Here structural and cultural violence overlap. Through the development of specific structures in U.S. society, enforced by means of direct violence, whiteness and racism are established in the United States as a deep substratum of culture and become forms of cultural violence themselves. Yet the dominant cultural history of the United States serves to deny and erase these physical, structural, and cultural realities of violence. The formation of U.S. dominant history serves as a primary form of cultural violence itself.

The history between Euro-Americans and American Indians[33] that Ward Churchill describes is no less troublesome and disturbing than the history of slavery and the racial caste system in the United States. "In the United States, the native population bottomed out during the 1890s at slightly over 237,000 – a 98 percent reduction from its original size."[34]

Churchill details the precise processes by which this genocide occurred. Commonly portrayed, genocide is a matter of direct violence – outright physical slaughter. Certainly, this was a central feature of U.S. policy toward Indigenous peoples, which has played itself out in many different ways over time.

> The people had died in their millions of being hacked apart with axes and swords, burned alive and trampled under horses, hunted as game and fed to dogs, shot, beaten, stabbed, scalped for bounty, hanged on meathooks and thrown over the sides of ships at sea, worked to death as slave laborers, intentionally starved and frozen to death during a multitude of forced marches and internments, and, in an unknown number of instances, deliberately infected with epidemic diseases. Today, every one of these practices is continued, when deemed expedient by the settler population(s) which have "restocked" the native landbase with themselves, in various locales throughout the Americas. In areas where it no longer poses a "threat" to the new order which has usurped and subsumed it, it is kept that way through carefully calibrated policies of impoverishment and dispersal, indoctrination and compulsory sterilization. Insofar as native peoples retain lands in these latter regions, it is used as a convenient dumping ground for the toxic industrial waste by-products of the dominant society.[35]

Churchill writes that genocide is also a matter of the creation of an entire system of laws and other methods by which Indigenous peoples were destroyed by means other than outright murder.[36] Contrary to popularly held beliefs about the fairness of the U.S. justice system, the legal system itself has represented the interests of those in power; it has served as a basis for the establishment and longevity of injustice – structural violence. Beyond and including myriad instances of direct physical violence, broken treaties, land grants, Indian removal policy, residential boarding schools for children, and the reservation system, government violence eradicated American Indian nations and subjugated their land and labor.

Churchill's and Harding's historical accounts are not reflected in the prevailing narrative of U.S. history. The dominant construction and communication of history obscures and attempts to erase the memories of direct and structural violence by those who became elites in the white male, property-holding, Christian majority. The dominant U.S. historical narrative itself serves as a form of routine, cultural violence to those whose histories are marginalized and subjugated by it. Harding's and Churchill's delineations of U.S. history helps begin to deconstruct popular notions of violence in U.S. history and runs counter to the popular U.S. narratives of freedom, peace, equality, and justice. Historical narratives like theirs and the oral histories of militant working-class organizers and conscientious objectors to war gathered and published by the Lynds provide historical accounts of resistance to oppression and structural violence, which the popular historical narrative fails to recognize. B♀ commented on why the radical histories of authors like Churchill, Harding, Schulman, and the Lynds are so crucial: "That's why it's important to write down the history. And for *us* to write down the history. For *us* to write our stories down. Because we can't trust *them* to write our stories down. We're always the criminals and the killers and the... You know? What are they?"

The Rationalizing Mechanisms of Structural and Cultural Violence: Denial, Reversal, Entitlement

The interviewees identified several interrelated processes by which the dominant group reinforces its norms, including its normative, cultural versions of history. The first means of reinforcing the dominant group history is the *outright denial of competing versions*. Much of Churchill's written works expose competing accounts of dominant U.S. history. He contends that the denial of the violent history and destruction of whole societies and cultures in the establishment of the United States is so deep as to constitute the essence of U.S. culture.

But paradoxically, the U.S. socio-historical narrative succeeds in denying the violence at the core of its culture by projecting its violence onto the oppressed other. For example, Indigenous natives of the Americas are portrayed as savage, while the white immigrant brings them Christian civilization. Churchill pointed out that this inversion of violence is a pattern throughout U.S. history, applied to American Indian and Black men alike. "They're forever imputing what they do to those they do it *to*, denying that they've done it and claiming that the other guys *did*." Churchill described multiple examples of "these truly amazing inversions of reality," which were often racialized in the extreme. He explained the myths that stereotype the Black and Indian rapist, where the dominant culture insidiously asks, "You *know* what 'they' do to white women, don't you?" The dominant historical record doesn't bear this stereotype out, while "rape *was* endemic in the way white guys dealt with Indian women" and Black women. Churchill noted, "The bottom line is that the dominant society systematically projects whatever modes of violence it imposes on Others as something that is being or at least will be imposed by the Others on *them*, and then describes the violence as human nature."

Each interview demonstrated the extent to which the operations of structural violence are grasped by the dominant culture not as violence, but as the nature of things, the culture itself. The deeply structured, normalized, yet denied violence of the dominant culture is projected onto others as those who are portrayed as violent by nature. But to deny and mystify *its own* deeply structured history and practices of violence, the dominant culture must invert and project its violence. Those who appear different from the cultural norm – those who are not white, not Christian, not heterosexual, and those who are poor – are the violent ones. This *pattern of denial and reversal* gets repeated over and over again. Schulman described this "basic paradigm of reversal" – the process of making direct and structural violence into a projection and then an abstraction – in the following long description of gentrification in New York City neighborhoods. I have left the following narrative in its entirety to preserve the complexity of her argument because it reverses the "commonsense" understanding of violence in dominant culture.

> You have a nonhomogenous neighborhood, which is what urbanity is. Urbanity is the realization that other people are

different than you. Then, through city policy, through AIDS, through a number of concurrent social events, certain people are removed from that neighborhood and they are replaced by a homogenous group of people who basically grew up in the suburbs and are brought back into the city. Their parents were city dwellers who left on the G.I. Bill to the suburbs. They are children who grew up in gated communities and racially and class stratified privatized suburbs [who] are now being invited to move back into the city, so the city can expand its tax base. That's what gentrification is. So you take a neighborhood that has become dangerous to its inhabitants, because they are losing their homes. And it's described as a neighborhood that's getting better. And it's exactly that same flip. The threat becomes the people who live there, who are being displaced. They are being seen as dangerous to people who have a gated community mentality and are willing to trade freedom for security. And that's again people seeing their own actions as benign and not taking place and seeing the reaction as the assault. It's the false neutrality of the self.... So the way that it affects the way people think is that people think of themselves and conceptualize themselves falsely. They see themselves as benign and neutral, and objective, value-free, and natural and regular, and just the way things are, when, actually, their position has been highly constructed and imposed by force – of which they have no awareness....

You take four rent-controlled apartments and you throw out all those people and you knock down all the walls and you make a luxury loft. That becomes a desirable place to live, when, actually, it should be a very stigmatized, very anti-social place to live, because four families have been displaced so that you can have this loft. But its actual meaning is obscured by a false value so that the people who live there think of themselves as elevated, when, actually, what they are doing is debased. So there's a false sense of self. That's what gentrification of the mind is. Because the people you've displaced are not there to tell you what you've done to them. You never see them. You never know them. You never know what happened to them.[37]

Schulman described the various manifestations of reversal as "supremacy ideology masquerading as reality." In the case of gentrification, the poor (who are often racialized) become the danger when, in fact, they are the ones losing their homes. Schulman described "the flip," this same process of reversal and the abstraction of violence at work in the struggles of the AIDS Coalition To Unleash Power (ACT UP), as a movement that intersected with sexual orientation:

> Gay people are constantly being accused of being predators… But it is the opposite of the truth. There's always the story that they are going to get you, they are going to get your children, they're going to infect you with HIV… you know there used to be this whole thing that the gay person was going to bite you and you were going to get AIDS. You can't be in the army with them because they are going to sexually aggress you. They are constantly positioned as predators and yet there's no really historic evidence of openly gay people doing anything physically aggressive. Sexual abuse, by priests and whatever, has to do with profound closeting and repression situations. But openly gay people, no. It is just one of those strange situations where the opposite of the truth is the common stereotype.

In his book *Endgame*, Jensen makes Schulman's point about structural violence in one of the twenty premises he posits about industrial civilization:

> Violence done by those higher on the hierarchy to those lower is nearly always invisible, that is, unnoticed. When it is noticed, it is fully rationalized. Violence done by those lower on the hierarchy to those higher is unthinkable, and when it does occur is regarded with shock, horror, and the fetishization of the victims.[38]

Jensen offered examples of how this works. An inestimable amount of children in the world die every year from starvation as a direct result of debt repayment to so-called industrialized nations. Yet those children don't count. He said, "Violence only flows when it's flowing upward; then it's called violence. But it is often a time of intentional ignoring of institutional violence." Continuing his description, Jensen said,

> If the people of India burn down a building, a Monsanto headquarters, which they've done, that's construed as violence. But what Monsanto is doing, systematically forcing them off their land, or what Coca-Cola is doing by depleting the aquifer... that's not considered violence. It's that systematic, invisible violence. It's one of the things that I wrote in *Culture of Make Believe* – any hatred felt long enough no longer feels like hatred. It feels like economics, religion, just the way things are. And we can just substitute the word violence in there.

"Any violence felt long enough no longer feels like violence. It feels like economics, religion, just the way things are." This dynamic is structural and cultural violence. It functions first through the denial of the violent history against those demarcated out by the dominant history itself as "others" – the poor, non-white, non-Christian, Indigenous other. Then in a projection of the denial of violence deeply embodied and embedded within, the perpetrators of violence are reversed. Those groups victimized by the dominant white, male, Christian culture are portrayed as the violent actors and threats within society. The question then is this: to whom or what are these "others" a threat? They are a threat to the material and psychological advantages credited to the dominant culture by virtue of its denied, violent past. These material and psychological advantages are referred to generally as "privilege" or "entitlement." I have chosen the language of "entitlement" because it emerged specifically from a number of the interviews.

Informal conversations with Harding have led me to ask questions about the adequacy of the term privilege itself. In conversation with Churchill, he suggested that a more accurate sense of the meaning and use of the word would be the "sense of entitlement." I use both terms throughout this book.

Rationalizing Violence:
Entitlements and "Only Some People Count"

A sense of entitlement is socialized into dominant culture persons, as Jensen puts it quite plainly:

> Why is the problem the culture itself? Because this way of life is based on exploitation, domination, theft, and murder. And why is this culture based on exploitation, domination, theft, and murder? Because it is based on the perceived right of the powerful to take whatever resources they want. If you perceive yourself as entitled to some resource – and if you are unwilling or incapable of perceiving this other as a being with whom you can and should enter into a relationship – it doesn't much matter whether the resource is land, gold, oil, fur, labor, or a warm, wet place to put your penis, nor does it matter who this other is, you're going to take the resource.[39]

Part of the mystification of domination and power is that many persons may be agents of power and reproduce domination without feeling that they have power, or even feeling privileged. Nonetheless, specific social locators confer psychological dominance and material advantages upon members of the favored groups. These advantages show up as a fundamental psychological sense of superiority. In the case of white privilege, author and professor Diane Goodman describes that

> Superiority is not always conveyed in blatant and intentional ways. In reference to racism, bell hooks… calls this type of superiority "White supremacy." She defines it as the unconscious, internalized values and attitudes that maintain domination, even when people do not support or display overt discrimination or prejudice…. This sense of superiority extends from the characteristics and culture of the dominant group to the individuals themselves. Oppression is commonly defined, in part, as the belief in the inherent superiority of one group over another.[40]

Certain persons and groups are valued more highly than others. A preponderance of the interviewees' information pointed to the notion that the underlying framework of this country is: some lives matter more than others. Most often, the worth of those lives is valued in economic terms. Jensen reported his discovery of a little-known United Nations' resolution called "Responsibility to Protect" (also known as R2P) in which "governing bodies have a responsibility to protect people from genocide, from mass rapes, from various atrocities." In a panel on war crimes in the Republic of Congo, a co-panelist with Jensen described that the application of this resolution, nearly ten years old now, doesn't go anywhere. The mainstream makes virtually no reference to it. It doesn't matter. It is not enforced. Why? Because of the system, the systematic violence of capitalism. For instance, atrocities in the Congo are allowed because the Congo has essential minerals used to manufacture cell phones and laptops. These resources are considered more important than the Congolese. Schulman said that although more than 80,000 persons died of AIDS in New York City alone during the epidemic, these people "are just a blank." Meanwhile:

> Every person who died at 9/11 has their name read every year. That's the thing about some people's lives matter and some people's lives don't matter. It's so obvious in the way this is all handled. Of course people died of AIDS because of the U.S. government. People who died in 9/11, you know, it's who's the perpetrator? That also affects the way the death is treated.

Schulman writes, about the "centerpiece" of supremacy ideology:

> It is the centerpiece of supremacy ideology, the idea that one person's life is more important than another's. That one person deserves rights that another person does not deserve. That one person deserves representation that the other cannot be allowed to access. That one person's death is negligible if he or she was poor, a person of color, a homosexual living in a state of oppositional sexual disobedience, while another death matters because that person was a trader, copy, or office worker presumed to be performing the job of Capital.[41]

Privileged status implies an inherent sense of superiority, conscious or unconscious. This sense of superiority leads to the understanding, positionality, and practices of entitlement. Time and again, members of U.S. culture have demonstrated that our right to material advantages and comfort is more important than the lives of the Congolese, the Iraqis, farmers in India. As Jensen never fails to bring to light, human lives are always valued as superior to other-than-human lives:

> What do all of the so-called solutions to global warming have in common? Saving capitalism… that's the independent variable. That's what must be saved. And the dependent variable is the natural world. The natural world must conform to industrial capitalism. And that goes to A: that's insane and B: that has to do with the question of identification. Who are you trying to save? There's another damn article in *The San Francisco Chronicle* a couple days ago. It was about how the salmon have gone down like ninety percent in the last ten years in California. All they mentioned was the economic effects. It's always the identification with that…. It's so clear, and this goes to the heart of everything. It's like, what are you trying to save? They are trying to save the system and, frankly, if we're really honest, also trying to save their own privilege.

The material entitlements and comforts of a consumptive lifestyle of civilization go about destroying all life as we know it. Yet, most people prefer their entitlements over ending the violence upon which the life of U.S. civilization is structured. Churchill echoed that the right of "consumption overall and a set of expectations that go into the nature of the economy" defines entitlement "for even a working-class quality of life in this country."

Schulman distinctively articulated that, within the gay liberation movement, there are deeper demands beyond matters of economic privilege and material entitlements:

> It's a different kind of revolution. It's a behavioral revolution at some level. It's transforming social custom. It's not a power; it's not regime change…. What gay people want is not that gay people run the world. It's that straight people change the way

they think about themselves. So it's a completely different kind of social demand.

Gay, lesbian, bisexual, and queer communities face structural and direct violence. But transforming injustice with regards to sexual minorities also addresses cultural violence, with its political, economic, and legal dimensions. It includes other dominant social institutions such as Christian churches, the media, and the arts and entertainment industries that select and control the portrayals of gay and lesbian lives.[42] With homophobia, the family plays a particularly critical cultural role as the family is often the first place in which people learn what it means to belong within dominant, heterosexist normative understandings.[43] The transformation of homophobia requires change at a deep cultural level, implying tangible losses that heterosexism demands as privileges. Schulman makes the loss of entitlements in the case of heterosexism clear:

> I believe that the most ethical position for straight people, in the age of homophobia, is to relinquish all their privileges until we have them too. It is the sexuality version of boycotting grapes. If a critical mass of straight people withdraw from discriminatory social institutions until they are available to gay people, those institutions will cease to have social currency. They will not be able to function until homophobia is eradicated.[44]

Schulman's analysis of homophobia makes clear that modes of structural and cultural violence control and keep in place the dynamics of oppression in smaller units of society. With violence, all forms – denial, reversal, and entitlement – play out throughout dominant society at every level. To genuinely address cultural and structural violence, to dismantle them through any means, violent or (non)violent, would result in privileged people losing entitlements ranging from a profoundly held psychological superiority to extensive material costs. Power and Churchill both defined entitlement as including "a presumption that [members of dominant identities] have the right to be in control" at every level, no matter what – economically, culturally, psychologically, spiritually. Entitlement is not only a result of structural and cultural violence, but it becomes a motor that justifies its active and passive resistance to fundamental socio-structural transformation so that privileges may be kept in place and not be lost. A comprehensive practice of (non)violence must address violence at these structural and cultural levels or it fundamentally cannot claim to address violence.

"Justifiable" Violence: Repressive State Violence and Response

Once we begin to grasp the interlocking nature of violence, we see that certain forms of violence by oppressed and exploited individuals and groups may be understandable responses to their experiences of structural and cultural violence. Yet because of the processes of denial, reversal, and entitlement underlying cultural and structural violence, this violence is rarely conceded as justified in the dominant moral imagination. On the contrary, this violent behavior is usually labeled and judged to be immoral and wrong.

Meanwhile, other forms of violence are justified. Brazilian Roman Catholic Archbishop Dom Hélder Câmara outlined a causal model of the relationship between the structural-cultural violence of oppression to other acts of violence as responses. A founder of Latin American liberation theology, he called structural violence "everywhere the basic violence." Structural violence is injustice. It is "Violence No. 1." "Violence No. 2" is the violence of revolt, when "conflict comes out into the streets." When violence No. 2 tries to resist violence No. 1, the authorities consider themselves obliged to preserve or re-establish public order, even if this means using force. This is "Violence No. 3." This repression completes the cycle Câmara referred to as the "spiral of violence."[45]

Generally speaking, the dominant culture regards the use of Violence No. 3 as justified. It is not often referred to as violence, but as "the use of force." This is Max Weber's classic formulation of violence as central to the institution of the state itself:

> [T]he state is a human community that (successfully) claims the monopoly of the legitimate use of physical force within a

given territory.... [T]he right to use physical force is ascribed to other institutions or to individuals only to the extent to which the state permits it. The state is considered the sole source of the right to use violence.... Like the political institutions historically preceding it, the state is a relation of men dominating men, a relation supported by means of legitimate (i.e. considered to be legitimate) violence. If the state is to exist, the dominated must obey the authority claimed by the powers that be.[46]

Câmara describes the growing self-awareness of oppressed people and their resistance to "legitimate" state and cultural exploitation, dehumanization, and repressive violence. Given the extreme levels of state repression against movements for liberation, and while consistently advocating nonviolence alone, Câmara counsels grappling with why oppressed persons may consider the use of Violence No. 2 (riots and rebellions, organized and spontaneous forms of self-defense, and armed struggle) as the only justifiable solution to their structural oppression. Câmara's nonviolence "is not a condemnation of violence," but an insistence that for "his" people "violence would be suicide." He wrote, "I respect and shall always respect those who, after thinking about it, have chosen or will choose violence."[47]

Those interviewees who accepted and advocated for social change "by any means necessary" spoke about the possible justification for the use of violent tactics in the midst of intractable structural violence, repressive violence, and oppression. They confirm the possibility posed by white, North American, liberation theologian McAfee Brown:

That structural violence can become *so* deep-seated, *so* powerfully entrenched, and *so* destructive and despotic that there remains no way to overthrow it short of physical violence. The need to overthrow it by such means is not only permissible, but is *demanded* in the name of justice, equality, and love.[48]

What justice or peace looks like for different groups in any context of social struggle will always be contested terrain in the field of seeking social justice. Moral frameworks for social action are rarely fully agreed upon, maintaining the peace of the current order with state violence is not understood as a moral choice or moral end (though such violence is disguised as such) for all members of a culture or society. Any exploration of violence makes it more difficult to clearly demarcate the difference between what constitutes legitimate and illegitimate violence. The use of violence by different groups within the culture, besides the state, cannot be universally condemned.

Furthermore, if we consider the liberation of the oppressed as a just end or goal, this may imply the justifiability, or justifiable consideration, of various means to achieving such an end. Just *the recognition* of such realities in a world of oppressive and repressive acts of violence would be a step forward for advocates of (non)violence.

We turn to a few examples in U.S. historical context to understand these complexities.

"Justifiable" Violence: Individual and Community Self-Defense

The interviewees' discussions of the justification of the use of violence by oppressed communities in social struggle included primarily two forms: individual and community self-defense and armed conflict. Here we delve more carefully into self-defense. Self-defense may act both as a means of resistance to the three forms of violence and serve community efforts for self-determination and social transformation.

Churchill and Umoja both noted examples of armed self-defense during Black liberation struggles in the United States to describe how organized, armed self-defense is a justifiable form of resistance to structural and cultural violence. Here, Churchill talks about voter registration in the 1960s, rural Alabama:

> The pre-existing condition down there was endemic Klan violence intended to keep Blacks "in their place." So much so that the nonviolence people wouldn't even try to organize voter registration in the area. Stokely [Carmichael] went in there pretty much *by himself* – other people came in, so he

wasn't the only SNCC[49] person there – but, in any case, Stokely didn't tell Blacks to turn the other god-damn cheek when these night-riders came, because he knew they were lethal. Lethal, but not brave. So he told people to arm themselves, and that they probably wouldn't have to kill anybody because once the Klan knew they'd shoot back, the nightriders wouldn't even show up. And he was right. The rate of Klan violence dropped off dramatically. Those on the receiving end, not repudiating "resort to violence" and instead preparing for it, not only caused the actual level of violence to abate very quickly, it instilled a sense of empowerment in local Black folks. They lost the fear which had prevented them from asserting even their most basic rights, and the number of registered Black voters – which had been almost nil – went right through the roof. That's how it works.

Churchill suggests that white supremacist racial violence was so vicious in certain parts of the South that armed self-defense was not only a justifiable but a *necessary* response, often essential to a community's very survival. Armed self-defense, in this case, resulted in a decrease in white violence and a space in which some Black residents felt it was safer to register and vote. It was both a means of survival *and* a means of change. Churchill suggests that armed self-defense both unveiled and disarmed, to an extent, direct and structural violence in this context.

Churchill goes on to illustrate a similar pattern of direct-structural violence in the 1960s–1970s Oakland, California, leading to the development of the Black Panther Party for Self-Defense. The Black Panther Party used armed street patrols, wherein Black men openly carried weapons and law books in hand. California law gave them the right to carry arms, and, by doing so, they challenged the discrimination and brutality of local, white law enforcement towards Black people. Churchill reported that under this strategy, the level of police violence in Oakland dropped nearly 40% in one year. Alongside other cultural and material community efforts in Oakland, this particular means of resisting police violence became a means of reducing direct violence and promoting self-determination to end structural (economic and political inequality) and cultural violence (racism).

Umoja explained several reasons why organizing for self-defense was predominant in specific communities in rural Mississippi. In the first place, individual self-defense was a means of survival for many rural, Southern Black people. Umoja described debates between Robert Moses, the first person in SNCC to go to Mississippi, and a farmer he stayed with, E. W. Steptoe, about Steptoe's carrying guns. Moses described that when Steptoe went to register to vote, his wife would have to pat him down because he'd have a little Derringer in his sock. Moses and Steptoe's wife had to plead with him when he went to Washington, D.C. to speak to Congress not to carry a gun into the congressional chambers. But of Steptoe, Umoja says, "That's who he is; that's how he's been surviving in this small county in Mississippi where he had known people who had been shot down on the street. He just had that type of survival mentality."

Members of SNCC initially believed that (non)violence would effectively change structures in the South, as did many prominent groups with the Southern Freedom movement. Umoja believes that differences over the justifiability of self-defense arose within SNCC not on a philosophical basis (whether either violence or (non)violence was justifiable in principle) but on a strategic one (what would be most effective in voter registration campaigns and changing these communities and society as a whole). At a point in time, organizers believed they were going to get support from the federal government. They believed the federal government would intervene to get Black people registered. But the Democratic Party held conflicting interests in Blacks being able to vote while not offending white southerners. SNCC and CORE[50] believed early on that (non)violent direct action was going to ultimately bring some change by forcing the federal government's hand.

In the following lengthy passage from our interview, Umoja describes the complexities of the situation. I include the following extensive direct quotations in their entirety, as they serve to address a historical narrative of the Southern Freedom movement not commonly held in the knowledge or memory of the dominant culture:

> On [one] level, we don't think other forms of struggle are going to be viable, and we have to get the support of the federal government. And we have to get the support of Northern liberals. We don't want to offend them, and we know that the image of Black people with guns scares the hell out of white people in American society. So we don't want to do anything that's not going to get their support. So that's why I think it's a turning point for some elements of the Black Freedom struggle when they say, "Look, the cavalry ain't coming! We're going to have to protect ourselves because the cavalry's not coming." So by the time of 1966, it was SNCC and CORE saying, "No, we've got to have the Deacons on the march." You know, the Deacons for Defense have to protect us. We can't rely on the [feds]... In fact, in that particular march... the federal government wasn't going to come and protect them anyway. It was going to turn the protection of the march over to the state of Mississippi, which they didn't feel like they could rely upon to protect them when they were going to certain areas of the state. In fact, the state troopers would attack the march in Canton, Mississippi, tear gas them and beat folk. There was a conflict over whether they were going to camp. They wanted to camp at this Black high school, which was state property – or really property of a local municipality. And the local municipality said, "No, we are not going to allow you Negroes to camp here." And they said, "We're going to camp there anyway." That created a conflict, and state troopers came and beat 'em up. Tear gassed them. King and others told people to stand down and the Deacons not to fight and confront them, so a lot of people were hurt that night. But they really felt the state troopers were the enemy. And they weren't going to get any federal support that night because Johnson didn't want to offend white voters in the South by sending federal troops down there at that

particular time. So they weren't a reliable ally. I think that march pushed people even further over in thinking like, "No, we're going to have to protect ourselves. We're going to have to defend ourselves." You know it's at that march where the slogan "Black Power" really becomes popular, and the thinking is, "We need our own power to neutralize white power." So I think that even radicalizes folks even more, and pushes them in a position around self.

Umoja's narrative reveals how the Black community understood that the realities of violence had been reversed. In essence, white people considered Black persons with guns a threat to white supremacy when in reality, Black people were armed to defend themselves from white violence. There was also a more profound sense of the historic reality that the U.S. government could not always be depended upon to serve and protect all of its citizens. The comfort, political support, and appeasement of white citizens mattered more than the human and civil rights of Black people.

Umoja defines himself as a New Afrikan and not as African-American because he believes the United States has not atoned for centuries of slavery and decades of apartheid (segregation) and allowing genocidal pogroms (lynchings) against communities of African descent. Moreover, he believes that historically, a significant portion of the African descendant population has desired to be self-determining, and the U.S. has denied the right of self-determination. Defining himself as "New Afrikan" represents a consciousness that the descendants of enslaved Africans must view themselves as a nation with the objective of self-determination and not just a minority of the U.S. empire. In this sense, individual and community self-defense 1) undermined the entitlements of white superiority to marginalize Black participation in democracy and 2) prioritized Black allegiance and self-dignity. Umoja further described how self-defense aided other tactics of structural and cultural transformation:[51]

In Mississippi, from like '65 through '79 you had all these boycotts. I think it was more based on a self-reliance strategy. Really in Mississippi you never really had a lot of nonviolent direct action. As far as I know, it was maybe on like three different occasions where you had demonstrations utilizing a nonviolent [strategy]. In McComb, Mississippi, they had some sit-ins, and [in] Jackson, Mississippi, when you had the Freedom Rides, you did have a Jackson student movement that did some desegregation stuff utilizing nonviolence. Then in Greenwood, Mississippi, there was a nonviolent march down there in 1963. But other than that, most of it was voter registration work, and people just committed not to carry guns and things like that. So you really didn't have that tradition of nonviolent direct action. But I think it was under the same thinking that if they did carry guns or they did emphasize that in the movement, self-defense, then just the thought of Black people with guns would really be counter to... getting the support from the federal government. But I think when they saw that wasn't going to happen, they went on to a strategy of self-reliance which included them protecting themselves, but also saying, if we can convince people in the community not to purchase, that's something they could do on their own, and we could force these white power structures to negotiate with us on issues like employing Black people, about respecting Black consumers, about how the police deal with us... things of that nature. I saw those boycotts as being very effective at a local level of changing race relations.... But it just changed the dynamics. I think that the Black community felt more empowered from this. I think they had to respect them on a whole different level... because they demonstrated their power, at least on a local level.... The last significant boycott I found on this level [was] in '78–'79 in Tupelo, Mississippi, and towns smaller than Tupelo like Holly Springs, Mississippi; Okolona, Mississippi; Lexington, Mississippi – places like that. Some of them continued the struggle up to the end. All of those places had a strong self-defense component where a couple of people were attacked, and they were able to respond back and just scatter the Klan. One of the arguments I'm making in that period of time is whereas people would stay home and would be more fearful of the Klan when the Klan would come out to counter-demonstrate some of their demonstrations, you'd actually have Black folks coming out and heckling the Klan and fighting with them. It was just a whole different dynamic where they weren't as scared anymore. I think part of this decrease of fear comes from some people being armed in their communities.

Other scholars share with Umoja the idea of self-defense as tactic of resistance as well as an affirmation of the humanity and agency of Black persons.[52] Like the legal tactics of the Civil Rights era, self-defense was used by African-Americans as a means to demand that, according to U.S. constitutional and international law, Black persons were humans and had as much right to self-defense and to bear arms as white persons. These rights are true whether or not these acts of self-defense were self-consciously political.[53] This affirmation of Black humanity, dignity, and agency was central to all efforts towards Black Liberation. By way of affirmation of dignity, armed self-defense was a direct, internal refusal of the cultural violence of racism. Unfortunately, in attempting to reverse the entitlements of white supremacy, depictions of armed Black men also served to reinforce reversal – the accusation of violence by whites to censure communities of color.

Self-Defense: Denial, Reversal, Entitlement

Umoja notes that white people's fear of Black people retaliating against them violently with guns for the violence they have experienced is at the root of condemnation of Black people's right to self-defense. Whether for self-defense or in armed struggle, Black people with guns constitute a violent threat to white supremacy. This portrayal is a direct reflection of the trajectory of reasoning from denial to reversal to entitlement. It denies the history of white violence. Conflating all Black resistance as equally and immorally violent serves to reinforce historically false cultural stereotypes that Black people are violent and white people are not. Huerta described a lecture where she "heard this woman saying that you don't have to say the word nigger, nigger, nigger anymore.

Because all you have to say is the word, 'criminal,' and people already think of a Black person." The reversal of a source of violence has been attached to Black male bodies in a string of discriminatory social policies and practices. Umoja identified discrimination that ranges from education testing to racialized police profiling to Black incarceration rates.

Kelly made a related statement about how the war against the poor gets played out in prisons, how race and class reversals benefit the entitlements of the dominant culture through structural violence:

> With the war against the poor here, we just presume that youngsters, teenagers, are criminals.... It's a good education to go inside the prisons. You learn, in a way that it's difficult to pick up in other contexts, what the war against the poor feels like as it's played out between prisoners and guards, loved ones outside.... You know, we all drive past these prisons all the time. You are walking past them... and we don't really imagine what's going on inside: the racism of it, the ripeness for fascism, or a reenactment of slavery. There are so many companies making money off of this now. Every university graduates a glut of new lawyers. How are you going to keep all these lawyers employed? You have to have criminals... they are the raw material. And it goes unquestioned. We just keep it going whether it's discernibly solving the problem or not. That's not a question. You know, it's the economy. How are we going to keep all of our lawyers employed? How are we going to keep up with our fastest growing new industry, the prison industry?

As Jensen explained, in the dominant culture, structural violence is not violence. It's the economy. It's the nature of things. To many members of the dominant culture, all violence on the part of people of color is the same: it is unjustifiable. There is a failure to distinguish between various forms of violence and the reasons for violence by different parties. While self-defense may result in acts of direct violence, certain questions must be asked: What was the context? To what conditions is self-defense a response? Members of the dominant culture regularly fail to make such distinctions and ask such questions.

The portrayal of the violent-other serves another purpose: maintaining control. The dominant culture perceives and fears a potential loss of material and psychological advantages by the threat of violent mass insurrection against vicious inequality and its entitlements. In terms of Indigenous sovereignty, Churchill labels this "The Great Fear" – the deep-seated fears of white people that American Indians may take their lands back by force. This is interpreted to mean that "the immigrants will correspondingly be dispossessed of that which they have come to consider 'theirs' (most notably, individual homes, small farms, ranches, and the like)."[54] In relation to African-Americans, a similar fear arises from the real historical and imagined insurrections of slaves against their slave masters. The denial of the violence of U.S. history is part of what gives rise to such deep-seated cultural fears that imply (even if only imagined) real material losses, including the power to control psychological blows to perceived superiority (a sense of entitlement).

Churchill asked if I knew any professed radical, nonviolent activist or spokesperson who has spent any serious amount of time in prison in the United States. By "serious" time, he meant ten years or longer. I did not know any. He went on to outline the number of Black men from the era of Black Power who were served lengthy prison sentences or were still incarcerated: Geronimo Pratt, Jamil Al-Amin (a.k.a Rap Brown), David Rice, and Edward Poindexter. He named many more examples, including radicals who were killed.

Churchill explained the reasons why these persons were such a threat, including Martin Luther King, Jr., as a (non)violent activist. Germanic-European culture teaches, "There's a place for everything and everything should be in its place. Any other arrangement is considered disorderly and uncomfortable – not tolerated." This can be translated at the family level or the level of social organization.

> King was galvanizing a community in such a way as to bring it out of its assigned station. The dominant culture, which is largely Germanic, decrees that there's a place for everyone and

everyone is to remain in their assigned place. This, of course, extends to entire groups, typically defined by race, gender, and ethnicity. There's plainly a direct correlation between privilege and social station... the departure of any from its assigned place disrupts the order of things [and] is therefore not only resisted but deemed intolerable by those conditioned and comfortable with the status quo. The further down you are in the pecking order of assigned places, the less comfortable you are and the greater your need, or at least your desire, to disrupt the social order and the politico-economic order as well, by departing from your assigned place. And so the methods employed to keep you in that place become harsher and harsher, the further down you are. The principal lesson embodied in King's assassination is that it really doesn't matter whether your approach is violent or nonviolent; if you're effective in galvanizing the oppressed to improve their place, you'll be targeted for elimination. Period. That being so, the only valid question is which approach is most effective in any situation. That's the one you use.

Churchill noted that most of the Black Panther programs were not armed. The federal government targeted the Panther Breakfast for Children Program as a top priority for neutralization. Any efforts to organize and empower persons of color "another further step down" on the human hierarchy meant increased punishment. If you push or step too far out of place, "They'll simply kill you. They killed pretty frequently here in some of these communities. These are not abstractions. They don't kill white people and they don't even put them in prison for long periods of time. It's not that no white people ever get killed. ... it's not that it never happens, but it's so exceptional it proves the rule!"

Persons of color are dealt with more extreme repression and punishment than white people because they are disrupting their assigned place. Since persons of color are further down in the hierarchy of dominant culture, harsher methods are used to maintain them in their place. Extreme state repression towards people of color is evident whether those communities attempt to defy their assigned place by the use of armed struggle and self-defense, or by organizing communities (non)violently in such a way that threatens power. More than half the interviewees noted that these conditions of repression either have not changed or have worsened in the United States today.

Social Location:
The Justification of Violence

This chapter has argued that the way we understand what violence is and is not – direct, structural, and cultural – is very much tied to our social location. Whether or not we have experienced and can name the impact of these three forms of violence in our bodies and in our communities will influence our approaches to justifying the use of violence by the state or other individuals and groups. All justifications for the use of violence for social change or social control are just that: justifications. We need to be clear that these justifications are shaped, though not determined, by social location.

Individual and group identities are reflected in or othered by the dominant culture. This dynamic informs what we know and what we don't know about violence, particularly in its structural and cultural forms. The maintenance of dominant cultural arrangements, mainly economic, depends upon particular cultural narratives that deny the historical truth of violence as it has exploited and destroyed communities of color and poor communities. The portrayal of the perpetrators of violence is reversed – to justify the dominant culture's existence and ongoing dominance and exploitation of these same groups. In turn, those who benefit because their social location primarily coheres with dominant culture depend upon this denial and reversal to maintain whatever relative material and psychological entitlements these structures of violence bestow. In this process of denial, reversal, and entitlement, social location also shapes what we believe to be justified or unjustified manifestations and uses of violence in the perpetuation of, resistance to, and destruction of the structurally and culturally violent status quo. All of this is relevant to our understandings of (non)violence, for if (non)violence claims to address underlying conditions of violence, it must address all of these levels.

– 2 –

CHRISTIANITY:
VIOLENCE AND (NON)VIOLENCE

The Christian History of Violence

The previous chapter delineated Galtung's three-fold definition of violence in its direct, structural, and cultural dimensions and how denial, reversal, and entitlement enable violence in all its forms. This chapter discusses the relationship between dominant Christian history and theological traditions and the preceding analysis of violence. Exploring the connections between violence and (non)violence and their relationship to Christianity prepares the reader for a more in-depth analysis of specific topics in subsequent chapters.

It is impossible to claim there is one thing called Christianity, for there are many Christianities throughout history and in the world. Yet the interviewees were all able to speak of something called Christianity (both Catholicism and Protestantism, also not monolithic traditions or entities) that pervade and undergird U.S. dominant culture. U.S. dominant culture includes Christian norms, which, as previously defined, cohere with other dominant social locators such as whiteness, middle-to-upper-class position, gender-conforming maleness, and heterosexuality. It is of this general sense of Christianity as an aspect of dominant U.S. cultural norms that I write.

Christian Violence:
Direct

All twelve interviewees described in different ways that Christians, as individuals and as institutions, have been active throughout history and currently in perpetrating direct violence out of a conscious, stated claim to Christian identity. Examples of Christian direct violence in U.S. history repeatedly arose in the interviews. One such is the Christian perpetration of war justified as a righteous mission of God against non-Christian populations. B♀, Churchill, and Jensen spoke of direct violence as the attempted eradication and assimilation of Indigenous peoples by Christians throughout United States history. Huerta, Kelly, and Schulman made explicit references to Roman Catholicism contributing to direct violence against gay, lesbian, and transgender persons in this country. To the interviewees, the history of direct violence perpetrated by Christians was so pervasive and continuous as to be the norm. Most of the interviewees also stated that the predominant U.S. Christian culture uses its theological power to legitimize the authority of the state to perpetrate direct violence.

But direct violence was not the focus of any individual's comments vis-à-vis the role of Christianity in violence. The central tension that arose in the analysis across the interviews was whether or not violence and domination were intrinsic to the very nature of Christian tradition itself. Does violence of all kinds abide deep within the structures of Christian theology and experience? If so, might Christianity be fundamentally implicated as the source of direct, structural, and cultural violence in the United States today? While most interviewees clearly saw Christianity's role in perpetrating and legitimating all forms of violence, they rejected the notion that this violence was *fundamental* to the Christian religion. Nonetheless, its relationship to violence demands careful analysis.

Christian Tradition:
Structural Violence, Cultural Violence

Galtung touched on the role of religion in different articles on peace studies, demarcating religion as *a* but not *the* primary domain of cultural violence in which the symbolic sphere serves to justify physical, emotional, and psychological violence, both direct and structural. As for how and why Christianity is a primary foundation for violence at a cultural level, Galtung explains that Judaism and Christianity, as an inheritor of Jewish monotheism, are the first religious traditions to establish a transcendent God "as a male deity residing outside planet Earth." Christianity went on to enshrine the Greek philosophical, Western tradition of dualism, sharp hierarchies, and dichotomies where the "good" is associated with the dominant social class as chosen by and associated with the qualities of the one, transcendent God. Evil is associated with all else. This transcendent dualism justifies direct and structural violence, as described in general terms by the following table from Galtung:[55]

Galtung's Taxonomy of Religious Hierarchy

God Chooses:	And Leaves to Satan:	With the Consequence of:
Human Species	Animals, Plants, Nature	Speciesism, Ecocide
Men	Women	Sexism, Witch-Burning
His People	The Others	Nationalism, Imperialism
Whites	Colored	Racism, Colonialism
Upper Classes	Lower Classes	Classism, Exploitation
True Believers	Heretics, Pagans	Meritism, Inquisition

Understood in this way, Christianity not only legitimizes the structures of violence in economic and political orders. Its language and symbolism intimately tie it to the existence of structural violence by the development of hierarchical and dualistic ideologies derived from Christian texts and theologies. There is disagreement over whether or not these sharp categories arose co-extensively with Christian tradition or are more modern products of Enlightenment thinking.

The left-hand column of Galtung's table demonstrates what categories of people these texts and theologies privilege. Modern Western dominant cultures, their systems of law, education, government, and ruling economic principles all derived from Christian theological frames. Galtung explains that even if one believes that religion is dead and modern Western societies are primarily governed by secular thinking,

Christian-based ideologies continue through secular ideologies of "othering." These contemporary secular ideologies are found mainly in the realm of politics, where the nation-state becomes God's chosen successor.[56] The hierarchical foundations of the Christian worldview persist in secularism as the foundation of oppression and all forms of violence.

Galtung attempts to sort out the major world religions into a taxonomy in which those that promote violence in all its forms are referred to as "hard," and religions that promote structural peace are called "soft." The "hard" religions have characteristics that promote violence. Among these traits are chosenness as self-righteousness, aggressive missionarism, a vertical archetype reinforced by monotheism that implies the transcendence of good and evil, singularism (that there is only one faith), and universalism (that the faith is valid for everyone in the whole world or universe).[57] Peacemaking, from a religious standpoint, means strengthening the "softer" aspects of any tradition. The characteristics of a "soft" religion emphasize the unity and immanence of all life and an inherent pluralism, including plural gods. Though he affirms that all religious traditions contain hard and soft elements, Christianity falls into the "hard" category for Galtung.

The interviews echoed some of these "hard" aspects of the Christian tradition that Galtung delineates as central to the promotion of violence. Churchill said of Christianity, "This is a monotheism that is proselytizing in the extreme. There's all sorts of enjoinders in church doctrine and the text itself to proselytize. It is the 'one, true religion.'" In other words, it is the essence of Christianity to define and defend a transcendent, vertically organized order of the universe and impose that order on the world through privileged categories of chosenness and difference. By its dualistic good-and-evil nature, the imposition of order is carried out aggressively and violently upon those who are not chosen. Chosenness as Christian identity in the United States combines with other categories of dominance – in particular, whiteness, socio-economic class, and male gender – in the founding of the United States and throughout its history. Culturally, Christian theological justifications have been used throughout U.S. history to justify every major form of oppression: slavery and racism, homophobia and heterosexism, sexism, and poverty.

Power said that the United States was a theocracy until 1960 and all public policy and law until then "...arose from the uncriticized, unexamined beliefs of Christianity. Judaism was tolerated in a more or less respectful way. But that there would be any other moral order of the universe was unthinkable."

Calling herself once a "true believer," Power described how the notions of a right and moral order were instilled in her as a young person growing up in the Roman Catholic community in the 1950s. "I was really raised with the religious, the sense that the spiritual order and the moral order that proceeds from it has to be central. You can't just not pay attention to it. Your life has to be about that." On the one hand, she was taught that there was a spiritual impulse of infinite love and mercy that demanded right action, a set of behaviors in defense of the moral. But what constituted the moral order in society, as defined by the Roman Catholic Church, often conflicted with the loving, ordering impulse she felt to emanate from God. Power described a deep desire as a child to "experience the congruence" of a spiritual impulse with the moral order. Yet "how to live rightly" meant in practice conforming oneself individually to the proper order as the church defined and defended it: the one, true religion. She recalled being taken to the Colorado legislature by the nuns at her Catholic high school to oppose the liberalization of divorce laws in the 1970s. The Catholic moral order defended and attempted to impose on society a hierarchical divine order defined by gender submission and heterosexual normativity. To Power, this was an example of Christian cultural norms imposing and justifying the structural violence attendant with gender and sexual minority oppression. Any articulation of cultural and structural violence and the church's role in this violence was absent.

In college, Power's deep desire to find congruence between her sense of God's love and order manifested itself in joining a militant group that attempted to "right" the unjust racist and imperialist, structurally violent order of the United States through the use of revolutionary violence. At the time, she believed her actions revealed a love for the oppressed in the

United States and Vietnam and a commitment to their liberation. Her efforts contributed to the murder of a police officer in the midst of a bank robbery intended to amass funds to support the revolutionary movement. After twenty-three years of fugitive status and six years of prison time, Power came to understand that the congruence of the impulse to love, found at the heart of the divine order and "right action," must be tempered by humility. "That impulse, when that impulse is married to overconfidence, to hubris, that's a really dangerous mix. Because that's religious fanaticism. Or dogmatic fanaticism." For Power, humility comes by "letting go of the idea that anything we think has any absolute truth."

> I know that being a true believer is a blinded position. It's a dangerous position to act from... when people are acting in the world with a religious fervor... righteousness can really blind them to human finitude and to the fact that we are all culturally situated. We cannot see. I think any time that religion, religious fervor, identifies an "other," it's a heresy. It's coming from a set of very confident, very powerful teachings. Catholicism is extremely confident. As a political order it imposed Christianity on much of the world. Despite the way that it was transformed by the more modern thinking of the Protestant Reformation or revolution, Christianity is shot through with a sense of dominance mission. So every tradition is going to have all of these clunky incorrectnesses, incompletenesses of vision. If we take them as "from God" with that level of authority, commanding us to act with that level of authority in a human world, disaster will ensue.... I think that if there's a virtue that Christianity is desperately in need of, humility would be it.... I feel like this is exactly where I was wrong and caused a lot of wreckage, [being] so confident... and acting on that without the restraint that humility brings.

Power's reflections on humility can extend to a number of insights about Christian social location and power. She cautions Christian believers to remember that religious beliefs are culturally situated. They are connected to identities, and those identities interconnect to systems of power, dominance, and oppression. While Christianity may not be the official state religion, a white, Christian moral order pervades U.S. cultural thinking. Despite a U.S. ideology claim that religious freedom is at the heart of its politics, dominant Christian understandings of individual and social morality and order take on the proportions of an all-encompassing, normative worldview. This Christian normative worldview is tied to racism, classism, sexism, heterosexism, and genocide that were present in the founding of the nation. To divest oneself of this personally and nationally normative, supremacist ideology is to begin to divest from the entitlements which this ideology justifies. Such divestment requires humility and sacrifice and has direct implications for Christian practice in social movements.

Christian Violence:
Denial, Reversal, Entitlement

The dominant white, U.S., cultural, Christian norm is to deny the role of Christianity in the structural and cultural violence of the United States. As described in Chapter One, this denial is essential to the perpetuation of violence. A false sense of the classed, white, U.S., Christian self and community denies the connection of Christian theology to the creation and maintenance of the economic-political status quo that is grounded in the social identifiers of race, gender, class status, and religious identity. Adapting Schulman's language from Chapter One helps us to think about how Christians adopt "the false neutrality of the [Christian] self."

> So the way that it affects the way [Christian] people think is that [Christian] people think of themselves and conceptualize themselves falsely. They see themselves as benign and neutral, and objective, value-free, and natural and regular and just the way things are… when, actually, their [Christian] position has been highly constructed and imposed by force, of which they have no awareness…. So that [Christian] people think of themselves as elevated, when actually what they are doing is debased.

Since Christianity is the cultural norm in the United States, Christians do not see the imposition of their worldview as doing violence, but simply "the way it is." Commenting on a protest in which the AIDS Coalition To Unleash Power (ACT UP) interrupted mass at St. Patrick's Cathedral in New York City,[58] Schulman explained this reversal:

> The Catholic Church got on local public school boards and passed a thing saying that public schools could not give out condoms. Now we don't care what they do in Catholic schools.... But we felt that people would die as a consequence of this policy, and, for that reason, we were justified in going to and interrupting mass. Now the problem is when they construct us as interrupting mass as violent, and them causing people to die as benign. It's very, very distorted. It's a kind of paradigm where the perpetrator depicts themselves as the victim when they are actually causing the pain. So their actions are not described. They are seen as neutral, and the response is created as the assault. That's how that event was described. Because people were more offended that mass was interrupted than that people would die because of their policies.... Of course, the people who interrupted that mass, many of them did die.... Their perception was that gay people should grin and bear it. If we did something, they were suddenly threatened. But when our lives were threatened, it didn't have any meaning. Because their lives mattered and our lives didn't.

Another example of this false construction of the self is the way, as Churchill described it, "Christian theology has been used in a manner to support property interest. Pure and simple." Jensen speaks of this throughout his written works:

> The early Europeans faced much the same problem we face today: their lofty goals required the destruction of these forests and all life in them, but they couldn't do it without at least some justification. The first two claims to virtue were the intertwining goals of Christianizing the natives and making a

profit. These embodied a bizarre yet efficient exchange in which, as Captain John Chester succinctly put it, the natives gained "knowledge of our faith" while Europeans acquired "such ritches as the country hath." Both the natives and the "ritches" – were quickly cut down. Soon the claim to Christianization was dropped, and the rationalization became "Manifest Destiny," the tenet that the territorial expansion of the United States was not only inevitable but divinely ordained. Thus it was God and not man who ordered the land's original inhabitants removed, who ordered the destruction of hundreds of human cultures and the killing of tens of millions of human beings, who ordered the slaughter of 60 million buffalo and 20 million pronghorn antelope to make life tougher.[59]

Euro-American, Christian theology undergirded multiple arguments for the eradication of Indigenous nations, including manifest destiny, the portrayal of American Indians as uncivilized, inhuman savages, and the *terra nullius* argument.[60] Similarly, white Christian theology and biblical texts also justified the inhumanity of Black persons of African descent, encoded their being as three-fifths of a human being in the U.S. Constitution,[61] and thus their legal enslavement as property. Christian theological justifications of genocide and slavery were the basis for the accumulation of property and wealth by white Christian men. Yet the particular role of a racialized and classed Christian theology is denied and obscured by the dominant white, Christian culture even as the theology continues to undergird an ongoing legacy of political and economic oppression of Indigenous persons and African-Americans, among others. The cultural situatedness of belief about which Power spoke is denied. The reversal expresses itself in a false and abstracted nationalistic value of being a benevolent, freedom-loving, democratic, Christian nation while marginalizing and othering whole groups as debased.

Christian Violence: Pacification and Reversal

Churchill described the repressive violence against people-of-color social movements as "disrupting their assigned place." He said, "Society functions on: there's a place for everyone and everyone in their place." As described in Galtung's table [page 57], Christianity has been a significant – if not the principal – cultural source to legitimate the violence used to maintain the assigned place of the oppressed. It plays another role in violence by attempting to mitigate threats to the established order before they break out. This appeasement is Christianity's role in pacification.

The Christian emphasis on pacification values claims of peace over demands for justice. Argentinian, liberation theologian José Míguez Bonino traces Christian institutional support for political order to Augustine, who solidified the theological relationship between the Roman Empire and Christianity in the late fourth and early fifth centuries. Augustine understood that justice and love were the foundations of the heavenly city and that the principles of justice and love were meant to impinge upon and judge the wrongly ordered earthly city.[62] Míguez Bonino interprets Augustine in the following way:

> Injustices should be corrected whenever that can be done without endangering order and peace. But if any redress of wrong threatens to become disruptive, it should be avoided. The premise of Augustine's position in these cases is quite clear – peace understood as order. Society is an organism that must function harmoniously. The chief purpose of societal organization is the suppression of conflict and tumult. Changes, or the respect for personal freedom or for justice, might endanger that order. Whenever an alternative emerges, therefore, the Christian ought to work for the best possible solution, the most just and generous one, *short of endangering the existing order.*... Peace, therefore, understood as order is the basic direction, the ultimate ethical key. Theologically, justice and love are supreme, but historically both are subordinated to order.[63]

Christian liberation theologians seek to upend the subordination of justice to order. Míguez Bonino wrote that the most important question for social transformation is not to what extent is justice harmonious with the peaceful maintenance of the existing order, but "*What kind of order, which order is compatible with the exercise of justice?*"[64] If justice defines the end of violence and the liberation of the oppressed, then social change is "not change just for the sake of change," but is for the sake of achieving a new order that is not based in violence as the current order is.[65] The establishment of a just order will require a disruption of the mirage of peace.

Yet the churches of the dominant culture have consistently supported pacification over disruption. B♀ said she regularly saw Christian churches covering the realities of direct and structural violence with calls for peace:

> Religion always kind of is the cover-up. Oh, it'll be okay. God loves you…. We have police shooting up communities all over this country. Then the churches all come out and say, 'Oh, let's have peace.' But people still get shot by the police! I don't think it's working very well. I think the success rate is a little whacked there.

In other words, when there is a threat to the order, Christianity often serves as a form of pacification to hold entitlements in place and falsely portray the oppressed as the primarily violent actors in society.

Jensen claimed that the development of urban culture was attended by the birth of the religions of civilization and the pacification of conquered peoples through these religions. Civilization, or life in cities, required the importation of massive resources into urban areas, extracted from those places where the resources exist. Jensen notes that at the heart of the pacification of Indigenous populations, Christianity divorced the spiritual life from the material realm. Christianity removed all meaning from the land, "excised it from the tree, excised it from the soil, and put it on some, you know, big God-Daddy out there." The earth as material and not spiritual is not a home. It is only a place where believers wait out their bodily days until reaching an eternal home in heaven. Christianity imposes a spiritualized worldview wherever, and on whomever, it seeks to dominate in order to separate populations from literally life-sustaining connectedness to their material landbases.[66] He views the colonization of the American Indian population in the United States as a process of pacification achieved through Christian theological support. "We can really talk about the process of colonization as a process of pacification. I love the fact that pacifism is the same word essentially as pacify." For the colonial project in the United States to succeed, white Christian colonialists had to find means to take land and its resources. The general means of pacification of native populations through Christian evangelizing practices partnered with the more directly violent means of assimilation, elimination, and eradication.

Jensen points not only to historical processes and concrete means of pacifying oppressed populations. He suggests that (non)violence from a Christian social location (and other dominant social locators) as a demand for social change often serves the same purpose of pacification in modern conflict and social change contexts as well as in colonial contexts. Compared to developing strategies of resistance and non-cooperation with violent structures, Christian (non)violence appears to pacify eruptions of conflict and anger occasioned by the vicious nature of structural violence and the false, reversed portrayals of who the perpetrators of violence are. In eras of both historic colonization and contemporary social change, (non)violence as pacification reinforces the material order and entitlement rewards of the dominant culture. When they serve the dominant culture's need to enforce pacification, white Christian calls for (non)violence are forms of cultural and structural violence.

A Uniquely Christian, Cultural Substrata of Violence

Some of the interviewees' perspectives suggest that because Christian monotheistic traditions are the basis for liberal, Western democracies, they cannot be usefully separated. The Christian religious worldview (as well as the more obvious institutional collaborations between church and state to support violence of all kinds) must be considered as a unique cultural and structural source of the direct violence attributable to both Christian and secular entities. In this argument, white Christian theology is not only reflective of a given historical context and its dominant culture, but is the very essence of a Western worldview whose cosmological foundations render it fundamentally violent. Galtung touches briefly upon the idea that the very cosmology of what he terms "occidental" [Western] culture may serve to justify structural violence:

> The cosmology concept is designed to harbor that substratum of deeper assumptions about reality, defining what is normal and natural. Assumptions at this level of depth in the collective subconscious are not easily unearthed, not to mention uprooted. And yet, it is at this level that occidental culture shows so many violent features that the whole culture starts looking violent.[67]

Along with the aforementioned notion of chosenness, Galtung includes a list of occidental "deep structures" that lead to privilege:

- dichotomous and deductive thinking,
- hierarchy,
- arrogance toward nature,
- a focus on individual agency, and
- linearity and progress.[68]

From the interviewee data, the features of this worldview which render it so violent include human supremacism, progress, individualism, and abstraction. In considering arguments for the ways in which Christian tradition and theology are predisposed to violence at its underlying core (substratum), (non)violence may also be implicated. Though advocates of Christian (non)violence may understand it as an attitude or practice that is completely at odds with violence of all forms, it is nonetheless a part of the same tradition of Christian thought and practice which creates and sustains violence.

Christian, Cultural Substratum I:
Human Supremacism and Progress

Galtung notes that an ecologically balanced planet is the basis for all human survival and thus a prerequisite for peace.[69] He includes the human species first among all of God's chosen in his analysis, resulting in ecocide. He also admits the natural world has been left out of his definition of types of violence and that his analysis of violence is anthropocentric.[70] Despite "speciesism" being at the top of Galtung's table, all of the types of violence associated with direct and structural violence relate only to human oppression. The only matters under consideration in the search for peace address the denial of basic human needs for survival and human well-being, identity, and freedom.

In their interviews, both Churchill and Jensen argue that the alienation from nature is inherent in the Christian mindset and constitutes the fundamental basis for legitimating all forms of violence. Churchill speculates that the description of the flood narrative in the book of Genesis is a response to a half-mile high wave that crashed into the center of Minoan civilization on what is now the Turkish coast of the Mediterranean Sea. This cataclysmic event triggers a traumatic level of alienation from nature. From that point on there was a comprehensible response by the community – "this absolute compulsion to figure out how to get a handle on nature so that it can never do this to you again, at a cultural level."

As a result of this event, Churchill explained that the need to control and to dominate nature becomes a Christian mental disorder, a pathology "that is put in terms of a theology." This theology has been refined and extended to the point where people don't even want to remember where it came from. Nature becomes the ultimate perpetrator of violence in a reversal where the earth itself is the destroyer of life rather than the creator-mother and life-giver. Humans become so obsessed with controlling the natural world that anything associated with nature also is an uncontrollable threat identified for elimination. In contrast:

You encounter Indigenous traditions, which conceive of the place of humans as not something apart from and working its will upon nature, but rather as integral to nature. They see themselves and are seen by Christians as being *part of* nature. This must be subdued and transformed into other than what they are – or eradicated. But that's a transformative process in the Christian mind, too. The Western mind, we should call it. I don't know how you distinguish the Western mind, so-called, from Christianity.... So the interface between Christianity and colonialism – they are absolutely inseparable. The Western outlook, worldview, is impossible without 1) Christianity and 2) the colonizing drive of Christianity to convert the heathens into Christians.

Though Christianity is distinguished from other major religious traditions by its extreme proselytizing, the fundamental core of Christianity is related to this primary alienation from nature. This alienation is so deep that it might be understood as a form of denial, as was the case with the culture of denial in U.S. history. However, this alienation from nature has severe implications for the rest of history. According to Churchill:

The dominant culture – the colonized mind – is at war with nature and so, by definition, is at war with all peoples of nature. The more natural the people, the greater the degree of hostility the dominant culture manifests towards them. This is an alienation so profound and so virulent that no one in the dominant flow of things wants to acknowledge that it even exists. Theirs is the normal and correct ordering of consciousness to relate to the world they say – they assert – they insist. So long as they look at it that way, there can be no admission of pathology. It follows that, absent an acknowledgment of the pathology, there can be no cure. What's necessary is for people to come to grips with the tradition into which they've been conditioned, and for these people to want to get out of that.[71]

The implication of Churchill's idea is this: Christian social location is one that is inherently about domination and control, in its text and theology. Christianity's fundamental alienation from nature is deeply structured into its worldview which, whether explicitly "religious" or not, is the dominant Western worldview. God creates the human and gives the human dominion over the earth: "And God blessed them, and God said unto them, 'Be fruitful, and multiply, and replenish the Earth, and subdue it: and have dominion over the fish of the sea, and over the fowl of the air, and over every living thing that moveth upon the earth.'"[72] Even when the biblical command for humans to "have dominion" over the earth is interpreted as more benign stewardship and care, the earth and its creatures are still the patronized, unequal, and dominated "other." Humans are superior to the being/s of the entire natural world. It is not only the other-than-human natural world that is the focus of this domination, but those creatures that come to be associated with nature: Indigenous persons of all nations, and all women and children generally. Jensen refers to this as "the death urge" of civilized culture:

> From birth on… we are individually and collectively enculturated to hate life, hate the natural world, hate the wild, hate women, hate children, hate our bodies, hate and fear our emotions, hate ourselves. If we did not hate the world, we could not allow it to be destroyed before our eyes.[73]

Churchill makes historical references throughout his works as to how this worldview, deeply embedded in the Western mindset through Christianity, has played out historically. He spoke of the occupation of the Pine Ridge reservation by the American Indian Movement in 1973 and the grappling among American Indians and their allies about why the government of the United States brought such intense firepower and focus to the repression of the occupation:

> Trudell actually said … "They had to kill us. They *had* to kill us. They didn't have any choice." [The] American Indian Movement (AIM) and he's talking about Pine Ridge.[74] "No, what are you on about? They *had* to kill us. It's the nature of the relation." He's talking third quarter of the twentieth

century.... "Why are you so mystified about what they were doing? Of course they did that; they *had* to do that."

The Christian tradition in the dominant culture serves to reinforce categories of chosenness and otherness, strengthening the isolation among categories of humans, and the human and not-human natural world. These differences become understood as natural and create the pretext for justified violence against oppressed communities and the earth.

Jensen placed further emphasis on the inherently anthropocentric nature of the Christian tradition. He said, "In a culture that's narcissistic enough to believe that *man and only man* was created in God's image, there might be just a wee touch of narcissism that's going to run everywhere else." Jensen was clear: the core problem with Christian tradition is, within its many hierarchies, the privileging of human life over other forms of life. While all of creation is described as good, only the human being in the Genesis story is created in God's image. When asked if he regarded the concept of *imago dei* as a central problem, Jensen responded, "Well, I don't have a problem with it as long as in the next sentence you say that the banana slug is made in the image of God. And so is the red-legged frog. And so is the redwood tree. And anybody who doesn't see God in any of those has got some problems." Jensen gave various examples about the profound difference between Indigenous and Animist worldviews (he does not equate the two) and the Christian worldview:

> One of the Indigenous people that I was just talking to a couple weeks ago, his people were people of the salmon and they have one song, "We are the salmon. The salmon are us. What happens to the salmon happens to us." He says his people have absolutely failed because they've allowed the salmon to be harmed. He says there's a sense in which they're not blaming the dominant culture. They hate the dominant culture. That's a given. But, in addition, they're accepting that they have failed in not resisting sufficiently. You see the difference? ... instead of singing "Jesus loves me, this I know for the Bible tells me so," it's like, "I'm in love with the

redwood and the redwood loves me." How different would that be if those were your songs? From infancy?

Human supremacism and human exceptionalism are central issues in discussions of violence and (non)violence for Jensen. "This form of narcissism – that only human (and more specifically some very special humans, and even more specifically the disembodied thoughts of these very special humans) matter – is central to this culture."[75] He used the following example, speaking of where he lives in northern California:

> The crab season is very short. The crabbers work very hard here. The local harbormaster was saying why they work so hard. He said, "Each crab is worth a dollar-fifty." Now imagine if there's all these envelopes all over the ground and each one has a dollar-fifty in it. You're going to run around picking up as many envelopes as you can, as fast as you can. Well, you know what? They're not actually envelopes full of money. They are actually living beings. And I don't have a problem with eating crab. But it's the recognition that you're not picking up an envelope full of money. How would he like it if there are these space aliens running around going, you know, "Each human is worth a dollar-fifty, and you are running around killing as many as you can so that you can get a dollar-fifty each." Suddenly it's violence.... I don't see any right now but the birds that were flying outside the window earlier … their lives are just as valuable to them as mine is to me. And those trees, their lives are as valuable to them as mine is to me. And the bacteria whom I'm going to defecate out, their lives are as valuable to them as mine is to me. That doesn't mean that we don't kill. It just means that we recognize that it's not an economic transaction.

That human beings are created in the image of God is a beautiful notion for humans, but it becomes the basis by which every other creature is devalued.

This view of the Christian tradition throws into question whether the tradition itself can actively redeem its way out of violence if its fundamental disposition toward the earth and the earth's creatures is domination and death. The anti-nature worldview of a dominant Christianity renders the tradition fundamentally culturally violent, justifying structural and direct violence through its basic theological claims to *imago dei* and natural dominion. Churchill acknowledged there have been many good Christians motivated by a liberationist understanding of their tradition who have contributed meaningfully to liberation struggles. Yet the dominant alienated, hierarchical, anti-nature worldview remains in place.

In my analysis of the interviews, there was nothing that served to counter the violently anthropocentric focus of the Christian tradition as portrayed by the preceding analysis. Two interviewees who advocated (non)violence alone mentioned the horrible destruction of the earth. Yet in literature related specifically to (non)violence, there is almost no material which suggests that the structural and cultural (non)violent transformation of inequality and injustice would include any subject for consideration other than human. From my research and experience in (non)violence thought and practice, there is little to nothing to address this critique. There may be many good Christians who, within a rubric of (non)violence, are engaging in earth-friendly practices and resisting the structures of environmental destruction to varying degrees. But until the anti-nature, Western, progress worldview is addressed, much less dismantled, (non)violence has little to say or do with addressing such culturally embedded violence within the U.S. Christian tradition. To fully engage such culturally embedded violence would expose the material entitlements which come to members of the dominant culture, including advocates of (non)violence, as a result of the destruction of the earth.

Attendant with human supremacism is the valuation of human progress. In the Christian worldview, humanity stands at the apex of the Christian vision of salvation history – the history of the whole world. Christ comes as the premier and final divine-human to reaffirm the theological hierarchy as the victor over earth and time through his redemption of *all creation*. In the Christian tradition, (human) history moves along a linear trajectory in which all manner of things are progressing towards a triumphant end. For Jensen, the first part of the narrative in the book of Genesis establishes both human supremacism and the progress worldview: to be fruitful and multiply, to fill and subdue *all* the earth.

> One of the central myths of this culture concerns the desirability of growth, a parasitic expansion to fill and consume its host. This was manifest from the beginning.... In the Western-Christian worldview, the world is forever moving towards a glorious end when all of creation will be redeemed. Progress is a premise so fundamental as to become invisible.[76]

The entire presupposition of industrial capitalism is human progress, improvement, consumption, and growth. The cultural justification for human wealth and progress at any cost results in the direct and structural violence and, according to Jensen, this progress worldview is fundamentally tied to a Christian worldview.

The progress myth is deeply embedded within dominant U.S. social change history. Reflecting dominant cultural sentiments, many interviewees indicated the notion that the inequalities of social arrangements are getting better, that we are progressing as a society and world in dismantling structural and cultural forms of violence such as poverty, sexism (heterosexism and homophobia), and racism. The question is: Is that true? The myth of progress serves the mechanisms of the dominant culture's denial and entitlement on both the right and left.

Christian, Cultural Substratum II: Individualism

What further extenuates an inability to see how Christian thinking and practice are implicated in the processes of structural violence is the problem of radical individualism. Galtung addressed that issue:

> In general it does not seems rash to assert that Christianity has been a 2,000 years-long exercise in structural blindness.... To Christianity, society has been a set of individuals all equipped with free will and a soul to be saved, whether by Catholic or by Protestant means, and the world has been a series of

nations, all free to set their goals; for instance to choose the Lord (and the more temporal lords serving by his grace), or to reject Him. That there should be structures of exploitation, fragmentation, and penetration tying individuals and nations together has not been apparent to Christianity. Christianity has focused on the individual actor, human being or nation, not on the structures tying them together.[77]

For example, Galtung notes that individual Christians may object to the individual husband who beats his wife, but Christianity has never fully objected to its own theology, texts, and structure as the basis for violence – the subjugation and domination of women.[78]

Christian Individualism, Sin and Violence

Dear described that the U.S. cultural obsession on individual acts of "immorality" as sin serves precisely to distract the Christian and Christian churches from their complicity in direct and structural violence:

> The empire, the culture of war, the first thing they do is they always want to co-opt the churches and the communities of faith. And it works. This is the story of the Roman Empire and what happened to Christianity with Constantine. They tell us how to be church. They tell us what morality is, and they tell us about sin. "That person over there is in *total sin*. How dare [you]..." distracting us from the fact that we just killed 1.4 million people in Iraq. As if that isn't the definition of sin. This is an age-old thing, and the church goes right along with the culture.

Here Dear refers to the fusing of the religious and political orders in the fourth century, when the Christian religion became the official religion of the empire, serving to bolster its political and military agenda with theological justifications. Dear commented further about the effects of the individualist construction of Christian sin:

> You have to accept being a sinner and trying to be good, but, meanwhile, we're killing people. The people at Los Alamos all

know they're sinners and they're seeking grace, and they're confessing their sins, and they're going for it, and, meanwhile, they're building nuclear weapons! I mean, if you are really going to deal with sin, and I say this as a Catholic priest in the sacrament of confession, which goes back 800 years.... Don't come and talk about that personal experience you have. Tell me about how you are racist, sexist, supporting killing children in Iraq. That's the sin. You're part of the national sin, corporate sin, the global mass murder that's happening around the planet. Then we're getting somewhere. That's the gospel language. Whatever you do to the least of these, you do to me. That's the measurement.... I don't think we deal at all with social sin.... Maybe if you talk about social or national sin, that might help us.

The Christian individualistic view of sin, violence, and punishment stands in contrast to an Indigenous worldview articulated by Churchill. From an Indigenous perspective, individual behavior, positive or negative, is construed with a construction of balance and harmony of the entire natural order that can sustain the next seven generations. He said, "You can do anything you want as an individual, as a group, within that paradigm of understanding as long as you don't violate it. You can be as imaginative [and] creative as you want, so long as you don't fundamentally disrupt the natural balance." In this view, violence works within a whole community to potentially unbalance and rebalance.

Osage elder and scholar George "Tink" Tinker[79] also described how violence and (non)violence from an individualist point of view makes no sense in an Osage worldview. Tinker's reasoning is so unfamiliar to the Christian mindset that it is included here in its entirety so that its meaning and contrast to Western individualism and its connections to violence and (non)violence might be fully comprehended.

For American Indians, nonviolence immediately forces us to go into a discussion of our culture and our understanding of the world. Nonviolence is an impossibility. If we were to take absolute nonviolence seriously, we'd all die. 'Cause we couldn't eat. Because eating involves perpetrating an act of violence –

one has to pick the corn, kill the buffalo, in order to eat. And those are genuine relatives of Indian people. My brother is a member of the *wazhazhe udsethe* (Osage Nation) of the *thoka towanton*, the Buffalo Bull clan. Their responsibility was always to maintain the relationship with our siblings in the Buffalo nation. As a result, even though the Osages relied on buffalo protein for our subsistence, the Thoka people were not permitted to eat buffalo. Except in a ceremonial context. That is true of Thokas yet today. So my brother and my oldest son are Thoka, are not able to eat buffalo. Because it would be for them an act of cannibalism, because they maintain that close a relationship with the buffalo on behalf of the rest of the people. Now we have permission, the rest of the people, to hunt buffalo, but to do it in a particular way that absolutely shows respect for Buffalo Nation as a sibling nation at all times. One way we do that is to have a clan that helps us maintain that relationship. And of course, corn is one of the three sisters for many, many nations across the southern two-thirds of the U.S., along with beans and squash. Those are all considered relatives.... Even down in Mexico, even down to the Mayans, down into Central America, people are clear that corn is one of the mothers of human beings.... Corn is one of our relatives, too. In order to eat, we have to do violence to the corn. So for American Indians, nonviolence is an impossible ideal. Instead, we would rather talk about mitigating violence with ceremonial acts that restore harmony and balance to the world. So before hunting buffalo, there is a rather lengthy ceremony that the people must perform before the hunters can even leave the village. It might take twelve days to perform this ceremony. They would do it at least twice and maybe three times a year, for three hunts of the people. That's one way of maintaining harmony and balance. Then when you kill the animals, there is a ceremony that has to be done on-site, before and as you butcher the animals. Same for corn. When the women plant corn, there's a ceremony to prepare the ground before they plant it and a ceremony at the time when they harvest it.

Here we see certain aspects of an Indigenous worldview that stand in contrast to a Christian worldview. First, the members of the other-than-human world are equal to the members of the human world. Direct violence against the members of the other-than-human world is as serious as direct violence against the human. Further, whether against the human or other-than-human, no act of direct violence is understood in purely individualistic terms. Certain acts of violence are understood to be necessary to survival. All acts of violence are understood to affect the entire structure and culture of Indigenous societies, which includes the other-than-human world.

As the above material demonstrates, a Christian cultural disposition to individualism keeps the focus of violence on direct, observable, individual, interpersonal acts among humans. As long as the cultural substratum of the Christian worldview is individualism, structural and cultural violence will never be fully exposed or understood, and neither will direct violence substantially abate. Individualism, particularly in light of human exceptionalism and supremacism, is part and parcel of what creates the illusion that violence and (non)violence are essentially separate phenomena. Violence is one thing (direct acts of individual injurious force against another) and (non)violence its opposite – the repudiation and avoidance of acts of physical force.

As Dear's analysis suggests, individuals who do not engage in physically violent, interpersonal acts do not see themselves as violent. This reinforcement of the commonsense understanding of violence as primarily individual behavior absolves the individual, who does not do (or thinks he does not do) violence, from further self-examination. This is denial. Such a person and such a culture of individualism fail to engage the realities and broader concepts of structural and cultural violence in which all individuals participate in this country. Individualism contributes to the practice of denial and supports the entitlements born of unacknowledged structures of violence.

Communalist, Indigenous views understand violence to be at the heart of many acts of living and survival. They do not seek to disavow these acts of violence, but to mitigate the injury or damage done to the community as a whole by such acts. They seek to restore harmony and balance. A cultural disposition to individualism keeps the focus of (non)violence on individual behavior. Exploration is needed regarding whether or not individual practices of (non)violence, as important as they may be, serve to fundamentally expose and confront violence at the level of structures and culture or perpetuate it.

Christian, Cultural Substratum III: Abstraction

As the foregoing analyses emphasize, (non)violence in thought and practice must be set within a broad understanding of violence within historical context and communities. While (non)violence in theology and practice may seek to counter or may perhaps reduce the pervasive existence and practices of violence at all levels, (non)violence does not, as such, negate violence.

Christian (non)violence advocates suggest that (non)violence is something that, in fact, exists and exists in opposition and as separate from that which we refer to as "violence" because theologizing itself serves as an abstraction from historical context. A main difference between Christian and Indigenous traditions is that Indigenous traditions are land-based – individual and community ethics and morality relate to specific places and events. This way of living and thinking contrasts with Christian ways of thinking, which have been abstracted from their original land-bases and universalized. Part of the cultural violence of Christianity is the imposition of ideals claimed to be Christian onto persons and circumstances regardless of context. Within the context of calls for (non)violence, Christian ideals of the peace and love of Jesus Christ have often demanded the repudiation of violence under any circumstances. Many times these calls for (non)violence have served or have been perceived to serve the purposes of the submission, repression, or pacification of a purportedly "violent" threat to the white, Christian, economic order. When Christianity's history of direct or structural and cultural violence is reported, such reports are often discounted as distortions of the essence of the gospel of Jesus Christ.

Jensen, in particular, decries (non)violence as a Christian principle and as a disembodied morality. He takes issue with a universalized ethic consisting "of commandments from a God whose home is not primarily of this Earth and whose adherents have committed uncountable atrocities." He challenges his reader to develop a morality that originates in a contextual, material realm which is imbued with the spirit of all living beings.[80] He points out the hypocrisy of resorting to Christian ideals in the face of history. Appeals to abstraction appear as a form of denial that may serve to perpetuate violence in all its forms.

> Christians... can point to a theoretical Christianity that does not attempt to express "dominion" over the earth and its inhabitants, that does not give other humans the choice of Christianity or death, that does not cause the hatred of women, children, life.... But we have to ask ourselves how these religions are expressed *on the ground, in the real world* – I mean both of these literally – how they play out in the lives of living, breathing human beings and others. What have been the effects of Christianity on the health of landbases? Has biodiversity thrived on the arrival of the cross? How has the arrival of Christianity affected the status of women? How has it affected Indigenous peoples it has encountered?... Not how they play out theoretically, not how their rhetoric plays out, not how we wish they would play out, not how they *could play* out under some imaginary ideal circumstances, but how they *have* played out.[81]

Jensen emphasizes that all morality and all effective action depends on a particular context.[82] This is particularly true when these ideals are written down, whether in the scriptures of religious traditions or in secular laws derived from the same religious traditions. Jensen notes that when certain "ideals" are applied to contexts, the applications almost always favor members of the dominant culture and serve the status quo itself.

Part of the examination of the context includes scrutiny of the social location of the individuals or the groups investigating and participating in the project of historical transformation. Míguez Bonino helps to deepen our understanding of this primary point:

> [Political and theological options] are themselves partly conditioned by our "location" within social reality and they in turn condition our analysis. We cannot, therefore, avoid the question: Who are the Christians – or the Christian theologians – who confront this fact of political reflection and decision? Whence do they derive their knowledge? To whom are they accountable? What influences their method and the conditions of their work? The response to this question must begin with the recognition of a "double location"... On the one hand there is the theologian's location within a theological discipline with its particular epistemological conditions and demands; on the other hand the theologian is also a social agent within a particular social formation.[83]

In matters of violence and (non)violence, theologians and actors must take social location into account with the utmost intention. Here social location includes the immediate historical context, the literal and material earthly location, and human identities. Action is critical, and theology is a second step to interpreting the realities of social struggles. Social location, individual and community experiences (in concrete movements for liberation and everyday life) predispose us to particular views of both the morality, justification for and effectiveness of the use of violence and (non)violence by different actors. Christian social location includes its intersection with other identity markers. If someone's social location primarily reflects the dominant culture, then it is very likely his or her own commitments are also reflective of a certain investment in the history and entitlements of the dominant status quo, and thus, in violence. Speaking out of his revolutionary context of Latin America in the 1970s, Míguez Bonino makes a statement that is still relevant. Whether or not to "use" violence from a so-called neutral point of view is a false construction of reality.

The point scarcely needs to be made that in a continent where thousands perish daily, victims of diverse forms of violence, such a neutral situation does not exist. *My* violence is direct or indirect, institutional or insurrectional, conscious or unconscious. But it is violence; it objectively produces victims, whether I intend it subjectively or not.... A significant discussion of this issue can therefore be only a discussion on the *violences* and the conditions of violence in our concrete situation. It has to do with who inflicts these different violences and who suffers from them, with the purposes of these different violences, and how these purposes are accomplished (or not) through their use. We must resist all hypostatization of *la violencia*, either to defend it or attack it. ... Such sentences as "we are against violence, wherever it may come from" or "we reject all forms of violence" may be quite "seductive for human and Christian sensibility," [but] they are only hypocritical self-justification or unconscious cooperation with existing oppressive violence. They can only make sense on the lips of people – who do not usually employ them – who are actively and dangerously involved in the removal of prevalent violence.[84]

Míguez Bonino points to the broad implications of direct, structural, and cultural violence for all persons. White, middle-class, U.S. Christian, (non)violent activists must be clear about the contradictions and inherent violences of their theological, economic, and political interests and entitlements.

The dominant culture's tradition of Christianity has been fairly indicted by the foregoing analysis. Not one of the interviewees denied that Christianity has been a source of all forms of violence. Whether or not one considers a Christian worldview and theology fundamentally violent, as a matter of historical practices, the Christian tradition and its dominant, white theology and practice in the United States has been predominantly violent.

But eight of the twelve interviewees who claimed some current or former relationship with the Christian tradition did see within it several threads that provided for Christianity to be a much-needed source of resistance to violence. There are radical strains rising from the margins of the Christian tradition that provide powerful examples of resistance to the status quo of religious partnership with direct, structural, and cultural violence. Further, they considered Christian (non)violence a possible source for exposing the denial of violence, reversing the social order, and undermining dominant cultural, psychological, and material entitlements.

The interviews suggest the possibility of a practical theology of social change based in Christian (non)violence. Yet, there may also be practices of organized, direct violence that may effectively contribute to the transformation of violence in all its forms. The task is to imagine how these practices might inform a critical, practical theology of social change that strengthens (non)violence.

− 3 −

LOVING-THE-ENEMY

Social change necessarily entails contending parties and interests engaging one another. Activists regard and take on the opposition in contexts of social struggle in different ways and use different terms such as "adversaries," "targets," and "opponents," as well as "enemies." Interviewees' specific references to the Christian scripture "love your enemies" and other scriptures such as "turn the other cheek" triggered "loving-the-enemy" as a normative concept within the tradition of Christian (non)violence.

White, liberal Christian scholars and activists commonly refer to "love your enemies" and its surrounding passage in the New Testament text[85] as normative for 1) a theological basis for (non)violence and 2) certain kinds of (non)violent practices in relation to a perceived enemy. In this chapter, interviewee descriptions of opponents in social struggle are used to deconstruct and reconstruct the notion of loving-the-enemy as a theological discourse and Christian (non)violent practice. I establish the normative Christian understanding of the scriptural injunction to love your enemy by briefly describing the interpretations of two of the most well-known, paradigmatic white, liberal Christian scholars in this area: John Howard Yoder and Walter Wink. Their work is referred to so often in popular and academic (non)violent circles that they represent the nucleus of the white, Christian (non)violent theological tradition.

Interviewee data surfaced inter-related critiques of traditional notions about loving-the-enemy. These critiques demonstrate where loving-the-enemy falls prey to the three previously identified substrata of Christian cultural violence: *human supremacism*, *radical individualism*, and *moral abstraction*. These perspectives demonstrate ways in which loving-the-enemy serves an ideological function: privileging and demanding certain actions and dominant groups while excluding others. Interviewee points of view require activists to clarify their motivations for (non)violence and to analyze the impact of their speech and practice of loving-the-enemy as (non)violence as it relates to direct, structural, and cultural violence. To be effective, loving-the-enemy as a discourse and practice of Christian (non)violence must also address denial, reversal, entitlement, abstraction, individualism, and human supremacism.

The Normative, Christian (Non)violent Theological Tradition

Representatives: John Howard Yoder and Walter Wink

John Howard Yoder and Walter Wink are to the modern scholarly, white, liberal, Christian theological and scriptural tradition of (non)violence what Mohandas Gandhi and Martin Luther King, Jr., are to the contemporary, popular tradition of (non)violent activism. There is very little discussion of Christian theological (non)violence without them. It is difficult to do justice to their perspectives in a concise fashion; however, this is what I attempt to do here. Their (non)violent readings of the New Testament center around two pivotal areas: Jesus' teaching in the Sermon on the Mount, paired with interpretations of Jesus' actions during his arrest, trial, and crucifixion. The relevant passage from the Sermon on the Mount is found in Matthew 5:38-48.[86]

> "You have heard that it was said, 'An eye for an eye and a tooth for a tooth.' But I say to you, Do not resist an evildoer. But if anyone strikes you on the right cheek, turn the other also; and if anyone wants to sue you and take your coat, give your cloak as well; and if anyone forces you to go one mile, go also the second mile. Give to everyone who begs from you, and do not refuse anyone who wants to borrow from you.
>
> "You have heard that it was said, 'You shall love your neighbor and hate your enemy.' But I say to you, Love your enemies and pray for those who persecute you, so that you may be children of your Father in heaven; for he makes his sun rise on the evil and on the good, and sends rain on the righteous and the unrighteous. For if you love those who love you, what reward do you have? Do not even the tax collectors

do the same? And if you greet only your brothers and sisters, what more are you doing than others? Do not even the Gentiles do the same? Be perfect, therefore, as your heavenly Father is perfect." (*New Revised Standard Version*)

Loving-the-Enemy as Christ Did: Revolutionary Subordination

For the theological academy, Yoder's 1972 book *The Politics of Jesus* became a foundation for the white, liberal Christian tradition of (non)violence. Within the Mennonite tradition of discipleship, Yoder's project was to develop an understanding of Jesus' "way" to follow. This way is the cross, a political alternative to violence, which includes voluntary servanthood and suffering, and a rejection of the empire. Jesus subjected himself to the violence of the Roman Empire to demonstrate another way, not conformed to the violence in this world.[87] Part of the witness of Jesus Christ's (non)violent action was what he *did not do* in the face of his arrest, trial, persecution, and crucifixion. The non-retaliatory speech and behavior of Jesus throughout these events pairs with the words attributed to him in the loving-the-enemy text to assert that Jesus' way is (non)violence. The paradigm of the cross is the paradigm for loving-the-enemy. If the task for Christians is to be like Jesus, then Christians must follow his example of (non)violence. The particular practice of (non)violence in Jesus' way is non-retaliatory non-resistance to violence.

Yoder's term for the New Testament (non)violent way was "revolutionary subordination." Reading both within and beyond the gospels of the New Testament, Yoder delineated various texts which suggest that the apparent call to replicate hierarchical, patriarchal, and slave-master structures actually contain an element of subversion where "the *subordinate* person in the social order is addressed as a moral agent…. Here we have a faith that assigns personal moral responsibility to those who had no legal or moral status in their culture, and makes of them decision-makers."[88] Furthermore, the individual in the dominant cultural and structural position in the relationship is called "to a kind of subordination in turn."[89] This is a potential seed for resisting through non-resistance and revolutionizing structures of violence by refusing to conform to their normative status in the world.[90]

Walter Wink depends upon Yoder's analysis for Wink's popular interpretation of the "love your enemies" passage to support a (non)violent ethic for Christians today. Wink is more well-known outside of the academy in white, liberal, Christian activist circles than Yoder. According to Wink's explanation of the Matthew text, the moment of non-retaliation towards a violent attacker is a moment of revolutionary subordination. Jesus tells persons who have no status within the ancient Roman Empire that they have the agency to turn the tables on the status of the violent offender by asserting their humanity. Jesus describes events of being slapped, sued, and conscripted to carry a pack as encounters with power in which the non-retaliatory action of the offended party robs the oppressor of power. For example:

> The person who turns the other cheek is saying, in effect, "Try again. Your first blow failed to achieve its intended effect. I deny you the power to humiliate me. I am a human being just like you. Your status does not alter that fact. You cannot demean me."[91]

Through the non-retaliatory assertion of humanity, loving-the-enemy unmasks the dehumanizing structural and cultural violence by which the system of domination operates.[92] Wink claims that this affirmation forces the one in power to no longer see the oppressed as the other, (re)humanizing the one dehumanized by the violence of the empire. Wink and Yoder's primary point is that loving your enemies by refusing to do them harm mutually affirms the human dignity of both the victim of violence *and* the victimizer. Wink, however, does not see non-retaliation as non-resistance, but as active resistance.

Loving-the-Enemy: Affirming Human Interconnectedness

Loving-the-enemy affirms the interconnectedness of life, affirming even the broken connection between the victims and perpetrators of violence in domination systems. Dear used the particular language of loving-the-enemy most repeatedly to make this affirmation:

> The theology of it is the most political revolutionary teaching in the entire Bible. "You have heard it said love your neighbor and hate your enemies. But I say to you, love your enemies." The second part of that is the most profound description of the nature of divinity.... You love your enemies because "God lets the sun shine on the good and the bad, the rain to fall on the just and the unjust." We don't want that. We don't worship a God who lets the sun shine on the good and the bad. A God of universal love, who loves everyone. Jesus embodies this nonviolence.... If your spirituality is of nonviolence and the theology is of a God of nonviolence, then you'll give your whole life for all your sisters and brothers around the planet.

Here Dear points to one of the most central tenets of loving-the-enemy, echoed by other interviewees. As humans created in the image of God, God is in all of us and loves all of us. Therefore we cannot do violence to any other beloved person in the family of God. As the Matthew text suggests, loving-the-enemy means perfecting oneself in loving all people, as God loves all people.

> Nonviolence begins with the truth that we are all one.... Every human being on the planet is your sister and brother. We're all united, we're already reconciled, all one, all life is sacred. The gift of peace was given millennia ago. The nonviolent culture is already created. We're actually one with creatures, and creation, and creator.... Nonviolence is remembering and recalling that, returning to the truth, every day, every morning in meditation.... Violence is just forgetting that. Violence is forgetting or ignoring who we already are – sons and daughters of the God of peace, one with all of humanity and all of creation.

When we see all creatures as imbued with the divine essence of life itself, we will treat all creatures as the divine. If the enemy, the "other," an opponent in social struggle is understood as someone I am related to in the family of God, then I can do that person no harm. Interviewees expressed that the interconnectedness of life is the heart of all forms of religious (non)violence, including Christian.

Harding shared how he came to this understanding during his military training. Away from his home church and family for an extended period for the first time, he took time to read the Bible and think. He became drawn to the Jesus of the New Testament. Soon Harding began to sense his connection to Jesus and that what Jesus taught about loving-the-enemy stood in contradiction to his training to kill the enemy:

> In basic training, I was learning how to fire a rifle at a bulls-eye. Throughout my life, I enjoyed sports and outdoor stuff a great deal. I found myself enjoying myself out there in the dead winter of the cold Fort Dix, New Jersey. And felt that someone was talking to me and essentially saying, "You enjoy this, huh? You think that the army is spending this money on you so that you can enjoy yourself? But no, you are being taught how to kill a man without him being able to see you. And what does this have to do with Jesus?..." The second thing was in that same period, and it was in some ways even sharper – learning how to use a bayonet because that was practice for really face-to-face engagement with another human being and learning how to quickly rip his guts out. I found myself saying, "Well, Jesus loves the little children, all the children of the world. And when they grow up, you're going to kill them, if your government tells you to."

Loving-the-Enemy in the Christian Tradition: Critiques

Critique I:
Human Supremacism

The love of others as the basis for (non)violence assumes the interconnectedness of all life. Only those interviewees who did not speak from an explicitly Christian faith perspective noted the connectedness of human and beings other-than-human. As one of the substrata of Western culture, the paradigm of "loving the enemy" appears invested in human supremacism. There is nothing in the scriptural framework of loving-the-enemy that deals with the other-than-human natural world. As previous analysis demonstrates, even under a rubric of Christian care for the earth, nature is objectified as fundamentally other. Loving a human enemy reinforces an understanding that violence against some beings – humans – counts more than violence against others who are not human.

If one of the deepest truths about loving-the-enemy reveals the truth of interconnectedness, this relates intimately to the matter of who matters. In the Christian tradition, other-than-human life is not considered conscious in the same way that human life is. In general, human persons do not see themselves as connected to other-than-human life as they do to other human persons. The violence committed against the other-than-human natural world isn't considered violence in the paradigm of loving-the-enemy. Jensen writes, "The murder of whales is not really violence, nor indeed is the murder of oceans. The same is true for trees, forests, mountains, entire continents." This means that within the concept of interconnectedness, as it relates to the other-than-human natural world, "all talk of accountability makes no sense: there's nothing to be held accountable for."[93]

The unacknowledged human supremacism at the heart of Christian (non)violence, mainly through the normative phrase of "love your enemies," undermines (non)violence as a meaningful concept or practice. If the fundamental power of loving-the-enemy lies in its affirmation of interconnectedness, then, somehow, Christian practitioners must reckon with what appears to be an insurmountable obstacle in its thought and practice: the hierarchical dualism of the human over the other-than-human. It must also confront the problem that an affirmation and practice of love and interrelatedness on an individual level, while important, still fails to rise to the challenge of transforming structures of violence.

Critique II:
Individualism
If We Just Love Enough

Jensen agreed to a certain extent with the sentiment of pacifists when they say, "If we just love enough, then that'll solve all problems." The problem is how love is individually applied, only demanded of the self and not the enemy, to humans and not to other-than-humans. The individualist, non-resistant, (non)violent emphasis on love excludes a whole range of other coercive tactics (be they violent or (non)violent) for change, which might also fall under the idea of love. Jensen urges broadening the understanding and scope of who we love, how we love, and who or what the enemy is. According to him, if humans loved their bodies and the earth, then they would not allow the destruction of the planet and the toxification of the environment that is killing everyone and everything. The individualistic insistence on loving-the-enemy and non-retaliation may serve structural violence by denying the thorough-going violence of systems. In practice, not retaliating against violent individuals and structures may amount to perpetuating their violence. Jensen asks, what does it mean to love our family members who are dying from a toxic environment? What does it mean to love the salmon? The subsistence farmers in India? The landbases where we live? The bodies we inhabit? For Jensen, loving the oppressed, marginalized, and destroyed of the earth means to privilege loving those who suffer over an individualist love of the enemy. Furthermore, this love may or may not necessitate the use of more violence.

Positive Anthropology and
the Realities of Structural Violence

The underlying anthropological assumption of loving-the-enemy is that human beings are good and seek the good. As a human, the enemy can be convinced to do the right and just thing. Yet communities primarily identified with the dominant culture in the United States have narrated a history wherein their acts of violence are either denied or justified in the name of progress and the collective good. The functioning of the reversal of violence creates a false impression that the perpetrators of violence are also good. An insistence on an overly-positive anthropology within the Christian tradition contributes to this denial and reversed portrayal.

Contrasting interviewee perspectives displayed the ambiguity over whether human nature is violent or (non)violent. By far, of all the interviewees, Dear held the most positive view of human nature, stating that his "anthropology is that we were created to be nonviolent."

> I think God is nonviolent, and that God is nonviolence. To be a human being is to be nonviolent. We were actually created that way. I see that in the baby; I think the baby is nonviolent. I see that in the myth of Adam and Eve, which was a culture of nonviolence. Audiences all over the country always tell me, "Oh, John, that's just ridiculous. You have a wrong anthropology. To be human is to be violent. We're all violent; we always have been; we always will; this is not possible."

Dear believes the essence of both human nature and the heart of God have been so skewed by culture, structures of violence, and churches, that the essential nature of the Christian religion has been lost. He says, "This is the scandal of Christianity."

Most interviewees believed that our human natures are a more complex mix of violent and (non)violent tendencies. Churchill said that in the first place, "violence is a natural phenomenon" that manifests differently within the same being in different times. It is a real thing, which can be dealt with through a variety of social practices from football to war:

> [Violence] is an innate impulse with which the species as a whole is endowed, but which manifests probably most strongly in young males because of testosterone and aggression and all of that. It serves some kind of function – to understand what it is and how to deal with it.

Alice Lynd agreed there is something innate to the impulse to act out violently. She learned this as a young mother and sees this phenomenon in the prisoners whom she serves:

There would be certain things that a child would do that would make me so angry that I would actually strike one of my own children. I had the feeling, you know, there are not very many people walking this earth who believe in nonviolence as much as I do, and what am I doing striking that child? Yet it just pops out. I think a number of the prisoners that we know have that in them that when something occurs, they instinctively strike out. Then they think about it afterward, "Oh, what did I do?" It just happens. And in a sense, it's beyond their control.... But at some point, a certain unpredictable set of circumstances will all come into play at the same time and "phsssht!" You know – the button is pressed; the reaction happens. I don't know how we can avoid that.

Power spoke about the human biological state and human nature as "inevitably in contradiction, inevitably causing suffering," and "imperfect." She said, "Our need to survive is, in a sense, in contradiction to other beings' need to survive." Humans have been trained, like animals, to dominate when threatened, or there is scarcity. Such a "head-to-head" disposition affects human thinking, reducing the ability to interpret long-term effects. But Power also believes the human-animal is created with an ability to enlarge its vision beyond its immediate need. The human being has access to a "heart-to-heart" state, a condition of affinity, physical closeness, cooperation, expansiveness, trust, and longer-term thinking. Humanity has the possibility to discern the moments when and if dominance is the truth.

In the thought and practice of loving-the-enemy, an overemphasis on a positive anthropology can mask the complexities of natural, human-animal instincts. Alice Lynd and B♀ both saw that violent tendencies that may be rooted in biology are inflamed by the pressures and deprivations of structural violence. Alice Lynd explained:

One thing [Romero] says may be justified, although unfortunate because of the consequences, is unplanned, spontaneous violence in self-defense or defense of loved ones or neighbor or community. He can understand and accept that as being inevitable, although, you know, then you have to deal with the harm that was done as a result. I'm very sympathetic to that. It's not that I would say that self-defense is justified. But I do believe that self-defense is something that you have to expect people to do.

B♀ commented:

Every experiment they ever did, whenever you put too many rats in a cage, they'll turn on each other. Whenever you create those kinds of conditions, that kind of response will occur. You can only shit on people for so long, you know. There's been rebellion throughout the history of this world.

The impact of structural violence on human-animal instincts creates a problematic mix of factors, which an appeal to loving-the-enemy cannot address. Umoja described instances in Mississippi and Los Angeles when spontaneous violence erupted. He said, "When people have been oppressed so long, sometimes you have this rage." It is very difficult to stop this rage once it is triggered. Umoja noted that with the charismatic leadership of someone like Dr. King during civil rights, small groups of persons "could be disciplined to a certain degree. But if you're just talking about people in general? Something is liable to happen." Umoja said that on one level, it appears easy to condemn violence, but if a community responds to the brutal conditions of their oppression, "It's dicey territory." Traditional interpretations of the loving-the-enemy scriptural text fall back on individualism and an appeal to human goodness. When they do, none of the above factors are taken into account.

For example, Wink uses a commonsense understanding of direct violence in interpreting the Matthew text. He focuses attention on the agent of violence and a victim. The occasions are discrete, interpersonal events of overt physical violence. The description of non-resistant action takes place within an interpersonal encounter. How an interpersonal act that appears to reinforce subordination can actually expose and disrupt cycles of structural and cultural violence remains a question, and in the realm of the hopeful. The enemy and the victim, in Wink's (non)violent interpretation of the text, are individuals whose ethical behavior transcends their historic context. When Christian theology posits a positive anthropology, as most white, middle-class, liberal (non)violence does, it assumes that there is also a "basic minimum level of decency present in any society."[94] The pervasive existence of structural and cultural violence questions the legitimacy of that assumption. How one understands loving-the-enemy, what constitutes love, and who the enemy is, is shaped by individual and community experience. Framed as the "revolutionary subordination of Christ," to oppressed communities, (non)violent practice may sound and appear like a demand for continued submission to oppression and the furtherance of structural inequality. In this way, the discourse of loving-the-enemy appears to function ideologically; in other words, it may conceal as much as it reveals. It appears to contribute to historical denial and reversal. Furthermore, if the goodness of human nature implies a belief in and practice of (non)violence, then loving-the-enemy as (non)violence is also equated with human goodness.

Writing in the context of Black Power in the late 1960s and early 1970s, James Cone was one of the first U.S. theologians to expose how (non)violence might be invested in the entitlements of dominant white culture and theology. The white tradition of (non)violent theology emerged from nineteenth-century liberalism, which emphasized the goodness and worth of humanity, including the goodness of "the powers that be." [95] From an African-American historical perspective, Cone delegitimized a theological anthropology that took for granted the innate goodness of white people and emphasized the vicious nature of white people's historic oppression of Black people. Such a theological perspective, particularly when applied to power, legitimized the white status quo. It played a part in the denial of the historic direct, structural, and cultural violence of the dominant white culture against the African-American community in the United States. In *Martin & Malcolm & America: A Dream or a Nightmare*,[96] Cone demonstrated how the tensions between a commitment to "loving the enemy" and "by any means necessary" within the Black Liberation movement partly reflected different socio-economic class locations within the Black community.

These differences were revealed in the Civil Rights and Black Power movements, as represented by Martin Luther King, Jr. and Malcolm X, respectively.

In Malcolm X's life experience and speeches, we hear the echoes of reversal and how "loving the enemy" might be perceived by oppressed communities as a further call to dehumanization and submission.[97] The Martin Luther King, Jr. and Malcolm X example shows how violence and (non)violence are shaped, though not determined, by social location. During the latter half of *Martin & Malcolm & America*, Cone demonstrates that King and Malcolm X's positions seemed to moderate and have a mutual influence. King realized the limitations of (non)violence among poor, urban Blacks in the North, and a trip to Mecca gave Malcolm X a broader vision of racial solidarity for social transformation. Even within the shared structural and cultural violence experienced by one historically oppressed community, intersecting identities affect perceptions of (non)violence and loving-the-enemy.

Individual Non-Resistance or Collective (Non)violence?

Wink's and Yoder's interpretations of the Matthew passage on loving-the-enemy circumscribe (non)violence to an individual *not* acting in retaliation when one is the victim of direct and structural violence. Even if Jesus did suggest non-retaliation as a practice of social struggle that has persuasive, moral power, it is important to mark the difference in potential for persuasion between individual non-retaliatory non-resistance and collective non-resistance. There is historical evidence that non-retaliation has played a part in persuading specific agents and structures of power to decrease or end their violence. However, in the context of social struggle, these acts of non-retaliation are most often collective and preceded by collective intention and training. Huerta said that she saw the individual and social transformation of "enemies" time and time again during the Farm Workers' movement. Huerta described the following incident:

> We were picketing down in Los Angeles at the produce market, and we had all these young women that were helping us out. Peace activists mainly came to help us. We were

picketing in front of these produce markets and [people] would come up with their dollies, iron dollies, and hit the women on the shins with the dollies, you know? [The young women] just stood firm. After a while, they just couldn't continue doing it. So I talk about the strength of it…

Notice that this situation has a collective dimension: female peace activists, trained in (non)violence, standing together against a group of perpetrators of violence. Huerta believes that enemies in social struggle will eventually be persuaded to stop perpetrating violence by the example of a victim's willingness to not-retaliate and to suffer. Huerta did not articulate the practical dimension directly, but every case she used demonstrated collective effort and public witness. The willingness of an oppressed community to publicly suffer and show love to a communal enemy, an entire structure of violence, is part of what persuades people within structures and a culture of violence to change. Individual witness does have power, but rarely enough power to challenge structures of violence.

Staughton Lynd was in the South during Mississippi Freedom Summer while Alice was settling their children in their new community in New Haven. During this time, they were exposed to thinking about and acting within the context of mass, public (non)violence. Years later (non)violence opened itself back up to them when they learned about covert U.S. warfare in Nicaragua in the mid-1980s. They both recalled casually watching television one evening when they heard an interview with a Quaker woman who was working with the organization Witness for Peace in Nicaragua. Alice said, "I was over near the stove, and I just stopped still and watched. I thought, "This is what people have been talking about – a nonviolent army, to get between the fighting forces. [I] was just dumbfounded." Staughton continued the conversation,

I remember about the same time (mid-80s) reading an editorial in the *New York Times* of all places, which said the Nicaraguan revolutionaries are different at least in this way: they have treated the soldiers of the army of the government they overthrew in a new way. They quoted Tomas Borge, one of the older and more disciplined Sandinistas who had had the opportunity to confront the man who had tortured him in prison. [It could have been his wife who was tortured; I'm not sure.] Borge said, "Well, now it's my turn. You punished me." And he said, "I'm not going to touch a hair on your head." He said, "I'm going to let you go." And I thought, "Wow."

At the level of public mass action and public consciousness-raising, such practices of loving-the-enemy take on a more significant potential for conversion and exposure of who the structural perpetrators of violence are, and therefore greater potential for persuasion at a structural and cultural level. Galtung notes that (non)violence must be communicated "from group to group" until the pressures and demands on the structures reach the nucleus of power.[98] Then social change happens. This shift is different from the individual, interpersonally persuasive, non-resistant encounter typically described by the notion of loving-the-enemy typical of much Christian (non)violence.

Furthermore, within the context of historic social struggles, even as a collective practice, non-retaliation has been only one dimension among many tactics and strategies of change. If loving-the-enemy as non-retaliation is granted as a form of (non)violent resistance, certainly it must be recognized as only one practice of (non)violence. (Non)violence understood as a broader constellation of passive and coercive practices arose in the time of Gandhi. It is anachronistic to equate loving-the-enemy as non-retaliation with the breadth of possibilities within (non)violent practice and to project the vast breadth and depth of modern practices onto Jesus' time. New Testament scholar Richard Horsley refutes Wink's exegetical analysis of the Matthew text as indicating a universal ethic of (non)violence in a modern context. Horsley grants that in the first-century, local context in which Jesus spoke, individual non-retaliation towards an enemy is a more appropriate label than (non)violence.[99]

Critique III:
Abstraction
Who or What Is the Enemy?

The demand for context and analysis of structural power and violence was evident throughout the interviews. Such an evaluation includes concretely determining who or what "the enemy" is. In some cases, interviewees described the enemy as an individual with whom one had a personal conflict. But more often, the identified opponent was specific to a community's concrete struggle and was not an individual: local, state, and national governmental entities and policy-makers, along with corporate interests, their executive officers, and money-lenders. Generally, the enemy was perceived to have political-economic power that the community of struggle did not and does not have.

Often human enemies served a hierarchy, possessing the ability to perpetrate violence of all three forms – direct, structural, and cultural. For Umoja, the opponent was the social group and its representatives that oppose a community's economic and racial liberation and self-determination. For many interviewees, these persons represent massive racial and corporate economic interests. B♀ used the language of "enemy" regularly to refer to any person or corporate interest that effectively serves to wage war on the poor of this country or another. Enemies are the people who "control the food; they control the banks; they control the water; they control the electricity. You know, they control everything." Kelly also used the language of perpetrators of economic warfare. Therefore, the United States, as a nation-state, was described as an enemy through its foreign and domestic policies, laws, and systems of enforcement from the courts to repressive police-state violence, and military. The enemy was also described as an opponent in war-time, both a nation-state and its people. Dear stated that in the original Greek of the New Testament, by "enemy" Jesus "clearly means 'nation-states': the people declared expendable by your nation." Therefore, groups of people and states declared by the United States as enemies are those whom Christians are called to love.

Certainly, as activists and scholars described the increasing complexity of socio-political and economic structures within the context of social struggles, the identification of concrete opponents grew more difficult. Schulman's language of "the powers that oppose you" is the best general, abstract definition for various terms used by the interviewees to describe the extensive nature of specific enemies. Enemies oppose individuals and communities with systems of violence such as industrial capitalism and imperialism or the cultural violence of racism, sexism, homophobia, and anthropocentrism. The enemy was also the culture of denial of violence itself and anything that prevents people from acting for change within the culture: entitlements, comfort, apathy, indifference, fear. Power saw the enemy as any person or group that another individual or group sought to "other" – anyone or anything put outside of being sacred, including individuals, an economic order, or a state.

Since the agents of violence are often obscured in structural violence, enemies often seem abstract. Yet the interviewees all described particular social action practices by which specific targets – individual and collective, organizational and institutional – were identified and held accountable. In various ways, all interviewees note:

1) the failure to research and identify concrete agents within structures;

2) when such agents are identified, they are, with rare exception, members of dominant cultural groups; and

3) those agents are rarely held accountable for their actions and oversight of pervasive acts and conditions of violence within their personal relationships, their organizations, or the public.

Schulman explains that ACT UP was successful in large part because of its "politics of accountability:"

> If someone hurts you, you have the right to respond. Your response is the consequence of their violating action. Pharmaceutical executives, politicians who have pledged to represent and serve the American people, religious leaders who claim moral authority – anyone who interfered with progress

for people with AIDS was made to face a consequence for the pain they caused. To do this, ACT UP had to identify what needed to be changed, identify the individuals who were obstructing that change, clearly propose courses of action that were doable and justifiable, and then force the people with power – through the tactic of direct action – to do something different than what they wanted to do. Making people accountable is always in the interest of justice. The dominant, however, hate accountability. Vagueness, lack of delineation of how things work, the idea that people do not have to keep their promises – these tactics always serve the lying, the obstructive, the hypocritical.[100]

Schulman writes, "The true message of the AIDS crisis is that making people with power accountable works."[101] The problem is that the message of accountability is obscured, even falsified as reversal plays itself out in the claims of the dominant culture to being victimized and oppressed when they are asked to be held accountable.[102]

Analyzing who and what the so-called enemy is in the midst of social struggle is critical to figuring out what it means concretely to "love" that individual, group, or structure of violence. For example, if the enemies of fundamental economic transformation are the structures of capitalism, how are they to be loved? How are they to be persuaded to stop their violence? These are not rhetorical questions. Violence is not always perpetrated by an individual directly present or even known to the victims. Normative interpretations of loving-the-enemy in the Matthew text incorporate few of these issues or address how to deal with them. These questions of "who is the enemy," challenge the abstract notion that fundamental social change will come about universally through loving-the-enemy as the tradition of Christian (non)violence suggests.

Turn the Other Cheek and You Get Two Bruised Cheeks

B♀ offered a different interpretation of the outcome of non-retaliation, which she derived from her experience growing up as working-class poor. "I have to say I'm not too fond of 'turn the other cheek.' I think you just get two bruised cheeks. That's my experience in life. And many other people." She described how poor the families in her town were and what it was like when they tried to unionize a timber plant in town where her father shoveled coal:

> They had no union there. They had no nothing there. We had no insurance. We didn't have shit. If they didn't inoculate us in school, we would never have been inoculated. Then the union came. There was bitter, bitter, *bitter* labor struggle around getting that union in there. My father would come home with a bump on his head or a black eye or whatever. This went on for quite some time. I was young, seven or eight years old. It was a physical battle. My parents always [said] they had a class consciousness even though it wasn't in educated language. I knew that the bosses were the enemy. I knew that from my house. I knew that from my neighborhood. I knew that from my life.

This childhood experience taught her about the world and who the enemy is:

> The thing that I know is rich people ain't never going to give it up. That's what I know. They're never going to give you a raise. They don't want to give me medical care. There was a whole polio thing that went on, and we couldn't get shots. And clearly, they didn't care.

A similar dynamic existed in prison:

> If you're in prison, you know that prison guards… you never trust them. There are some good ones, but you never trust them completely. It's the whole class thing. There are some good bosses but most of them… you don't trust them. It's that basic kind of thing.

From an actual social location, B♀'s perspective challenges Wink's theoretical analysis. What causes someone to believe that when a victim of violence asserts his or her dignity by offering the other cheek, this action will register with the offender and so "create enormous difficulties for the striker"?[103] Is it not just as likely, as B♀ suggests, that the one who turns the cheek (and is already considered less than human) will be struck again? This result comes not as an abstraction, but from the social location of one who has experienced the structural and direct violence of poverty. Wink admits that a "nonviolent orientation is premised on a power seldom recognized by oppressor and oppressed alike."[104] It is a form of power that "those inured to violence cannot comprehend."[105] Yet Wink still hopes that a violent offender, who is backed by and benefits from a system of denial, reversal, and entitlements, will be awakened to the oppressive nature of the structure and the humanity of the one he violates. How does this happen? B♀ suggests that it does not – that the victim's revolutionary subordination proves mutual human dignity to the enemy may or may not be accurate. Non-retaliation may do little more than reinforce the superiority of the one in power. The very structure is invested in preventing agents of violence from accepting its true nature.

(Non)violence and Moral Abstraction

In this contemporary context, loving-the-enemy through non-retaliation based on the example of Jesus' teachings and crucifixion must not be equated with (non)violence in general terms. Furthermore, loving-the-enemy as non-retaliation must divorce itself from an insistence on equating (non)violence with a moral high ground. The preceding analysis has shown that traditional conceptions of Christian (non)violence ignore the complexities of history, power, and culture. The various forms of violence are rarely distinguished and dismissed under the discourse of moral-ethical, theological Christian imperatives.

Traditional notions of loving-the-enemy by doing the enemy no harm equates all forms of violent retaliation as morally equivalent, and all agents of violence as morally the same. The commitment to loving-the-enemy and (non)violence amounts to a moral belief system. Wink serves again as an example because his perspective is so typical of white, Christian (non)violent theology. Wink writes that when we respond to domination with violence, we speak and act on the system's terms. "We turn into the very thing we oppose."[106] Jesus offers a different way:

> … a way to fight evil with all our power without being transformed into the very evil we fight. It is a way—the only

way possible—of not becoming what we hate. "Do not counter evil in kind"—this insight is the distilled essence, stated with sublime simplicity, of the experience of those Jews who had, in Jesus' very lifetime, so courageously and effectively practiced nonviolent direct action against Rome.[107]

Wink's final argument is that Christians are unequivocally called to (non)violence. Based on his interpretation of Jesus' words, Wink's assessment is that (non)violence is always, without exception, the more moral, spiritual, freeing, creative, open, and imaginative way to seek justice.[108]

Though Wink occasionally offers an apologetic for the use of violence based on context,[109] these statements ring hollow when the preponderance of his writing treats violence as "evil" and "what we hate." If Jesus' (non)violent example of loving-the-enemy is what is good and moral, and its opposite is evil, then (non)violent Christians are good and violent actors are evil. Furthermore, if Jesus' (non)violent example shows us "what is truly human," then those who act with violence are not "truly human." Here, Wink participates in the reversal of violence whereby the actions of (non)violent, Christian actors are seen as morally superior.

A problem comes when advocates of (non)violence put it on a morally higher plane. Christian activists reinforce a higher moral dimension by naming (non)violence as Jesus' "way." This moralist perspective regards all forms of violence as morally the same and excludes a comprehensive discussion of strategy based on an analysis of power and context. The oppressed cannot use violence because then they will become the oppressor and replicate their methods. The violence of the oppressed (self-defense, spontaneous rebellion, armed struggle) as a response to structural and cultural violence is equated with the violence of the state. Churchill called this abstract argument, "fruit of the poison tree:"

> What if you actually use the same sorts of methods and such as the people who are doing this to you? You'll end up in the same position as them. The woman who physically resists rape, therefore, becomes a rapist?... Fruit of the poison tree. Gandhi

did say something to this effect. If you overthrow your oppressor using the same means that the oppressor uses to oppress you, you will end up being a replication of the state because it's a moral defect. Inevitably you will end up being some sort of a totalitarian, ugly, evil, oppressive people in that domain as much as they were oppressed before. I'm not sure that's quite true on the facts. You've had some really unfortunate outcomes of revolutions through resort of arms that were made. I don't know of any of them that are worse than India. And that is the *Gandhian* revolution. You really want to put India up as a model of what you are trying to achieve? Which tree was it that poisoned that one?

Churchill counsels historical accuracy over abstraction, noting that not all persons who have employed the use of violence in self-defense or armed struggle have ended up becoming as violently oppressive as their oppressors. Nor has (non)violent revolution always resulted in less oppression or structural violence. Not all violence is morally equivalent, and (non)violence is not necessarily a more moral choice. (Non)violence is selectively preferred based on context.

Jensen draws attention to situations where the benefits of abstractions are chosen over real, live beings. Real, material contexts and relationships should determine courses of action for justice and not abstract, moral ideals.

One of the things that really upsets me about dogmatic pacifism: it's like, are you saying that it's not acceptable for a woman to kill someone who is trying to rape her? If they say, "No, that's acceptable." Okay, great, you are not really a dogmatic pacifist. Because now we're talking cases. That's the conversation I'm really interested in having. When is it acceptable and when is not acceptable, personally and socially? My definition of violence, the definition I like best, is "any act that causes harm to another." ... If I eat a carrot, I'm committing an act of violence against a carrot. The carrot was a living being. I pull it up, and I'm harming the carrot. So most of us, under most circumstances, know that it's morally acceptable to commit an act of violence against a carrot. Most of us, under most circumstances, would not agree to commit an act of violence against a human being. So I'm interested in talking about where we draw those lines.

Jensen gave another example where there are nine men in a room and one woman. Eight of the men are raping a woman. He said to a dogmatic pacifist, "You are the ninth man. It's not really going to help her very much for you to stand back and say, "I will not participate. I'm going to stop this by my own non-participation." The activist answered, "Yes it would, because that's one less dog," indicating he broke the cycle of violence by not sinking to the level of violence of the other men. Jensen responded, "No, that's not particularly helpful. The response is for you to stop them." Two questions arise for this discussion of loving-the-enemy: If loving-the-enemy morally excludes forms of violent coercion, thereby allowing the perpetuation of violence in all its forms, then is it love? Can it reasonably be considered (non)violence? In this and other specific cases, loving-the-enemy cannot be equated absolutely with (non)violence.

Churchill also cautions advocates of dogmatic pacifism who accept the violence of the state as moral or justified while condemning violence on the part of the oppressed as immoral or unjustified. He presented a hypothetical circumstance where a violent criminal kicks down the door of an unarmed, (non)violent activist's house. That person locks himself in a room with a phone. Churchill then asks these questions:

> Who you gonna call to help? You're going to call the police. You don't disbelieve in armed force? You just want to displace it on somebody else, preferably somebody you can say works for you. So much for your fucking moral principles.

Churchill points out the hypocrisy of absolute pacifists who support self-defense in the case of their community, but not in the case of others. They say, "'Well, that's different; of course, I'd defend my family.' Yeah, and you got a monopoly on how you define family." It is easier to condemn the violence of others when one's own family and community are not under attack.

The resort to arms in self-defense or organized armed struggle is not more morally pure or even more effective than (non)violence. All of the interviewees who affirmed "by any means necessary" acknowledged that there was no purity in either violence or (non)violence. Organized tactics of violent resistance have not always been effective to make meaningful small changes or to take state power. Churchill and Lynd both recognized there had been unfortunate outcomes by many groups that resorted to the force of arms. There may also be a devastating emotional impact of violence on individuals and communities who use it.[110]

Umoja pointed out that some particular organized acts of violence, both in self-defense and as strategic attack, have caused him to question the morality and justifiability of certain kinds of violence, even when he understands the root cause. Certainly, not all forms of violence serve the ends of justice, and violence often does contribute to ongoing cycles of violence.

> It shouldn't be that armed struggle is a principle, or nonviolence is a principle. It should be that we'd do whatever was necessary. I'm not talking about anything that's heinous, something *extreme*. My rational side tells me that doing stuff like that is just going to create this whole cycle that's going to continue.

Clearly, there are many good reasons not to use violence and to oppose it on a moral basis. A critique of Christian (non)violence is not meant to undermine its life-affirming, justice-seeking theological notions and practices. The critique urges context-based analysis over abstractions.

The portrayal of loving-the-enemy as equated with (non)violence as a moral position from within the Christian tradition fails to take into account that, when acting (non)violently, persons with dominant identities are still implicated in and by structures of violence. This implication is the reason for formulating (non)violence with parentheses. The practice of (non)violence does not negate the reality of violence in which (non)violent actors continue to be implicated, even as practitioners of (non)violence. Here is where (non)violence has the potential of becoming a form of denial in and of itself: when (non)violent actors claim absolution from the conditions of violence in which all members of the dominant culture participate and from which they benefit. Simply because a (non)violent activist from the dominant culture may not engage in direct violence, that person is not absolved of violence. It is precisely because structural and cultural forms of violence operate to obscure the agents of violence through abstraction, a (non)violent community from within the dominant identity groups must recognize that neither their discourse of (non)violence nor an inferred morality of their action will excuse their participation in other forms of violence. This confession is particularly true of a Christian (non)violent community. If Christianity is a substructure of violent domination in this country and world, historically and currently, attaching a moral imperative to Christian (non)violence smacks of hypocrisy, if not denial.

Critique IV:
When Loving-the-Enemy
Privileges Power and Enables Violence

A critique of loving-the-enemy reveals what Christian activists think they are doing through their (non)violent practices. Such an analysis also exposes the impacts of their actual practices and discloses deeper beliefs underlying these practices. Jensen suggests that moral calls for (non)violence may conceal more deep-seated fears of what breaking up the existing structures of violence might really demand. Covered-over fears may surface, no matter what one's individual or community social location is. Traditional Christian (non)violence suggests that through a non-retaliatory assertion of humanity, loving-the-enemy unmasks the dehumanizing structural and cultural violence by which the system of domination operates. As B♀ pointed out, this viewpoint and practice fail to consider just how self-interested the entitlements of structural inequality and religious, racial, and class privilege may be.

Jensen said what "oppressors really want you to do is to believe that they are invincible" so that a "state of dependency is fostered in almost every way possible." He likened the U.S. culture of violence to an abusive family dynamic. Abused women often do not leave their abusers because they have come to depend upon them for survival. Abused women say to themselves, "How will I eat, and how will my children eat if I leave my husband?" Women know they "are seven times more likely to get beaten when [they] try to leave." These are the same kinds of things people from all social locations think and ask when considering whether or not to fight systems of cultural and structural violence.[111] Both oppressed and privileged communities inevitably fear the ramifications of what changing the dynamics of the exploitative, abusive system might mean.

> On the larger scale, systematically, we are made dependent upon the system that's killing us. Does your food come from a landbase, or does your food come from the grocery store? Does your water come from a tap, or does your water come from a river? How would we eat without the system?

Despite possessing adequate knowledge about the devastating effects of the economy on the earth and the poor, virtually all persons in the United States depend upon this current way of life and the people who run its systems. Participants in an economic structure know a threat to the powerful is a threat to their livelihoods and expectations of the good life. The culture trains members of all social locations in aspiring to be members of the dominant culture and the American way of life. The culture has made desirable the material entitlements that destroy the planet and its inhabitants. To have those entitlements, we must deny the various forms of violence and deny that our benefits are entitlements. There are social rewards for going along. Resistance means that one may not receive social rewards and may even be punished. Under these circumstances, loving-the-enemy means not fighting the system. Non-retaliation works to preserve social structures. There is no challenge to consider the sacrifices to the privileges and entitlements implied by directly and coercively confronting the enemy – individuals and systems – in concrete ways.

As in an abusive relationship, everything in a system of destruction is designed to protect and care for the oppressors through structures of violence. The culture of historical denial and its narrative rejects that the structures of the whole society are violently unequal. "We are a land of equal opportunity." "The culture is good." "We are progressing as people and a nation." "We are a light to the nations." That there would be any other system of government or economy is inconceivable.

By privileging reverence for the oppressor's life over the oppressed, loving-the-enemy as non-retaliation may become part of the discourse of human and United States' progress, exceptionalism, and denial. Schulman addresses the myth of goodness and progress through the history and treatment of AIDS in the United States. She describes a program on National Public Radio reporting on how the American public eventually "came around" to accept people with AIDS and get them treatment and that "*naturally, normally* things just *happened* to get better. That's the way we nice Americans naturally are. We *come around* when it's the right thing to do."[112] The U.S. myth of goodness and progress destroys the history of the people in ACT UP who, through active, self-sacrificing, (non)violent struggle, forced people in power in the United States to "come around." It privileges the discourse, the entitlements, and the denial of the powerful.

Jensen often receives communications from individuals who question the need to fight back using violence if necessary. He said it is always easier to have this conversation about fighting back with people who have already fought and survived an individual abuser or a system of abuse "because their identification with the system has been broken." Privileged people, who are invested in their entitlements with little experience of abuse, respond predictably with "If civilization crashes what will happen to the people?" Jensen always responds to this question:

> Which people are you talking about? Are you talking about the hammer-head shark people? You talking about the Coos salmon people? You talking about the polar bear people? You talking about the subsistence farmers in India? I mean, all those people are better off immediately? When people say, "What's going to happen to the people?" they are talking about the global elite, which are the only ones that matter in this equation because we've identified with them. If you truly identify with the Delta smelt, the Delta smelt are suffering

right now. If you identify with the subsistence farmers, the subsistence farmers are suffering right now. They're dying right now.

Particularly for privileged people from various intersections of dominant identities, it is difficult to consider confronting the enemy because they are us. As analysis of structural violence suggests, all U.S. citizens are implicated in the devastation of the environment and the human beings who are exploited and destroyed to maintain the U.S. lifestyle. Jensen remarks that if space aliens were destroying the planet, humans would easily fight back because they wouldn't identify with them. If citizens of this country were to confront the systems that destroy human and other-than-human life, they would have to confront themselves and their material entitlements.

Yet Jensen counsels that while all people must be accountable for their investment in the privileges of the system of violence from which they may benefit, most persons should not over-identify with the oppressor as the enemy. While members of the dominant culture benefit from systems of violence and environmental destruction, the enemy is not always "us." For example, Jensen wants the proper share of the blame for environmental destruction to be placed at the feet of those who are most responsible for it. He uses the example of water:

> We so often hear that the world is running out of water. People are dying from lack of water. Rivers are dewatered from lack of water. Because of this, we need to take shorter showers.... Well, no! More than 90 percent of the water used by humans is used by agriculture and industry. The remaining 10 percent is split between municipalities and actual living breathing individual humans. Collectively, municipal golf courses use as much water as municipal human beings. People (both human people and fish people) are not dying because the world is running out of water. They're dying because the water is being stolen.[113]

Overly harsh self-criticism falls back on individualism and does not do an adequate job of identifying "the enemy" historically and currently

— those who are primarily responsible as the agents of decision-making within economic and political hierarchies for destroying life. Everyone in the United States is implicated in violence. We are not all, however, the enemy. Churchill spoke of the importance to never compromise one's commitment "to call things by their right names... [and] speak the truth as you see it." It is critical to name violence accurately as what it is, and not to "look for ways to make it comfortable to the perpetrators or the beneficiaries." A part of speaking the truth and calling things by their right names is the need to "make distinctions between perpetration and benefit."

A Reconstruction of Loving-the-Enemy

"Churches" are specific "cultures and structures" that create their own violence. Christians are implicated by all the forms of violence that The Church perpetrates on those they mark out as other. Though Christians may claim a God of Peace who loves and calls Christians to love all persons, including enemies, individual Christian and institutional Church practices reveal a theology that is, practically and theologically, violent. Dear states, "Trillions of dollars to kill everybody – now everybody thinks that normal. 'That's what God is;' 'that's God's will;' 'that's the way the world is supposed to be;' 'that's what it means to be human.'" Dear calls for structures and practices of worship and living in the world which reflect the loving God in Christ in whom Christians claim to believe.

A mere claim to the God of love or the command of Jesus to love the enemy does not make such a claim reality, nor does it negate the realities of violence. While practices of (non)violence may point to and participate in a theology of God's love for all by not participating in actions of direct violence (retaliation), those practices do not negate violence in all of its forms. Loving-the-enemy as a theological abstraction does not equal a transformational, (non)violent, social change and constitutes a highly inadequate view. It is an abstraction to believe this is so or to claim that the violent practices that have attended Christianity historically are somehow an aberration of the essence of Christianity. For as the critique of abstraction and the commitments of practical theology make clear, there is no essence of Christianity apart from historical practices.

Through a more thorough structural analysis of a given context of social struggle, a more robust notion of what loving-the-enemy means would better serve those who desire to remain committed to a transformational Christian (non)violence. Some aspects of loving-the-enemy within the tradition of liberal Christian (non)violence require more careful consideration and reconstruction. Three perspectives from the interviews aid the reconstruction of loving-the-enemy by confronting the problems of abstraction, individualism, and human supremacism.

Reconstructing Loving-the-Enemy I: Practice over Abstraction

All of the interviewees stated in some way that it is easier to hold rigid ideologies about both violence and (non)violence than to engage in the hard, slow work of practice, whatever that practice may be, and to accept the consequences of radical action. Loving-the-enemy can serve as an ideology over against a form of collective practice. As a theological fallback, loving-the-enemy is an inefficient shortcut to the difficult work of contextual analysis and strategizing. Radical and Christian liberationist perspectives critique loving-the-enemy, the abstract concept of love itself, and de-contextualized, de-historicized applications of scriptural texts. The historical context demands a definition of who or what the enemy is and what the enemy's concrete actions are before determining a meaningful response to various kinds of violence – direct, structural, and cultural. Normative theological demands for (non)violence in social struggle often obscure distinctions between the different forms of violence discussed so far and the operations of power and entitlement.

Loving-the-enemy in (non)violent practice currently means little more than a certain set of familiar behaviors to which liberal activists have become attached. While they appear as active behaviors and resistant to structures of power, their impact on structural violence amounts mostly to passive non-resistance: protest actions, sign-holding, marches, and so on. This is not to suggest these practices are useless or meaningless, only limited.

Churchill writes that in the United States' context of social change, there is an avowal of radical (non)violence with very little concrete engagement in such practices.[114] He counsels advocates of absolute (non)violence to spend time in communities that are under direct, structural, and cultural violent attacks to more clearly grasp the nature of their own stated commitments. Individuals should engage in a direct confrontation with state power in their home context in order to grasp the real effects of confrontational action that seeks to transform social structures.[115] Then activists should engage in a "period of independent and guided reflection upon their observations and experiences 'in the real world.'" The outcome of this process is "a formal articulation of precisely how he/she sees his/her values coinciding with the demonstrable physical requirements of revolutionary social action."[116]

Similarly, liberationist Juan Luis Segundo wrote that a theologian who would like to know how the gospel of Christ, such as loving-the-enemy, might be applied in a revolutionary circumstance should not consult the gospel first.[117] The application of a scriptural text first requires a context of struggle in which the activist-theologian is engaged, and out of which the text is interpreted and applied. That Jesus' command to love concretely requires wholly gratuitous love for the neighbor or enemy regardless of the circumstance is only one view.[118] Segundo's view is *efficacious love*: concrete love conditioned by the historical moment and resulting in the liberation of the poor. Liberation of the poor is not possible apart from the transformation of social structures, which cause poverty. Efficacious love is to be directed towards the poor, the oppressed, and the suffering – not towards their enemy. The dynamics of Jesus' commands to love, are not universal, but bent towards using "the least amount of violence compatible with truly effective love."[119] Therefore, some use of violence is implied. Efficacious love includes the potential for violence as a form of love in the effective transformation of structures and cultures of violence. Love that is not effective in transforming structures actually privileges the dominant culture and the maintenance of its structures of violence.

B♀ described how the George Jackson Brigade (GJB) engaged in organized violence to seriously disrupt structures and institutions of violence, while attempting to avoid doing violence to humans. B♀ offered an example:

> No one ever got hurt. We cased this bank for the longest time. Oh my God, forever. We got ready to do [it], and we realized that school started. There was a school down the street. We saw all these fucking kids. What did we do? We left. We never went back there again. We couldn't do it. It wasn't correct.

When she was asked to join the GJB, there had been a recent action where a bomb went off inside a bag of dog food in a grocery store. B♀ described the result of the bombing:

> There were a few minor damages, nothing serious. People got some cuts. But it was stupid, 'cause you don't do that. Take it to their power source. If you take that kind of step, you have to be the most-principled, the most-careful, and the most-determined-to-not-hurt-anybody person in the world.

I asked B♀ if all of the deliberations in the GJB were made in consideration of protecting human life. She answered,

> Yeah, absolutely. We even warned the police. They managed to disarm a bomb. We made a statement, "We suggest you guys not do that. It's dangerous when you do that." We understand that they're the working class, too. They're just the cannon fodder. Just like soldiers. That was always a discussion. How do we not harm citizens? Even during bank robberies. I was never in a bank more than five minutes. I would just say, 'Let's get this over with as quickly as possible. You don't want to be here, and I don't want to be here. Let's just do what we got to do and get the fuck on down the road.'

B♀ held together an interesting tension: an ability to identify and name the enemy on multiple fronts, to confront the enemy, to do material harm to the enemy, but not to destroy human life. For B♀, resistance and retaliation primarily in terms of destroying material property, fell within the scope of dealing with the enemy. These actions were also effective in giving her organization a platform from which to communicate publicly about structures and the culture of U.S. violence at home and abroad.

The purpose here is not to justify violence or its effectiveness in all cases. If loving-the-enemy can be reconstructed as a meaningful source for the theological tradition of Christian (non)violence, then it must be applied within a practice of social struggle in the community. Both Churchill and Segundo referred to revolutionary contexts in which organized violence for self-defense and armed struggle may be required. A given context of conflict may not call for the use of violence. The point here is for Christian activists and their communities not to predetermine action from an abstract, moral, scriptural, or theological point of view, but to engage struggle and structural analysis first. Analytic engagement is a prerequisite for a credible claim to loving-the-enemy.

Reconstructing Loving-the-Enemy II: Interconnectedness as a Practice

What makes a concept like loving-the-enemy potentially powerful is not only the belief but the practice of interconnectedness: recognizing the sacred, inter-related nature of life. As commonly and currently practiced, few routines of (non)violence get at the heart or potential power of loving-the-enemy as human. Harding said,

> I don't see nonviolence or Christianity or Marxism as in any way fully expressed through those names: they are simply indicators of our understanding of the struggle to become our best selves and to realize our deepest humanity.

For Harding, (non)violence is not an abstraction. Understood within the context of struggle, it is whatever most recognizes and nurtures the human-divine within and between humans. Loving-the-enemy as interconnected requires a concrete context of struggle in which living beings affirm interconnectedness by practicing it. Loving-the-enemy works against the disconnection of living beings, undermining individualism while it practices building community.

Harding talked about experiencing a moment when a Christian minister spoke to the audience during a memorial service on the anniversary of the Greensboro massacre. He reported that the pastor came out of the pulpit and started to pray for the people gathered, some of whom were "still deeply embedded in the world of Marxist-communism." Regardless of differences in belief, the pastor poured oil over the attendees and prayed for them, for Jesus to be with them. Harding interpreted this experience:

> To me, that's what nonviolence is about – wherever the stream of love comes from, you share it with whoever is there. If it's your enemy, you share it with whoever is there. If it's somebody who believes something totally different, you share it because they are humans before they are anything else.

Continuing to refer to this event, Harding went on to describe his definition of (non)violence:

> [Nonviolence] is the way of being that makes it most possible for you to accompany while hugging… and dancing and loving and sharing your best humanity. At our best, that's what we have to offer to each other. Our best humanity. That sometimes may come out in books and sermons and articles and speeches, but it comes out at its deepest level in creative relationships that bring life. That, for me, is what nonviolent movement is all about: life-sharing, life-giving, life-affirming…. For me, the deepest truth is the truth of our connectedness. The truth of our need for each other. The truth of our belonging to each other…. So, wherever you or I recognize a deep desire to acknowledge, encourage, and live out a movement toward our best selves, then nonviolence is simply a way of negotiating how to hug, how to walk together, how to build together, and how to create together. It's not a kind of a banner that says, "this is the banner that you have to march under…." We don't say that this is the only way, but this is what I have, and I'm so glad that we can be close enough so that I can touch you with it and that you can touch me with what you have. So nonviolence is clearly not an

ideology. It is what I find to be a wonderful way of sharing the human experience and walking with each other and massaging each other with healing oil.

Affirming the interconnectedness of all life, Power preferred the practice of non-othering to the language of (non)violence. She said, "I think what turns into violence is not the picking up of a gun. What turns into violence is the othering of the opposition. That's the origin. That's the first violent act." Enmity, or hatred, is othering. "It's placing this moment of this being-ness outside of what's sacred. I think that's the radical power of Jesus' dictum to love your enemies." In her experience, however right it may have viscerally felt to be an armed enforcer of a just order, it was not "the truth." She said, "It's just more true to be moving from a loving heart, even as you are witnessing horrors." For Power, activists who claim (non)violence are as prone to othering as are those who claim other means:

> There's a righteousness, a blind righteousness, among even practitioners of nonviolence, or there can be. Having the philosophy of nonviolence and the practice of othering, it's no guarantee. The philosophy of nonviolence is no guarantee that you won't do violence, or that you won't create enmity, that you won't act without a blind spot.... When people have a dogma of nonviolence, they hate violence. They hate the war. They *hate*. Still, in a way, I won't say hate, because that doesn't feel fair. They do other.

Regardless of our perspective, Power said we are called to expand what we hold in the vision of love and let go of the idea that anything we think has any absolute truth.

With theological justification for its direct, structural, and cultural violence, Christians from the dominant culture have historically identified marginalized others, destroying them to seek their own survival and dominance. The Christian political-institutional apparatus is unable to understand itself as racially and culturally situated, embracing its justifications for violence as religiously-based truths. The dominant Christian tradition has mostly failed in practice to extend its affirmation of the interconnectedness of Creator and creation beyond the individual. Yet the Christian tradition still contains an expansive and contradictory impulse and command to love. Power recognized it "has produced some really significant nonviolent moments right along with its attempt to seize state power...." Working against individualism, a reconstructed notion of loving-the-enemy as (non)violent practice would more intentionally seek to extend itself beyond moments of non-resistant, interpersonal encounter. Affirming an interconnectedness of all life, advocates of (non)violence would also accept the deep interconnectedness of all forms of violence. This would lead to engagement in collective practices of (non)violence that not only addresses direct violence but structural and cultural violence, including human supremacism. In a similar vein, advocates of Christian (non)violence would recognize they have the same potential for imposing hardened "truths" as any other ideological, politicized form of Christianity.

Direct, structural, and cultural violence depend upon othering. Structural violence requires denying the full humanity of individuals and whole groups who are marked out as different from the dominant culture. Reversal requires a false elevation of the dominant culture that relies upon debasing the marginalized as less than human. Once dehumanized, further violence can justifiably be carried out against them as threats to the entitlements held in place by the structural violence of the dominant status quo. If the U.S. Christian tradition is fundamentally violent, then practices of (non)violence would be constituted by practices by which others are rehumanized in their context. By refusing to other, both in theological principle and Christian practice, those whom the dominant culture has taught us to other can become leaders on a journey toward re-humanization. Through practices such as not othering, loving-the-enemy provides a potential starting point for reversing the false portrayal of the perpetrators of violence that is required by systems of violence. As Churchill addressed, (non)violence, as love, means an actual practice of connectedness through proximity and relationship with human and other beings that suffer the extremes of violence most profoundly, so that the impacts of both violence and the commitment to (non)violence might be better understood. The affirmation of interconnectedness in thought and practice allows for a deeper, renewed practice to emerge. When applied collectively, the potential for social transformation multiplies exponentially.

In their interview, the Lynds mentioned Barbara Deming's model of (non)violence.[120] They described Deming's "two-hands" approach as follows:

> In any nonviolent situation, one hand says, "You're just going to have to go through me if you want to do that." But the other hand reaches out to the person… what his interest is, and what his concerns are, what his feelings are going to be…. Barbara's "two hands," I just think is so important. That one hand is saying, "Stop what you're doing." And the other hand is reaching out to the person. And that you're doing both at once.

Deming's approach is an interesting way to conceive of loving-the-enemy and expands on Power's insight on non-othering and interconnectedness in the context of structural violence more thoroughly. Activists establish their sense of connection to the adversary in struggle while resisting actively through obstruction, disruption, and confrontation.

Reconstructing Loving-the-Enemy III: Vision and Practice

The abstraction of loving-the-enemy has been less a practice of fundamental social transformation than a vision for the world. While Segundo's concept of "efficacious love" showed that love may include the potential for violence, love of the enemy does not prefer any kind of violence. All of the interviewees indicated that (non)violence is, in fact, a meaningful ideal that serves the purpose of developing greater space for solidarity in the struggle for justice. (Non)violence creates greater possibilities among larger segments of the population for building a just society into the future. At the end of *Pacifism as Pathology*, Churchill wrote of (non)violence:

I would at last like to state the essential premise of this essay clearly: the desire for a nonviolent and cooperative world is the healthiest of all psychological manifestations. This is the overarching principle of liberation and revolution.[121]

Every radical and Christian liberationist encountered in this research supported (non)violence as a meaningful, positive, preferred option for social transformation. Liberationists do not counsel idealism but call for a utopian vision that envisions something new, that has enough substance to it to be both prophetic and to stimulate an imagination about new possibilities.[122] Moving toward a world based on loving-the-enemy requires, in part, a nurturing of the imagination about the possibility of a different world. Dear said, "Here in the United States, historically we are the blindest of the blind. We really have no imagination for peace whatsoever." Throughout U.S. history, there have been agents of (non)violent imagination that we must emulate in our own practices without falling prey to simplistic idealism. Dear continued with these words:

> In this world of 35 wars, 25,000 nuclear weapons, a billion starving to death, global warming, violence at an unparalleled level, one of the first casualties is the loss of the imagination.[123] Certainly, in the United States, it's gone. The Western, privileged world has lost the imagination. If you walk down the street of New York and say, "Can you imagine the United States without an army?" They're gonna lock you up. They may slug you. I mean, you just cannot imagine it. The heart of the work for peace and justice is to help people to reclaim their imagination for peace. My teacher is William Lloyd Garrison. He stands up, radically public, and he says, "Excuse me, United States, I am announcing the abolition of slavery." They all laughed at him! Then they tried to kill him and burned his house. They said to him, "There has always been slavery. It's in the Bible!" And he said, "No." He lifted up the vision of a new world of equality. A new world is coming; we're all going to be equal. He gave people vision. That's what the movement does. Susan B. Anthony: "All women can vote."

Dr. King: "I Have a Dream." The Berrigans: "We're going to end the Vietnam War." Helen Caldecott: "We're going to abolish nuclear weapons." What the movement should be saying is, "We are announcing the abolition of war, poverty, executions, racism, sexism, starvation, nuclear weapons, global destruction, and any form of violence."

Huerta said part of the rationale behind the commitment to use (non)violence in the Farm Workers' movement was establishing a totally new vision for relationships within the farm-worker community. She recalled one meeting in which organizers returned from a picket line where they had been physically beaten up by a union that opposed their organizing efforts. The organizers said, "It's one thing to be nonviolent against the employers, but these Teamsters were coming up and beating us up in front of the workers…" Huerta continued, "So then César [Chavez] made it very clear that we were going to continue using nonviolence, and that we were not going to use violence because if we did then we would be using it against each other. He made everybody take a vow." Chavez was as concerned about practicing a new vision of community within the farm workers as he was about loving-the-enemy.

Loving-the-enemy, refraining from the application of violent retaliation against injustice and its agents, has more transformational potential for creating a humane social outcome for individuals and societies. Harding describes this essential practice of visioning as knowing what we are for, not only what we are against. This mirrors Jensen's constant refrain that the main reason activists are unsuccessful in their efforts is because we do not really know what we want, and we don't think strategically.[124]

While there is a need to establish a vision, Staughton Lynd cautions:

> I do not think ordinary persons bleed and die for a vision that they have not experienced. I think the vision must be rooted in daily life, and if it is not, nothing will happen. If the vision is the seed, daily life is the soil.[125]

Interviewees support the need for certain kinds of ideals and models in order to hold out a vision of the future that is different from the pervasive violence of the present. Loving-the-enemy as an ideal may serve as part of such a vision. Once again, however, a meaningful vision cannot emerge outside of the context and community of daily, lived, practices. The creation of a (non)violent vision is not an abstraction. It is a collective practice based in context, grounded in analysis, and aimed at structural and cultural transformation. What constitutes a constellation of effective collective practices is the subject of the next chapter.

– 4 –

TACTICS

After a full analysis of the interviews, a theme I broadly label "tactics" contained the most data. No matter their perspective on (non)violence, the interviewees repeatedly talked about the effectiveness of tactics. Their differing views reveal a debate over whether organized violence or (non)violence, or a combination of both, is most effective for social transformation. They all affirmed that social change was achieved by the effective combination of multiple tactics, even within a tradition of (non)violence alone. The interviews underscored the conflict between the need for effectiveness and the reality that deep transformation is often not tangibly achieved in a lifetime. It is hard to know in the short-term whether or not social change tactics and strategies are effective in the long-term. Yet, the interviewees demonstrated that effectiveness matters. Though unique contexts necessitate different tactics, what has been effective in past actions can be known.

Christian activists often employ the notion that efforts for social transformation are meant to be "faithful, not effective." But the attention on effectiveness in the interviews posed the question: If Christian social action does not strive for effectiveness, then how is it striving for social transformation? If an affirmation of Christian (non)violence as an expression of faithfulness is desirable, then Christians must construct a theological point of view and practice of (non)violence that is either "faithful *and* effective," or a practice in which being "faithful" is not a hindrance to being effective.

Looking at Effectiveness in History and Social Transformation

The interviewees suggested that analysis of historical context was a part of helping to determine effectiveness today. This inquiry includes the study of other historical contexts for the effective deployment of multiple means of social change as well as differences among historical and cultural contexts of violence. Some interviewees pointed to instances of past denial within the tradition of (non)violence, addressing the naïve claim that (non)violence is always effective, whereas violence does not "work." Others posed challenges to whether (non)violence alone, currently or historically, has the capacity to create deep social change. Staughton Lynd, as committed as he is to (non)violence, said that, as a historian, he had to reckon with questions like, "How could slavery have been done away with in the United States without violence? It's not that I don't want there to be an answer, but I don't know what the answer is."

The historians in the interviewee group recognized that in specific historical contexts, fundamental socio-structural change has come about as a result of the forces of violence and (non)violence working together effectively or as polarizing influences within a social struggle. Churchill said Martin Luther King, Jr. was anathema to the white power structure until Black Power became a more prominent threat to white supremacy. Then King became "a great alternative to these guys." Churchill believed that even though King and Malcolm X had real philosophical disagreements over the use of violence and (non)violence, they were working together.

Similarly, Umoja didn't dismiss the influence of (non)violent direct action on the federal government during the Black Freedom struggle, demonstrating that resistance by multiple means created fundamental changes in the South and throughout the country. In Mississippi, there was some (non)violent direct action on desegregation, but, primarily, there was "voter registration work and people committed not to carry guns." There was always "a strong self-defense component" against white supremacist violence, as well as boycotts that were effective at demonstrating the purchasing power of Black people in communities. Change happened through Black people's agency in local movements using all the means at their disposal.

Churchill also described that Gandhi played the polarity of violent extremism in India to his strategic advantage during the struggle for Indian independence from the British Empire:

> The vaunted career of Gandhi exhibits characteristics of a calculated strategy of nonviolence salvaged only by the existence of violent peripheral processes. While it is true that the great Indian leader never deviated from his stance of passive resistance to British colonization, and that in the end, England found it cost-prohibitive to continue its effort to assert control in the face of his opposition, it is equally true that the Gandhian success must be viewed in the context of a general decline in British power brought about by two world wars within a thirty year period.[126]

Gandhi was proficient in firearms, served in the army as a medic (though he condemned himself for his complicity in war-making), supported pacifists empowering themselves with firearms training, and did not oppose establishing military bases to fight the Japanese in World War II.[127]

Churchill sees the absolutist refusal to accept the historic effectiveness of the polarity between violence and (non)violence as another demonstration of the U.S. culture and history of denial. The insistent claim that (non)violence work is "alchemy," means that pacifists cannot point to any evidence "where nonviolence ever actually worked in the context of real violence, but it will. We'll pretend that it did, and we'll go ahead with the expectation that it will." Jensen said that, in a social struggle, there is a need to recognize a role for people who are committed to (non)violence. "But what they need to do is they need to recognize the role of militancy as well."

The theological tradition and practice of white, Christian (non)violence has been a primary source for setting up, implicitly and explicitly, the absolute contradiction between violence and (non)violence theologically, and therefore historically. The dichotomous moral valuing of (non)violence over violence has suppressed the history of competing accounts of effective means. In our interview, I said to Harding that I sensed a contradiction between his deep commitment to (non)violent practice and his historical writings about all forms of Black resistance, violent and (non)violent. He responded, "In a deep sense for me, nonviolence and my connection to it was fundamentally a connection of struggle – learning how to carry out nonviolent struggle for justice and for a new society. And there's no contradiction." That Christian (non)violent activists are called to be "faithful, not effective" in practice often evades these historical complexities, setting up deeper levels of historical denial.

Effectiveness and the Problem of Control

Part of the conviction behind the commitment to faithfulness over effectiveness is the traditional Christian belief that God, and not humans, is in control of history. When the time is right, as determined by God, God will intervene in human affairs to set the world right. "Faithful, not effective" privileges God's time and action, devaluing human action in history.

Most interviewees were suspicious of dominant Christianity's role within the culture by

- reinforcing pacification,
- maintaining the order and status quo of the structures of violence, and
- removing agency from the historical realm.

"Faithful, not effective" is an example of a theme within Christian (non)violence that has the potential to do that. In an early book, Jensen mentions the notion of *kairos*: a time of destiny when the purpose of a person or culture is to be fulfilled.[128] He wrote about the "fine line" between "waiting for the arrival of understanding – *kairos* – and the need for action." With regard to the continuing destruction of the environment, Jensen has more definitively stated that now is the time for communities to push back with effective tactics or hasten this collapse. If not, Jensen contends, the eventual collapse of the planet will result in more violent, long-term consequences than the result of the use of violent tactics to hasten the end of environmental destruction. Forcing change by any means is more faithful to the planet and its inhabitants than waiting for God to intervene. Faithfulness to the earth means intentional human action toward a healthy world.

But individual interviewees were clear that deep social change cannot be forced. Schulman said that one of the lessons of politics and history is "you can't force the *zeitgeist*."[129] There are long periods of regression between progressive periods in U.S. history. These periods of backlash exact an enormous personal price on a large number of persons. "But you do know that the new period is going to come. But you can't force it, no matter how much you want it or need it.... In the meantime, it is important to keep rigorous thought and small, accountable action alive."[130]

Power said that a higher, spiritual perspective helps dominant culture activists to act humbly by accepting that they are culturally situated and are not "the ultimate actor." Power maintained that the use of violence to disrupt is a behavior that reflects the Western culture's need to control. She said that for social transformation to be effective, we have to "surrender the concept of 'make it' do anything."

> Prosperous Americans are accustomed to having a huge amount of control over the circumstances of their lives. It's part of their identity. It's part of our identity as a nation. We can end poverty. All of this dominating that we do all over the world. The perpetrators of that kind, they get away with it because it aligns with our sense of powerfulness as a birthright.... That's part of the Western civilization.... The hubris of Western civilization is the hubris of modernism. We can make things right.... We have a habit of mind. We've inherited a sense of entitlement and power.

Power also said, "For liberation theology to turn and say, 'Let the experiences of the oppressed be the source of our understanding'... was a very important move."

Power further reported that in the complexity of the world situation during the Vietnam anti-War and Black Power movements, the violence that her group employed simply was not going to liberate the oppressed and make the revolution come. It was an attempt to exert more power and dominance in the context of power and dominance. Her group did not realize that they couldn't "actually make that fantasy happen. We cannot 'make' the revolution." There is no way that anyone can know that violence itself is going to effectively lead to a revolutionary situation which is free from the power and dominance that violence inevitably employs.

Power explained that while any social context may appear to have strong tendencies toward specific outcomes, there is no way of knowing when a system will shift from an expected outcome to an unexpected result. Systems of dominance have fallen almost without warning, such as Soviet communism and the Berlin Wall. Such examples demonstrate that "dominance systems are not unchangeable." They can fall and be transformed. Since there is no way of acting in a definitive way that will ensure a desired outcome, there is never a guarantee of effectiveness.

While in agreement with Power's claim that Western culture is motivated by control, Churchill believes that the use of organized violence is not necessarily about control, but the effective alleviation of structural and cultural violence. Furthermore, if violent means of effective structural (versus individual) transformation are about control and coercion, so are effective (non)violent means.[131]

Interviewees stake out different positions over matters of coercion and control. Does effective action seize the moment of change or create it through force? Does "faithful, not effective" cultivate passivity by undermining human agency, thereby reinforcing privilege, in the face of injustice? Or does it keep patterns of dominance in check by challenging the instincts and needs of the members of the dominant culture to be in control? Is militant (non)violence necessarily less controlling and coercive than militant violence? Again, answering these questions is partly a matter of social location and context, including who the agents and communities acting for change are.

Effectiveness:
Negotiating The Liberal-to-Radical Divide

A strong divide among interviewees over what constitutes concrete "effective" violent and (non)violent responses to violence appeared to fall within what Jensen and others describe as a liberal-versus-radical divide. Traditionally understood, liberal political and economic goals accept that the institutions of this society are good and can be redeemed by (non)violent means to serve the interests of all people and the earth. Radical goals imply the complete dissolution of the institutions as agents of violence, which may involve violence to be effective. According to Churchill, the test as to whether (non)violence is revolutionary (radical) instead of reformist (liberal) is whether its principles of practice

> are capable of delivering the bottom-line transformation of state-dominated social relations, which alone constitutes the revolutionary/liberatory process. Where they are found to be incapable of such delivery, the principles must be broadened or transcended altogether as a means of achieving an adequate praxis.[132]

Yet the liberal-radical divide is not so clear-cut between choices of strategies of reform or revolution. Nor is it helpful to equate (non)violence with liberalism and violence with radicalism. Based on their analysis of the contemporary U.S. situation, the interviewees agreed that the United States was not in a revolutionary period. Therefore, most of them thought that organized violence was not a particularly viable radical option. Even if violence were justifiable, it would not be effective. There are a number of reasons for this. The general population is not prepared to understand it, prepare for it, or use it. Neither are most activists.

Primarily, the interviewees saw organized violence as ineffective because of the repressive violence of the state. Schulman said that she understood the need for violence in a revolutionary context. "It's not like I have a "no violence" position," she said, "…but in the American context, the state power is so overwhelming, practically, you can't really win. They can hurt you more than you can hurt them. So it's not a practical strategy." About those who decide to use violence as an organized strategy, Huerta said, "I think they're naïve…. First of all, you're outnumbered. You're not going to win. It's kind of a suicide." The state kills and jails activists and destroys movements that it considers to be a violent threat, using the cultural justification of "necessary" violence to maintain the social order. In the interviewee's opinion, the destruction of any radical element of an activist community at this time would not contribute to overall effectiveness.

If the United States were in a different period, organized violence might make more sense. In the meantime, Kelly admitted that she was not tuned into the debates over violence and (non)violence any longer because she thinks, "We haven't even explored the nonviolent tactics," which include a broad range of lifestyle change and political resistance in the context of radical, local alternative communities. She believes if communities of resistance engaged in both of these (non)violent aspects in a more committed and sacrificial fashion, it would have a significant effect on positive social change. Activists must try such means before resorting to violence.

With clearly different emphases, all interviewees affirmed effective means of action across the liberal-to-radical spectrum, in order to create the conditions for when a radically transformational moment might be seized, the *kairos* moment. Staughton Lynd writes about the difference in thinking through reforms that might be considered revolutionary or radical and reforms that are not.[133] About the various means of advocating for prisoners, Lynd wrote:

> Our maximum program has always been, Shut [the prison] down. Our minimum program has been, Make it into a maximum-security prison with a small supermaximum security section for prisoners who actually have committed serious acts of violence while in prison. We have accomplished the latter…. Presently we are taking up the demand for death-sentenced prisoners that they should have full contact visits throughout their time on Death Row…. This is a struggle we can win. We will conduct it both in the courtroom and on the streets, in the courtroom of public opinion. And if we do so

effectively it will not only seek to achieve an immediate human objective, but to make the public more aware of death-sentenced prisoners as fellow human beings: the perception that may lead, over time, to the abolition of the death penalty. Thus this "reform" – that a person sentenced to death be able to touch and hug members of his family – while it may not be revolutionary, will draw on the efforts of prisoners and their relatives as well as the effort of lawyers, and has a horizon, a penumbra that suggests that a different kind of world is possible.[134]

Embracing the liberal-to-radical spectrum works towards a goal of effectiveness by promoting the understanding that persons have varieties of experience with activism. Persons with different experiences in social change and from different social locations are going to exist with varying levels of ability, knowledge, willingness, and readiness to participate. For Alice Lynd, for example, effective social action always had to be something that was consonant with what she was able to do. During the early Civil Rights and Vietnam era, this had to do practically with the fact that she was a mother:

> My feeling was, yes, I'm willing to do this but as a live-in, not as a sit-in. I didn't want to be involved in things that involved getting arrested and civil disobedience and things of that nature. I was a mother of young children, and it was fine by me to live on the college campus and even to engage with white neighbors as I walked our son to kindergarten through the neighborhood. I was primarily a young mother rather than a civil rights activist. During the Vietnam War, early on, [friends] came to visit us, talking about how the Vietnamese women would go out at night to talk to soldiers and try to win them over to not fighting against the villagers. I had the feeling that I needed to find some equivalent, again as a mother of young children, that I could do that wasn't going to be picketing out in front of the induction center or something like that. But something that I could do consistently, with

being a mother and a teacher of young children as I was then, against the war. I discovered draft counseling.

Even as these scholar-activists primarily represent more radical visions for social transformation, they recognized that their capacity and desire to resist actively developed over time.

Particularly in light of the current era of non-revolutionary regression that the United States is in, the development of a broader culture of resistance requires several other elements, which might be considered more liberal than radical. Schulman likened the gay liberation struggle now to its pre-revolutionary days of an earlier generation, "when so much newly preliminary and yet foundational work can be done."[135] Individuals and communities need to be prepared for the seizing of revolutionary opportunities when they arrive. Therefore, identification of these tactics and strategizing and implementation of multiple means across the liberal-to-radical divide result in effective social transformation over time.

Collective Practices for Effectiveness

Because neither the vast majority nor a committed minority is prepared for the demands of radical action in the United States today, collective practices must work to meet different audiences where they are, seek to create communities of resistance, and prepare the ground for riskier action. Matters of effectiveness deal with how to meet people where they are, to encourage them to push themselves to a more wholehearted commitment to social change, and to hold persons accountable for making sacrifices needed to achieve the changes they claim to desire and seek.

Whatever their opinions on the justifiability of violent or (non)violent tactics, interviewees spoke about four areas in tactics and strategy that have potential as a constellation of effective practices for structural-transformational changes to systems of violence. These four areas focus on

1) Consciousness-raising within both oppressed communities and privileged communities in the broader dominant culture,

2) Organizing for people power,

3) Building alternative communities and lifestyles to prefigure a shift in the political and economic power structures, and

4) Sustained, direct action by a critical mass.

Every circumstance requires its own contextual analysis.

In general terms, holding the matter of the justifiability of violence and (non)violence in tension and suspension, I claim this overall portrayal, if it were collectively enacted within our identified communities of belonging, is faithful to and effective for achieving a profound social transformational end. These practices intend to confront violence at multiple levels, working towards effectively dismantling denial, reversal, entitlement, individualism, abstraction, and human supremacism.

Effectiveness 1 – Consciousness-Raising

Among many efforts, all of the interviewees were involved in consciousness-raising of many kinds: public lecturing, scholarly and popular writing, teaching, organizing educational forums. Since a critical element for the perpetuation of all forms of violence in the U.S. is a denial of its history, for the interviewees, breaking this denial through consciousness-raising is a tactic for social transformation. There are varying ways to raise consciousness, depending on the community.

Consciousness-Raising in the Dominant Culture

Kelly spends much time in the United States creating "some more heightened awareness either through virtue of speaking or writing of people who bear the brunt of our wars." This critical dimension of change humanizes the war-time enemy. Through truth-telling and humanization, consciousness-raising exposes the reversal of falsely identifying the so-called enemy (Iraqis, Afghans, Muslims, etc.) as "freedom-hating" and violent threats, while the invader (United States) is placed on a pedestal as the benevolent, "freedom-loving" liberator.

Like Kelly, B♀ made it clear how consciousness-raising was a necessary addition to other more militant forms of action with a revolutionary purpose. The tactic of property destruction was meant to raise critical consciousness. It gave the George Jackson Brigade "a way to talk." Sabotage created moments in which to raise the following primary point:

> We are at war. Most people don't want to say that or recognize that, but we are. We have an internal war that goes on every day in this country.... The new statistic for California is one in four kids is hungry in this state. One in four. That's the result of a war. A social war of the government against its citizens. So it lets the enemy know that we're aware that it's a war. It lets the people know, if you can write your information in such a way that it exposes those facts.... It lets us start talking about other things.

Consciousness-raising in the dominant culture intends to expose structural violence – how wealth and privilege depend upon the impoverishment, degradation, and death of others. This awareness on the part of the dominant culture is vehemently resisted, but profound social transformation is impossible without raising this basic awareness.

Churchill said the notion that privileged persons will have their consciousness changed by information and then act on that basis, "is to be extremely optimistic." Yet he holds some optimism for the possibility that people can change. Here Churchill noted that "tactical considerations" are not only about revolutionary, material, and structural shifts but influencing "root-level apprehension" of the conditions and thought-structures which have led to endemic structural and cultural violence.

For example, B♀, Schulman, Huerta, and Jensen all spoke directly to the need to raise consciousness about the nature of racism endemic to U.S. history within the dominant culture. Consciousness-raising in the dominant culture may serve to address white denial, racist reversals, and white people's sense of entitlement about their material advantages. Social justice in the United States will never be achieved without dismantling racism at this root level. Yet raising consciousness about racism in the dominant white culture has not effectively eradicated its psychological and material effects. Jensen states that there must be corresponding revolutions on the inside (perceiving, thinking, being) and the outside (breaking down of current system structures).[136] Consciousness-raising lays a groundwork within dominant culture for future possibilities to disrupt and transform structural and cultural violence.

Consciousness-Raising in Oppressed Communities

Schulman and Umoja stressed that just because persons live in oppressed identity communities does not automatically mean that they will have a political consciousness about the structural nature of oppression and violence.[137] Therefore, political consciousness-raising in marginalized communities is also critical. Umoja emphasized that the primary obstacle to the liberation of oppressed communities is their acceptance of the terms of their own oppression: they do not believe they can be free. Speaking about several communities from Blacks in the United States to Palestinians, Umoja said,

> People who are oppressed have to be ungovernable....[138] It's not just a question of guns or weaponry or anything like that, but how determined are the people to achieve whatever the political goal is. Look at struggles we see in Palestine. People are tremendously determined to assert their self-determination. Even if they don't have guns, they're throwing rocks. It appears that Palestine is not going to die because in the minds of these people, it is worth them sacrificing their lives for and putting their bodies and lives in jeopardy to disrupt this system they see is oppressing them. It's really a question of "what is the will of the people?" Not just a small group but the majority of the people. Are they willing to accept oppression? What are they willing to do to disrupt it? They have to see that the system that oppresses them is illegitimate and they have to feel that they have the capacity to

defeat it and they have the capacity to be in command of their own affairs.

Each community has to determine in each context what means are necessary and effective to defeat the system that oppresses them. But to assess those means, Umoja understands there has to be a consciousness in the first place:

People just have to have that type of insurgent consciousness. That's lacking right now.... In the United States, overall, there's a lack of insurgent consciousness. I look at my students today. Just the thought that there could potentially be a revolution is different from when I was a young man.... I thought we had more hope. Not just hope, but more feeling that there were radical alternatives and possibilities. Right now, I don't see that. That lack of imagination comes from just not seeing those possibilities. The world is different. The world I grew up in – you had Vietnam going on; you had these revolutions going on in Africa, Latin America. It wasn't just the United States, but all these places; you had all this insurgent activity. It's not like that right now. Something similar has to be there for us to even think a revolution is possible. To think that significant social change is possible is the most significant weapon we have right now: our own imaginations and minds.

Every interviewee saw that raising the critical, political consciousness of oppressed communities was crucial, particularly as socio-structural change does not emanate from the dominant culture of a society, but from and across the margins of society. Schulman explained:

Revolutionary movements are not born in suburbs. They're born in different kinds of places where different kinds of people are living in front of each other.... Mostly change, and this is true for cultural change and aesthetic change, starts in the margins. Then it moves to the center. Change does not start in the mainstream. The mainstream absorbs it from the margins. The most effective ways to make social change are from subcultures and counter-cultures. Then those ideas become mainstream ideas. New ideas are not produced in the mainstream in America, because the mainstream is so homogenous and can't conceptualize. That's why we're in so much trouble – because so many people can't conceptualize.

ACT-UP was a highly successful aspect of the overall gay liberation movement because it spoke from the margins. By contrast, Schulman's opinion is that the current gay liberation movement is so assimilated to the mainstream and conformed to middle-class norms such as marriage that their strategies today fail to make fundamental structural changes.

Schulman said that most radical, important work in this country takes place in and across marginalized subcultures in the United States. For example, Schulman raises consciousness about Palestinian self-determination within gay and lesbian subculture – who, like any other community in the United States, has no face for Palestine. "Most of the people who support the current regime only have received wisdom. They haven't thought it through for themselves."

> On any issue, there will always be hardcore people who will never change their minds on anything. But you don't have to persuade everybody, all you need is a critical mass. I think there are five communities in the United States that really want to move forward on Palestine and are looking for leadership: LGBT, secular Jews, African-Americans, academics, and artists. These are communities where, if credible leaders who they recognize – who are usually only subcultural – would give them permission to advance their thinking, they would. That's my responsibility right now…. The job for someone like me, who is a very low-level, subcultural organizer, is just to make my community more aware. Other people are doing it in their community. When the moment that certain kinds of policy things come up, then there will be various subcultures that are sophisticated about those things.

Effectiveness 2 –
Organizing for People Power

Information of all kinds serves as a corrective to denial. Information empowers oppressed communities – to engage in critical understanding and to act locally in ways no longer bound by cultural and structural denial. Schulman noted that story-telling and consciousness-raising are important but are not a substitute for other means of social change. People need more than stories and awareness; they need tools and collective power. Huerta said,

> We are a very uninformed society. Dangerously uninformed. The average person doesn't know how things work – government, political machinery. People don't realize that they have the power to have an influence in government. This is one thing that we teach our people: that we can get our Board of Supervisors to give us some money that we need for the sidewalks, and the streetlights, and the swimming pool, and things of this nature. Once they can learn that, then they sense that they can make a difference, that they can be in the decision-making. The average person doesn't have a clue.

To Huerta, poor and marginalized communities don't need abstractions. They need specific information and concrete tools by which to act. "You've gotta be specific. You really have to educate people. To generalize, you are not really educating them." Reversing the false portrayals of the oppressed will never be achieved without bringing people both critical awareness and tools by which marginalized persons can act together.

Consciousness-raising is not effective until it moves into collective action. Huerta said education and consciousness-raising serve a limited effect without the parallel process of organizing people for political and economic power. When I asked Huerta what she believed to be the (non)violent strategies that promote social change most effectively today, she answered, "Just organizing. I think just organizing and educating people." What constitutes organizing and education today is the same as in earlier movements:

- raising money,
- hiring and training organizers,
- going into the community,
- meeting with hundreds of people one-on-one,
- holding house meetings,
- creating neighborhood organizations,
- learning direct democracy,
- choosing and rotating leaders,
- teaching people how to research and plan,
- creating educational forums.

In Huerta's mind, educating and organizing is fundamentally about developing leaders. Organizing always starts with education that gives people empowering information and specific tools to become leaders in order to change their immediate circumstances. There are tensions and connections in severely marginalized and exploited communities like the farm workers in central California, between consciousness-raising and meeting basic community needs. She described varied small, local organizing efforts effectively organizing to get sidewalks, curbs, and streetlights in rural areas, passing bond issues for a local gymnasium and swimming pool. Small victories such as these allowed for more extensive efforts to raise consciousness and work towards increasing wages for all local farm workers. Financial literacy training led to matching grant programs, micro-enterprise loan development, and a larger understanding of economic power. Because dozens of small local grassroots initiatives had been successful, the organization was able to mobilize around broader issues such as health care. They brought together multiple strategies into one campaign: postcard and letter-writing to legislators, also picketing their fundraisers, creating forums with other organizations, media strategies, story-telling, even fasting.

Most local, grassroots initiatives require small victories to keep momentum and to believe achieving political power is possible. Schulman saw this necessary psychological component within (non)violent social change in disempowered communities. She said, "When you try a strategy, there has to be a chance that it can succeed.

Because if you don't have victories, you can't have a movement. Human beings need victories; it's a human thing. Even tiny victories." The "faithful, not effective" approach fails to recognize that even small-scale effectiveness motivates commitment to a longer-term vision of change in addition to, if not apart from, a faith perspective.

Moving from consciousness to implementing action is incredibly challenging. Schulman discussed how difficult it is to organize communities that have been historically disempowered:

> One of the problems of organizing powerless people or people who have been excluded from power is that they are not proactive. They don't have the feeling or experience that they could have an idea and that idea could actually happen.... When you're organizing people who are powerless, your job is to transform them into implementers so that they can actually take responsibility for having ideas and for following through and implementing. That's possible by creating positive environments and communities where people depend on each other and a culture of accountability; real leadership can be there.

Caution: Organizing versus Organizations

Umoja agreed that for the Black community, this moment in history is "a period of time of building consciousness and institutions and organizing people." Consciousness-raising and organizing prepare communities to agitate on issues like police brutality, health care, education, and prisons. Given the intractable nature of economic power, Umoja noted that even significant reform-oriented solutions eventually require significant social movements to make real change. Movement-building is significant in today's social change environment:

> Right now, we have organizations; we don't have a movement per se.... I remember when it was a movement. Everybody in my community knew what the Black Panther Party was. I can't say that about my organization, that everybody in my neighborhood knows about [it]. It's a different period.

Everybody knew there was a significant anti-war movement. I remember we were even thinking when I was a teenager, "Man, should we register or not?" If you have a significant movement, it puts it on everybody's agenda.

Umoja points to some of the problems with community organizing which have developed since the movement era of the sixties and seventies:

I see a lot of good, young activists who might be interested in particular things. But because they have these jobs working for non-profits – that becomes their agenda, whatever the non-profit's agenda is. I think that's part of the problem. These people in SNCC, they were working for pennies. I'm not saying people shouldn't be compensated, if we had a capacity to pay people. But a lot of times, I think they're working around things that are disconnected from what people want and need and desire, folks who are struggling. Look at our educational system. Or, people losing their houses right now. That's not necessarily where the dollars for organizing people [are]. For non-profits, it's not where the money is, so we don't have any activity around that.

Schulman concurs with Umoja, commenting that in the current era we have bureaucracies and not "real activism. ...there are no structures in place radical enough to be able to mobilize people to respond effectively" to any issue such as "budget cuts, lack of jobs, lack of educational opportunities, foreclosures, etc."[139]

Huerta also noted that organizing is different today than in more radical times. "Cesar never wanted the people who worked for the union to have more money than the workers. He wanted them to live at the same level of poverty, so to speak.... But that changed." Since then, the non-profit sector was organized differently. The Farm Worker movement had to compete for the best organizers, to professionalize and offer salaries. Union organizers were very well trained and began to receive "nice, big fat salaries." Furthermore, Huerta noted, the economy has become so stratified that individuals can no longer make the same kind of commitments that they once might have been able to make.

> The way that our country is now structured financially makes it very difficult for people to make a full-time commitment. Back in the day when we started, rents were forty dollars a month. Gas was 27 cents a gallon. People could afford to be committed. People hitchhiked everywhere. We have this whole fear ambience around our country now so that people are afraid to help each other out. People won't talk to each other. Everything is so expensive. So people can hardly afford to be a full-time volunteer. People have to work two jobs to pay the bills. It's just very expensive to fulfill your basic needs. So in the United States, I think it's very difficult for people to commit a lot of time.

Increasing levels of structural violence impact the ability to organize.

Staughton Lynd had an even deeper critique of organizing: there is an "implicit inequality" between the organizer and the organized.[140]

> I have come to the conclusion that everything we did in the 1960s presupposed a superficial and inaccurate conception of organizing. This was true of the labor movement, the Alinsky movement for community organizing,[141] SNCC in the South, and SDS in the North. The idea was... you come into a situation; you sleep on the floor and eat peanut butter sandwiches. Or you take a room in the motel or whatever. Your conception is that you are not going to be there very long. You are just going to help people form their own organization with leaders that are responsible to the rank and file. Once you've brought that into being, then your work is over. You leave. There are all kinds of statements from people to the effect that this is exactly what folks sought to do.

In the place of organizing by outsiders, Lynd counsels and lives an "intense localism." A given project should not be thought of

> ...merely as a tool for social change, but as a community.... The spirit of a community, as opposed to an organization, is

not, We are together to accomplish this or that end, but, We are together to face together whatever life brings.[142]

For Lynd, organizations – both non-profits and labor unions – promote a "complex and restrictive institutional environment that stands in the way of creative and spontaneous action from below" and leaves prominent power dynamics in place,[143] reinforcing the existing economic structures.[144]

Organizing and consciousness-raising may be particularly effective in bringing people together around shared concerns and actions in a non-revolutionary context. There is a greater possibility of bringing people into social change activism through such means as preparing and creating the understanding and conditions for later action. Those uninitiated to social action may be provided better critical tools to understand more radical actions, even if they do not take them. No matter the social location or length of experience of activists, organizing and consciousness-raising should be ongoing tactics aimed at radical social change, to deepen critical analysis at all levels of engagement and to renew veteran activist circles.

Effectiveness 3 – Alternative Communities

Radical transformation is rarely achieved without a long-term investment in community-building. No matter what the interviewees believed about the use of violence or (non)violence for social transformation, all agreed that resistance to a culture of violence, particularly economic, could only be nurtured in community. While religious institutions are fraught with inconsistencies and hypocrisy over matters of violence, certain religious communities were viewed as examples where resistance to popular culture was made publicly manifest. When I asked Kelly about where the particular sense of (non)violence began to be nurtured in her life, she described how the nuns in school and church showed her:

> You could be reasonably happy and fulfilled without having the slightest interest in acquiring personal wealth. They shared

everything in common; they wore the same outfits in common. They worked for no salary whatsoever, did good work, and we always presumed they were doing more good work for people who were less well-off than we were elsewhere…. They were pretty astonishing, educated women, given the resources available to them. That, to me, was a fairly heroic example of how a life could be organized with other people to try to accomplish certain, writ large, works of mercy as opposed to works of war. So that part of Christianity as it was mediated to me is really important.

As in much literature on Christian (non)violence, Kelly and Dear pointed out that a Christian tradition existed outside of the political and economic order prior to the adoption of Christianity by the Roman Empire. Kelly referenced early Christian communities' "300 years of witness" and active consideration "of the risk to give in to the military." There is scriptural evidence that suggests these early Christian communities shared economic resources across class boundaries. This usage of historic Christian origins as examples for counter-cultural, anti-institutional communities served as one of the strongest currents in defining the possibilities for an effective Christian (non)violence that offers real alternatives to structural violence.

Christian community provided Dear with a basis for making radical commitments. For five hundred years, his Jesuit order has taken seriously preparing for life-long vows. During preparation for taking vows of poverty, chastity, and obedience, Dear and three fellow ordinands decided to prepare an additional vow, modeling it on Gandhi's vow of (non)violence. Dear described the years of practicing, praying, studying, and experimenting about (non)violence. In his years of obeying the vow, he has been "scared to death and shaken," beaten and mocked, and went to prison. He put himself in many of these positions:

> In some very dark moments, I did not respond with violence because I said, "I professed a vow." So something happened to me…. There's a tradition in our Catholic, Christian, Western spirituality for two thousand years of taking these holy vows to God. In Christian language, there is a grace there….

Dear believed that the depth and length of such a process in Christian communities could have a greater transformational impact.[145]

Harding put his growing interest in (non)violence into practice when he joined a faith community in the Chicago area and became a part of its pastoral team:

> It was in that context that my whole sense of the meaning of nonviolence began to grow. In '58, some of us from that congregation began talking about what was going on in the South. And began asking ourselves about the brotherhood and sisterhood across racial lines that we said we were so glad to represent on the South Side of Chicago. We kept asking, "Well, what if we were in the South? What would it mean there?" The Mennonites have chosen this term of "discipleship" as a way of identifying their way of being, and we were asking – what would it mean to be disciples in the deep South? Some of us… said, "Why don't we go and find out what it would mean?".… So five of us, three whites and two Blacks, got into a station wagon and promised that we would do our best to remain committed to our conviction that we were brothers and that no human laws could separate us.

This smaller group began to ask questions within a larger Mennonite community:

> What do nonviolence and nonresistance do or say in the light of the struggle going on in the South? What do nonviolent Christians have to say to that?

In other words, alternative communities are not meant only for their own improvement, but to impact the violence and (non)violence of others.

Though Quakers, at the time of their interview, the Lynds described the surprise with which they found themselves attending a number of primarily Christian groups to discuss current issues of concern and action, as well as spiritual practice. Staughton Lynd tried to explain why they found themselves in such communities at this time:

After all these years of struggle and befriending this group and that group, we find ourselves going to three different sets of meetings with religious seekers. Now, why are we doing that? … It's as if you don't pick these people. It's that they are called to something that you are also called to – the ardor, the sense of being devoted to something that is speaking through all of us.

Lynd said it was difficult to know the role of such entities, particularly in a time when it is unclear if the nation is headed towards greater openness or fascism. As a historian, he noted that in some of the longest periods of barbarism, Christian monasteries and desert communities "were indispensable to the human spirit." Neither he nor Alice

had the faintest idea of why we're meeting with these people…. It has something to do with the fact that capitalism has destroyed Youngstown…. Under such circumstances, the different kinds of voices that "crieth in the wilderness… Make plain the way of the Lord" [Isaiah 40:3] are important.

People need concrete communities in which to resist and act against the structures of violence in the culture. These communities are meant to work against individualism, sustain voices against violence, and actively refuse to go along with the structures of economic violence that destroy communities. This work happens through various practices of shared living, studying, spiritual rituals, and direct confrontation.

Many alternative communities have a critique of the economic structures that are at the heart of their vision. The critique is lived out in sharing economic resources. Huerta described the union headquarters at La Paz at the Farm Workers' movement. It was formed on the basis of Gandhi's concept of the ashram, where all things were held in common:

From day one of the organization, we discussed a lot about Gandhi, how [César] wanted to form the union. [Gandhi] had ashrams… That was the concept that began the headquarters of the union. We called it La Paz, peace. It was a community. Now looking back, I don't think we could have built the union any other way. No one took salaries – like the ashram concept where people work, and all of what they earned went to the organization. That's pretty much the way that we lived. Whatever money we raised went towards the union, to build a union. At La Paz, we had a community kitchen where everybody ate together.... We had several trainings, and we would bring all the farm workers up there to live so that they could get trained. So everybody lived together, and we had a community kitchen. It was that concept from the ashram concept that we did that. People lived off food stamps.

Kelly is committed to creating shared community, nurtured outside of formal institutions, focused on just economic living as a form of (non)violence:

I want to be part of that effort within the peace movement that links change of lifestyle to the possibility of pacifism. 'Cause I don't think it is appropriate to talk about pacifism if we are not willing, almost in the same breath, to talk about simple living and sharing resources and preferring service to dominance. If we don't accomplish those changes, then I don't see how we can have a pacifistic relationship to other people, because our lifestyles are so inherently violent in the American way of life.

Kelly posed a series of questions about learning to practice resistance to economic domination through communal living and lifestyle changes:

How am I going to travel? ... Am I in the habit of tilting increasingly towards actions that carry small little slap-on-the-wrist penalties rather than something that would really cause a change in my patterns and some measure of sacrifice? To what extent am I willing to say that I should be part of, at least have some agrarian component in my lifestyle, so that the hard work of planting and cultivating food is something I am familiar with?

Power concurred that resistance includes looking closely and candidly at our economic behavior:

To the extent that we can openly and honestly reflect on the inadequacy of our old tools, our given modes, to that extent, that's how much this can take hold, and we can participate in it. The model in my life is again coming face-to-face with the fact of the outcome of violence and integrating that – literally "paying the price" for it, acknowledging the harm and suffering we have caused. Instead of righteously condemning everybody else, you are looking more clearly at your own effects. If we can do that really honestly and wisely, we are going to be more effective. People have said, "What can you do?" I say, "Well, you know, here's a really simple one: Take moral responsibility for every relationship that you are involved with by reason of economics." Just do that. That will do it. That will become overwhelming, so choose one. I will not consume alienated products. Or fair trade. I will know the person who wove this cloth. Whatever. Find your answers to that. This is a creative process. We're all in denial about what we're stealing and who we're murdering – human and other-than-human. We have to look at that.

To adequately claim (non)violence as a method of social transformation, communities (whether secular or Christian institutions or alternative communities) must look clearly at their economic behaviors. Ultimately, the transformation of violence implies sacrificing the sense of entitlement around an economic lifestyle that comes with the economic privileges and material advantages of structural violence. This kind of collective, anti-economic approach to (non)violence is rare and rarely achieved outside of community.

Caution: Lifestyle Activism Does Not Equal Social Transformation

Most changes in lifestyle, even in concert with others, offer little by way of actual challenge to structures of violence, and have a weak claim to being effective (non)violent tactics; that is, addressing violence at its multiple levels. Staughton and Alice Lynd have a life-long commitment to living in community and creating community resistance to local economic injustices. For Staughton Lynd, we need to experience what a new society might be like with "prefigurative[146] experimentation, the construction and nurturing of new institutions… a horizontal network of self-governing local entities comprising a 'dual power' that begins to manage our common affairs in a new way." When and where these parallel institutions have been created currently in the United States, they have yet to be sustainable or to provide substantive alternatives to actual structures of power.[147] He wrote:

> In the area of economics, participatory democracy cannot provide a full alternative to established institutions except by capturing and transforming them.… Can we not agree that participatory democracy, understood as a movement building new institutions side-by-side with the old, cannot provide bread and land? Failure to face this problem realistically will result in the poor turning for help to those who can provide it at least in part, and the co-optation of protest movements by the Establishment.[148]

SNCC's radical efforts to organize Black voters in the deep South reverted to democratic party politics. This resulted in the demise of SNCC itself, partly for "ignoring the need for an economic program" to help Blacks "find their way beyond desperate poverty and economic dependence."[149] Lynd encourages alternative communities to actually think through the development of sustainable local institutions versus the current reality of alternative communities serving as opportunities for privileged people to change their lifestyles. Staughton Lynd cautioned against a kind of naïve optimism about what alternative living and "green" efforts really contribute in light of the barbarism of capitalism:

> I am darned if I'm going to be a middle-class tree-planter and market-gardener and this sort of thing, as if that were any sort of any kind of real solution to kids growing up in the inner city. This doesn't mean that we don't have a garden right about ten feet from where you're sitting. But people who have put all their energies into such things and who, worse,

conceptualize them as a real road to the future, I think are deceiving themselves.

Churchill and Jensen also mounted a substantial critique of "alternative" lifestyles. The inherent individualism of lifestyle activism bears little to no effect on structures of violence and are often co-opted by the systems to which they are alternatives. Recycling is not a "bad thing," Churchill said, but economic structures have turned it into a profit-making business. Many things that people recycle probably "ought not to have been used" in the first place. Riding a bicycle or

> getting your own wind generator, which presumes you could afford one, doesn't alter the fundamental disparity and resource distribution and so forth that make the baseline expectation of what quality of life should be in this country any different.

In the dominant culture, lifestyle activism takes the current economic system and human supremacism for granted. Churchill noted how "green jobs" and "green technology" is still a structurally violent point of view that "leaves the fundamental genocidal equation in place," as far as justifying the destruction of the earth and those most closely associated with it. There's nothing in the green revolution

> that suggests that somebody, who's already having so little impact that they happen to be in the upper Amazon region in Venezuela, shouldn't be dispossessed and their land put to better use – so that other people can continue to enjoy the level of affluence they happen to enjoy right now while having a lesser environmental impact.

Therefore, within the context of eradicating structures of violence, they are not actively, disruptively (non)violent. Overall consumption and the set of expectations that go into the nature of even a working-class lifestyle in this country create incredible disequilibrium throughout the earth and world. From an Indigenous perspective, the knowledge of environmental destruction calls for balance in all relations and beginning to bring things back. For Churchill, this is a fundamentally anti-economic, anti-growth point of view.

Jensen said that personal lifestyle change might be important, but it is not enough:

> People forget that personal change is not social change. There are no personal solutions to social problems. If you put this in another context, it becomes really obvious. I mean, does anybody really think that composting would have stopped Hitler? It's like, let's all ride our bikes to work to stop capitalism. It's just crazy.

The confusion about what real change looks like plagues environmentalism today and connects to Jensen's previous analysis of learned helplessness. He said,

> There's a lot of people who end up stuck on this notion of "if I change myself that'll change other people." That has absolutely destroyed any potential for social change the environmental movement may have ever had.... The notion there is only personal change has so metastasized across social movements that a lot of people can't even conceptualize the notion of organized political resistance. They think that recycling is environmental. They think that green consumerism is environmental. Vegetarianism's going to save the world.

Alternative communities and lifestyles may appeal to a large portion of the general population. They may nurture and sustain a community through actual resistance to structures of violence as bread and land are offered in real ways. Currently, these efforts have limits to actually confronting and transforming violence or offering real alternatives to the status quo. Alternative communities and lifestyle activism should not be a substitute for organized resistance, but sites for its development and enactment.

Effectiveness 4 – Disruptive, Direct Action

At the level of activism where persons and communities are already involved in some degree of social change, interviewees all affirmed that fundamental socio-structural change demands increasingly radical tactics that effectively and collectively resist and transform power. The central aspect of this effectiveness is to disrupt the control of the systems of cultural, structural, and direct violence. A critical element of effective disruption by small groups is the collective ability to sustain it.

Dear referenced something he heard from Daniel Berrigan, "In the end, positive social change happens when good people break bad laws and accept the consequences." Dear went on to reflect:

> All the movements from the abolitionists, the suffragists, civil rights movement, labor movement, anti-war movement, were all hopeless throughout their whole life, and then, suddenly, there was a breakthrough of hope. Why? Because ordinary people kept at it. They didn't go away. There was no sign of change. There was no way they were going to get rid of slavery. There's no way women would ever get the right to vote. There's no way Jim Crow is coming down, or the Vietnam War is going to end, or the Berlin Wall's gonna fall, or apartheid's going to end, or nuclear weapons are going to be dismantled, or women will be ordained. It's hopeless, and they work for it anyway. Thousands of people kept at it, and that's how change happens. Then if you go farther, in the end, leaders, ordinary people, committed civil disobedience and suffered, and suddenly there was a breakthrough. And you go, "Well, it was a miracle!" No, the miracle was that they kept at it. The challenge is to keep at it, and some people have to really take risks…. If you are talking about social change, I find that exciting – ordinary people, keeping at the day-to-day work, doing one or two things for some area in the struggle, not giving up even though there's no sign of hope. And then some people also crossing the line and actually engaging the law, which upholds the structure of violence and oppression. You have to engage the law at some point. That's how the change happens.

Elements of Collective, Disruptive Action 1 – Discipline, Persistence

Umoja said that (non)violence is an effective means of social transformation when it is disruptive and disciplined:

> I don't think I ever really believed that you could just create an army and just be able to seize power, but we used to say stuff like armed struggle would be the fundamental way that oppressed people would be able to gain power. It creates the type of image that you are going to have an army that's going to come do this, an army of the people. But really an army is a disciplined formation. I think the major question [is] if you are actually going to have fundamental social change, because you've got interests that are not willing to give it up freely, that you are going to have a capacity to disrupt their control. And people have to be able to resist that through whatever means that they have. That might be that they're not going to go to work. That might be that they're not gonna purchase. It might be that they're going to do stuff to make sure that the system's capacity to do those things don't take place. All that doesn't involve somebody picking up a gun.

Umoja affirmed that the sacrifice, organization, discipline, and training required by (non)violent, mass disruption impose extremely difficult demands:

> Nonviolent direct action requires a tremendous amount of discipline. It requires a lot of commitment. I describe to my students the sit-ins. I said, "Think about this. Somebody's cursing at you. Pouring something on you, pouring milk or whatever on you, spitting on you. You gotta maintain your discipline through all that. You can't react. You can't curse the person." To a class of fifty, I said, "There are probably three people in here that could do that...." Practice over a period of time! So you got to get a massive amount of people to do that.

Elements of Collective, Disruptive Action 2 – Research, Training, and Organization

The ability to disrupt systems in a sustained manner requires several other elements to be effective. Schulman remarked how ACT UP's strategy was like that of Martin Luther King, Jr.

Basically [King's strategy] was

- you educate yourself, so you are totally informed on your issue;

- you make proposals that are winnable, doable, and reasonable;

- when the powers that oppose you refuse to act, you do self-purification, which in our case was nonviolent training or [civil disobedience] training; and

- then you do a direct action.

Those are the four steps. He lays them right out.[150] That's exactly how we operated. There's no point in making a demand that's not winnable and doable. Your demands have to be reasonable. You have to be an adult and show how it can be done. That's what we did. We were like: this is how you study this drug. This is how you develop this insurance policy. We did all the groundwork – for needle exchange, for housing for homeless people with AIDS, for everything. Then we presented everything to them, *fait accompli*. Then we did actions to make them do it. And then they did it. But that's the winning strategy.... It always works. It works in life. If you are really clear and understand more than your opponent, ultimately, you have an advantage.

Schulman described the massive amount of education, training, and administrative work that went into (non)violence as an effective group of tactics that supported disruption. Working across movements, women from the no-nukes peace movement provided (non)violence trainings for mass civil disobedience: "People learned how to be carried away, how not to resist, how not to fight back, and all that kind of stuff." In addition,

We had a hugely complex structural infrastructure because we had very sick people getting arrested. They had medications and they had all kinds of problems. We had a really great system where every person who was arrested was noted, and everyone was watched out for... but it took a lot of organization. There were people in ACT UP where that's what they did. That was a very, very, very strong part of the whole thing. It had to be.... Especially when you had people whose health was so compromised.

Sometimes disruption occurs spontaneously. But interviewees agreed that disruption is most effective when it is disciplined and organized, supported with a structure and training.

Caution:
Effective Disruption is Always Opposed By Power

A community of struggle will know when a (non)violent witness has been effective in the face of oppositional power. Staughton Lynd noted the difference, historically, between (non)violence as a moral witness and (non)violence as an effective disruptive tactic. Important (non)violent witnesses usually fail to produce any substantive structural change because they pose no real threat to systems of violence; for example, conscientious objection to war.[151]

The existing law of conscientious disobedience to military orders is framed for Quakers, members of the Church of the Brethren, Mennonites, Jehovah's Witnesses, Amish. People who come from a pacifist background and who the powers-that-be know are never going to amount to anything other than a hill-of-beans – numerically. So it's a perfect illustration of what Herbert Marcuse had called repressive tolerance.[152] "Oh, we're broad-minded. This is the United States of America. We're going to let you Quakers deal with bedpans in some hospital. We're not going to force you to fight. We know that's against your religious training and belief."

This approach stands in contrast to the way the government deals with individual conscientious objectors who object to fighting in specific wars today (versus objection to war in general) on the basis of specific objections to the unjust nature of a particular war, or because of the nature of the crimes they have witnessed being committed by the U.S. military. These individuals "don't get any kind of break" and pay a tremendous price for their disobedience. The U.S. government cannot allow for such contextual objection, as any mass resistance to service would constitute an effective collective disruptive threat to the U.S. military.

Significantly disruptive (non)violence is always opposed by power. When it is not a threat, it is tolerated. Lynd has written about why the (non)violent legal right of workers to strike has been attacked by economic elites: because worker strikes have the strong potential to disrupt economic systems.[153] The government and labor unions have worked against the (non)violent right to strike in both legislative and collective bargaining processes. Union leaders wanted the economic advantages of contracts to assure government and corporate interests they were not a threat and to control the rank-and-file workers. Unions have bargained away the right to strike in the life of given contracts, while various levels of government legislated against mass picketing and for replacement workers. Systems of structural violence effectively denied working-class people access to a disruptive, (non)violent tactic, precisely because it was effective. The withdrawal of an effective (non)violent tactic potentially results in increased violence:

> The stage is set for working-class violence. A handful of strikers are expected to watch passively as carloads of strike replacements are escorted by the police into their place of work, to labor at their machines or desks, and take bread from the mouths of their children. When workers decline such institutionally choreographed masochism, they are discharged by their employer and hustled off to jail by the authorities. They may also be denigrated by middle-class supporters as "impatient" and "impulsive" persons, who "ill-advisedly" took matters into their own hands, rather than trusting their lawyers to produce victory through the Labor Board and the courts.[154]

Caution:
The Disruptive Power of Property Destruction?

If opposition by state power is an indicator of potential effectiveness, then property destruction might be considered a form of effective disruption. Without a doubt, those activists who employ or even threaten property (destruction, trespass, occupation) as a means of resistance have met with more repressive violence and severe state punishment than any other community of resistance in the United States. Many of the debates over violence and (non)violence in current social-change activism in the U.S. center around the practice of property destruction.

The matter of property destruction has been a tense debate within (non)violent activist circles. Dear talked about a Plowshares action in which he trespassed on a military base in 1993 and hammered on an F-15 nuclear fighter bomber:

> The government said I committed violence. All the movement, the churches, the country, the *New York Times* said I committed violence. Everybody who was for nonviolence said I'm a practitioner of violence.... I'm arguing that I was actually beginning to get rid of a weapon! Of dismantling it! ... Is hammering on the nuclear weapon violence? No, I think you can knock over a table that is totally oppressing poor people.

Kelly recalled a (non)violent action from twenty years previous when there "was a big question about whether or not to pour blood" on a missile silo. She remembered a tremendous amount of questioning and anger around these contentious tactics. But Churchill questions why, when "the level of violence that is endemic to this system is so monumental and continuous" that "we have debates about whether or not it's violent to break a window at Starbucks in response?"

B♀ identified that the reversals and entitlements of all forms of violence are always, in the end, about power and private property ownership. Sabotage and property destruction strikes at the heart of structural, economic violence. Jensen notes that the smashed window of a corporate enterprise belongs to the rich and the rock to the non-rich.[155] Ownership of property in the United States has been established by violent force. "The acquisition and maintenance of the property of the rich is the central motivating factor impelling nearly all state violence."[156] Property destruction intends to raise awareness of this denial of violence. Repressive state response indicates that such questioning cannot be tolerated at this level. There is much debate over whether or not tactics of property destruction are effective. Nonetheless, these tactics appear to have more of a disruptive effect on the state and economic power than much current (non)violent action does.

It seems appropriate that the Christian (non)violence community takes a stronger role in analyzing structural violence and considers deeply the ways in which U.S. Christian theology undergirds the attitude toward the inviolable nature of private property ownership. As B♀ shared previously, there is a way to engage in organized violence for the disruption of power through attacks on infrastructure without intending to take a human life, while recognizing that there is no way to control for the possibility that humans may be killed through the destruction of property. Furthermore, the spectacle of property destruction gains public attention, which provides a platform for consciousness-raising about structures of violence. Nonetheless, property destruction as a tactic, like all forms of disruptive action, should be set within an analysis of structures and strategy of collective action. Property destruction may be effective, but activists must still ask: effective to do what?

Barriers to Effectiveness 1 – Habit and Embracing the Familiar

A fundamental problem with contemporary (non)violence as it is currently practiced is that it relies upon many of the same tactics of earlier protest movements. Protests are coordinated. There is little element of disruption or surprise. Activists and the police are so accustomed to the traditional tactics of (non)violent protest that they generally pose no real threat to the state and no substantial risk to participants. Umoja said, "Sometimes we get too committed. We think just by going there with signs and stuff, because that's what we're used to doing – things will change." Power noted that (non)violent action today has become a construct of repeated actions. (Non)violence is "no longer a word that emerges from the center of the chest… It feels so morally superior, there's a nice comfort in the protest action." She contrasts this with the kinds of actions that emerge from an experience of being in solidarity with the dispossessed in society and acting on that basis. In terms of re-using tactics, Schulman said,

> One of the problems is that people repeat losing strategies all the time because they embrace the familiarity. It feels comfortable to them. For five years, I worked on the St. Patrick's Day parade.[157] …I was arrested five years in a row trying to march in that fucking parade. I dealt with Irish people a lot. I went to Ireland. Here are the only white people that had ever been colonized. They'd been in this situation for 800 years. They have never found a strategy that could create change. They did the same thing over and over and over and over. This love of familiarity was greater than the desire for change. I kept saying to them, "Why do you want to do something that you know is not going to work?" And they just couldn't try something new. There are people who are like that; it's a human trait…. There are certain kinds of people who get tied into certain kinds of repetitions, regardless of their consequences. There are cultural passivities that are developed around repetitions. That's why they never won. That's why the situation has never changed. It's so absurd. Because they just wouldn't try anything that could win.

Barriers to Effectiveness 2 – Self-Interest (Entitlements)

Schulman described what made ACT UP effective in their actions was group willingness and ability to make the sacrifices necessary to carry on research and action over time:

> It just has to be a *zeitgeist* where a critical mass of people are willing to take a stand and make a commitment for a period of

time. It doesn't have to be a majority. In this country, great change is made by very small numbers of people. Very small. But they have to be extremely committed. … [There] are hundreds of people in ACT UP who were doing nothing but ACT UP. They were at ACT UP five days a week. Everything, all their friends were in ACT UP. They quit their jobs to work in ACT UP. People in ACT UP did not know what each other did for a living, and they didn't know each other's last names…. Of course, you can't do that forever. But you need a small group of people who can do it for a number of years, and then you can achieve huge social transformation. But if you don't have that, nothing's going to happen.

Schulman observed that the difference between the gay community of ACT UP and the queer community today in New York City is

separated by the gulf of action fueled by suffering on one hand and the threat of pacifying assimilation on the other. When the ACT UPers were in their twenties, they were dying. And the replacements for the dead, these young, were on the road to normalcy. The young had the choice to live quietly because of the bold fury of the old.[158]

Many people will not commit to radical action unless they understand their own self-interests are at stake. People at intersections of dominant social identities are less likely and less willing to understand the context of violence out of which other forms of violence grow and therefore may see little reason why their own self-interest may be affected by violence. Without experience, knowledge, or self-interest in other communities, most persons in the dominant culture will do little to nothing to disrupt their current social identity and comfort level in order to take almost any kind of action, much less seriously disruptive action. Huerta describes the disconnect between organizing some of the most marginalized people in the United States to act, while persons with privilege can't find time to make a phone call.

If we can get uneducated farm workers to get their congressperson to change their vote on healthcare, if we can get uneducated farm workers to knock on 2,000 doors on the census, my God, can't we get our educated people to do some of this? … Or just pick up a phone call, send an email, pick up the phone and call your congressman. It takes five minutes! Responsibility! I call it responsibility. That's what we teach our people. Nobody is going to do this for us. We have to do it for ourselves. If you don't step up to the plate and write that letter, sign that postcard, make that phone call, send that email, it's not going to happen. Like we always tell people, "The power that you have is in your person." This is the power that you have. This is all the power that you need.

As activists themselves, the interviewees critiqued the lack of risk-taking among already engaged activist communities – not only giving time and resources but, in particular, their resistance to any kind of confrontative action. In many of his books and in the interview, Jensen describes a typical response to his public lectures where he talks about the need to "fight back" against numerous forms of oppression, death, and environmental destruction:

When I talk about fighting back to people in different social locations, their response was many times very predictable by social location. Middle-class or upper-middle-class white people, especially, but other people too, would often put up what I've taken to calling a 'Gandhi shield.' They say the names Martin Luther King, Dalai Lama, and Gandhi again and again, real fast, to keep all evil thoughts at bay. It's a position of privilege. Many other groups, many people of color, poor people, gang kids, prisoners, especially Indigenous people, family farmers, survivors of domestic violence would not put up a "Gandhi shield." Instead, they would look at me like, "So tell us something we don't know. Let's go, bro." It didn't take me very long to realize what the difference was for these latter groups – violence is not some abstract philosophical, theoretical, theological question to be puzzled through. It's a part of life, and you deal with it. It doesn't mean you participate, and it doesn't mean you don't. But you deal with it.

Jensen clarifies this further in *Endgame I*:

> The direct experience of violence, on the other hand, often brings questions closer to the people involved, so the people are not facing the questions as "activists" or "feminists" or "farmers" or "prisoners," but rather as human beings – animals – struggling to survive. Having felt your father's weight upon you in your bed; having stood in clear-cut and herbicided moonscape after moonscape, tears streaming down your face; having had your children taken from you, land stolen from you that belonged to your ancestors since the land was formed, and your way of life destroyed; having sat at a kitchen table, foreclosure notice in front of you for land your parents, grandparents, and great-grandparents worked, shotgun across your knees as you try to decide whether or not to put the barrel in your mouth; feeling the sting of a guard's baton or the jolt of a stun gun – to suffer this sort of violence directly in your body – is often to undergo some sort of deeply physical transformation. It is often to perceive and be in the world differently.[159]

I believe Kelly would agree with the preceding analysis by Jensen. Our responses to violence are conditioned by "where we stand." But she lamented about accusations of privilege when it comes to a lack of social action. These indictments turn into one more justification for not acting for persons who may be disinclined to act in the first place:

> When people are anxious about what falls into a level of inconvenience in terms of becoming more active, or for other reasons don't really want to take steps, a good escape hatch is provided, I think, by [other] people who say you are exercising your white privilege... We would have had a much higher student-youth resistance to the United States invasion of Iraq in 2003 had it not been for students who had been coached to feel anxiety and to feel, "If I commit civil disobedience am I

acting on the basis of white privilege." ... Over the years, I've seen people not very much wanting to take that risk anyway. It is not really that much of a risk at all. Then finding the escape hatches created by people who would seem to be even further to the left.... That should be critiqued: the possibility that people who believe that they are espousing a more refined level of radicalism may be circumventing the opportunity for people to begin along that path in the first place.

There is a tension between how to get folks to act within their social location and encourage them to take greater risks.

Barriers to Effectiveness 3 – Fear and Risk

Human fear of sacrifice and loss is at the heart of why folks do not enter social-transformative struggles. The same principle applies to the general population as to veteran activists. People within the dominant culture who desire social change may not desire to lose the material and psychological entitlements that come with the consequences of more disruptive action over the long-term, violent or (non)violent. Schulman wrote, "... fear and discomfort must be separated from the decision to act. Fear can be acknowledged, but fear cannot be the decisive factor. Fear must be separated from action in order for some reach towards justice to be maintained."[160] Jensen described coming to terms with barriers to action, including fear:

> I must be willing and prepared to deal with the effects of my actions. Related to this, there's the fearful: I must be willing to cross barriers of fear, both tangible, real, present-day fears and conditioned fears that feel just as real and present but are not.[161]

Jensen asks all potential social change agents to recognize their fears and not to make a virtue of inaction or ineffective action.[162]

For those already engaged in activism, Kelly presents a powerful example of risk-taking. She measures what she believes is an adequate commitment to (non)violence by borrowing a phrase from Miguel

D'Escoto: "to seriously look at nonviolent actions commensurate to the crimes being committed." That meant "upping the ante for me in terms of risk" and raising "the question of trying to experiment with teams of people imposing on themselves the same risks required of soldiers."

Kelly learned from Daniel Berrigan to think of unarmed peace activists taking the same risks as soldiers in a war zone:

> Berrigan said one of the reasons we don't have peace is because the peace activists are only willing to give half a life or half a commitment, in contrast to soldiers who don't get a chance to say "well, I would but," I'm working on a career track or something. If [soldiers] are told to go, they go. We don't have that sense within the peace movement. So I wanted very, very much to be part of some group that might be an arrow pointing to – what would it be like if we did have people giving the same equivalent as is required of soldiers or that is in fact imposed on civilians who don't have a chance to flee?

Much profound transformational change is prevented by a general unwillingness on behalf of the general population to lose their comforts, much less to take major risks. Dear said,

> People can't hear or don't want to hear it. We're very, very comfortable in this culture. Even non-white, non-wealthy people are still very privileged in the United States, compared to Haiti and the Congo and what's happening in Palestine and elsewhere. There's great poverty and oppression here, but by-and-large, we're so comfortable, and we're just like, "uh, we just don't want to do any more." Change only happens if you're willing to struggle for it…. Being passive or thinking you can just vote your way into change, that's just not how it's worked historically. Change comes from grassroots movements of struggle.

B♀ echoed Dear's point about how privileged people are in the United States:

> We have American privilege. We can go out, and we can march around, and we can get tired, and we can go home! We

can eat. We can be warm. We can drive our car somewhere. There is that whole element of American exceptionalism. That's just part of our struggle. I don't think we can expect people in the rest of the world to make revolution, and we don't do shit. We have to do something. We have a responsibility.

Churchill critiqued privileged persons within U.S. social movements who engage only those tactics that remain within their own comfort zone and maintain their personal safety. He used the example of the primarily white anti-Vietnam movement. When the U.S. took ground forces out of Vietnam, the draft as it was known ended. Even though the war continued, with the U.S. "bombing the living shit" out of Vietnam and Cambodia for years, the protests stopped. Churchill commented that "as soon as the personal jeopardy was out of the equation" (the threat of being drafted), the anti-war movement basically disappeared. Then Kent State happened:

> You had four dead white kids! Four! Now that's horrible for the four dead white kids and their families. [But] you are supposedly going into this struggle because you understand that there's millions of people being turned into hamburger. But three of your guys get killed and…? The whole anti-war movement was based upon existence within a comfort zone…. It's privileged white kids who are the ones in school trying to preserve their comfort and protection in adopting a moral posture that, as soon as they're assured that their comfort zone will be extended without the effort, walk off and leave….

For Churchill, the comfort zone is being able to watch and protest the destruction of life, "like it's an action movie." The comfort zone is staying safe within a certain realm of (non)violent action that fundamentally threatens little by way of one's material or psychological comfort and, therefore, does not fundamentally address violence in any significant way.

Conclusion

Neither an orthodox theology of Christian (non)violence or any other practice of either (non)violence or violence is adequate to deal with the vast complexities and all-encompassing, inter-related nature of direct, structural, and cultural violence in any given context. There is a vast territory of what might be considered both faithful and effective, even if limited to (non)violence. Staughton Lynd made the following point. "People oriented to nonviolence sometimes think of a circle with a very defined border." For these people, certain things seem very clear-cut:

> If you refuse to serve in any war, you're still within the circle. If you transgress in this way or that way, then you're outside it. There are really two kinds of people. There are the nonviolent people and the people who are into violence to some degree.

He went on to say:

> I think that's the wrong way to think about it. I think the circle is not precisely circumscribed. I think the circle is a center which radiates and that there's all sorts of contested terrain further out. And so many things go with that, like not being so damned self-righteous.

International anti-globalization activists, particularly in the anarchist tradition, use the language of "diversity of tactics" to deal with the matter of "contested terrain" – differences of opinion and practice related to the use of violent and (non)violent tactics. A majority of persons are unlikely to engage in social transformation at the level of disruptive public action in the current U.S. context. Nonetheless, the spirit of the "diversity of tactics," an openness to contestation and real differences, is relevant and necessary to pursuing a theology of faithful and effective tactics for social transformation.

It seems possible to faithfully claim, strategize, and act within a paradigm of Christian (non)violence while admitting that there may be an effective role for violence and a commitment to solidarity with communities of struggle across differences. Certainly, it is faithful to the historical narrative to recognize that violence has been effective in creating some change for better and for worse. Furthermore, there are many active and committed groups working for peace, Christian and not Christian, historically and currently. They have negotiated different ways of handling differences of belief and practice around violence and (non)violence.

In particular reference to (non)violence, all the interviewees suggested there was a failure of imagination, a failure to strategize, and a failure to risk bodies and entitlements. For those desirous of continuing to claim faithful (non)violence, there are plenty of opportunities to work towards effectiveness before condemning violence as unfaithful, immoral, or ineffective. There is much within Christian scripture to address matters of fear, risk, loss of life, loss of material possessions, disruption, counter-cultural prophetic speech, transformation, and so on. Yet as the tradition of practical theology itself demonstrates, apart from transformational practices, scriptural commands and theology are hollow. Nonetheless, Christian community does provide one strength crucial to the work of social transformation, a dimension of social change that is often difficult to create: the existence of an already organized, concrete community in which to encourage interconnectedness and vision and to work against individualism. Jensen notes, "There is a role for our spiritual longings and for the strength that a true spiritual practice can bring to social movements."[163] These practices must be nurtured within a collective process, with broader accountability and solidarity with different communities of struggle. We turn to the practice of solidarity in the next chapter.

− 5 −

SOLIDARITY

A key question in my research was, "In what ways is it possible, and what factors make it possible, for allies from dominant groups to be involved in marginalized communities' struggles for justice?" This is an important question for me, personally. Throughout my research I have asked myself, "How do I and how can I hold a commitment to Christian (non)violence with conviction in the context of such deep and abiding violence? How do I act with integrity with persons who are most impacted by the structures of violence, whose oppression is a result of my own people's perpetration of violence and from which I continue to benefit?" Questions of allyship are important questions for social change, generally. All interviewees affirmed that any real measure of transformation of the structures of violence will only be accomplished collaboratively, across various kinds of difference: differences of identity, differences of cultural and material power, and differences in belief and practice about the legitimate means of change, violent and/or (non)violent.

Yet such alliances have been fraught with problems historically. In many cases, justice-seeking movements have replicated the very forms of violence, power, and privilege they have claimed to oppose. In this chapter, I will consider various responses the interviewees gave to the question of the practice of being allies. The language of solidarity was often used synonymously with allies. Ultimately, solidarity arose as the more useful concept and practice to inform a critical, practical theory of social change, especially when it comes to evaluating violence and (non)violence in the context of social transformation. In particular, Staughton Lynd's idea of "solidarity *as* (non)violence" is instructive of multiple practices by which structural and cultural violence may be usefully addressed and dismantled.

Reinforcing Violence:
Bringing Dominance into Movements

Commonly conceived, allies are persons with privileges and power emerging out of identities in the dominant culture who seek to align with persons and communities from oppressed identity groups to address grievances of an oppressed group. Whether it is men seeking to ally with women, white people with Black people, or straight people with the LGBTQ+ community, the problem with allies and for allies is that they "often bring that dominance with them into the movement."[164]

Most interviewees agreed that there has been limited evidence of truly shared relationships between social justice change agents from primarily privileged identity groups and primarily oppressed identity groups. Structures of violence and inequality, and patterns of denial, reversal, and entitlement replicate themselves in movements for social change. In relation to activists coming out of privileged identities, Churchill said,

> There is this absolutely intractable compulsion to be in charge! We're not working with anybody, no matter what our interest is, if we have to concede that they might know something that we can't tell them they knew.

In particular, women interviewees described many occasions of sexism and homophobia within and across their movements. Huerta, Power, Schulman, and B♀ all described ways in which women were marginalized by male leadership in social struggle. Power said that the Catholic and other religious anti-war left was so sexist that it "was no place for a self-respecting woman." Schulman described that the sheer trauma of the AIDS crisis, when gay "men became endangered and vulnerable," temporarily righted the sexist imbalance of the period:

> [Men] needed each other and women to intervene... They needed women's political experience from the earlier feminist and lesbian movements, women's analysis of power, and women's emotional commitments to them. They needed

women's alienation from the state. As men became weak, they allowed themselves to acknowledge the real ways that women are strong, particularly recognizing our hard-won experience at political organizing.... As protease inhibitors normalized AIDS, this relationship shifted back. Men began to regain their collective health and with that their patriarchal imperatives.[165]

Schulman wrote that as gay men regained their health, they began to marginalize the women who made their existence possible. As the history of AIDS activism remains invisible, gay men have no context for recognizing the role of women in their lives. Now, gay men "again feel superior. Now that *we* need *them* to let *us* into the power system of representation that they control, there is no reciprocity."[166]

Undoing Dominance:
Asking, Listening, Awareness of Social Location

The common experience of oppressed groups is that persons coming from dominant identities within U.S. culture come imposing their own ideas, dominant identity norms, and control. They tend to be largely unaware of these controlling behaviors and see their leadership and control as entitlements. These impositions reinforce structural and cultural violence. The interviewees, however, pointed to practices that helped to transform the danger of bringing dominance into movements.

Some interviewees vividly recalled past movement experience in communities seeking group self-determination when members of the dominant culture actually asked them what they needed. Huerta recalled a Farm Workers' march in Calexico, California, that stood out in her mind. "Ted Kennedy was with us on that march. We had gotten some rooms in this motel down there and he walks in and he says, "Okay, tell me what you want me to do." B♀ also recalled a critical instance. Not long after being released from prison the first time for a petty crime, she attended a workshop at a community college about women in prison:

These lovely Quaker women were trying to have this workshop and, you know, just being so nice and lovely and doing their little do-gooder thing. Which was not a bad thing, but it irritated the fuck out of me. So I just got mad and said, "You don't know what the fuck you're talking about!" So they said, "Who are you?" I said this is who I am and this is my experience. They said, "Do you want to give this workshop?" I said, "Yes." And that's the first time I ever did a workshop. So, bless those lovely Quaker women.

Because they were so rare, such instances of asking and invitation were memorable to activists coming out of marginalized identity groups.

On the other hand, Churchill expressed that when privileged persons constantly ask oppressed persons the same questions about what to do to rectify injustices, they often are not really seeking answers. Of his experience of public lecturing about Indigenous issues, he said,

> It's always a white person that asks, "What can I do? What can we do?.... My response is, "Can you pick up a fucking board and hit me across the head?" They just look all bewildered and confused. I say, "Are you willing to? Are you capable? You know you are! So why are you asking me the question? There is an infinite realm of things you can do. But you're not going to, are you? How did it become my responsibility to tell you what to do?" That, by the way, is a question that I am never asked when I am with people who have no education, no resources – outside this country and inside this country, too.

Often, when privileged people ask questions of what to do, it appears to avoid the critical step of taking action. Deciding what to do, doing it, and learning from the process of acting is more useful than continually asking others what should be done. From a position of privilege, there is a tension between asking persons within marginalized communities what would be helpful as an ally and how such asking always puts the burden of responsibility back on the oppressed to provide answers. Allies in struggle who find this problem both confusing and maddening must recognize that such tensions are also a product of the history and rationalizing mechanisms of direct, structural, and cultural violence.

Despite the hard lessons and failures of allyship during previous movements, interviewees agreed there were still obstacles to being an ally – an inability to ask, to listen, and to be aware of the patterns of dominance one's social location brings. These ongoing liabilities reinforce a sense of entitlement to know and to lead that privileged allies bring into movements. The unawareness of this potential for dominance also reaffirms the perception that privileged actors continue to operate under an illusion that denies the historic realities of structural and cultural violence. To affirm (non)violence as a practice of social struggle and solidarity means to understand the practice of (non)violence not only as physical non-retaliation, but to engage all practices which undermine the various levels of violence discussed in previous chapters.

Jensen's perspective on the possibilities of inter-species communication makes notions of being an ally – listening, awareness, accountability, and action – even more challenging. There is the need to transform human consciousness to recognize that other-than-humans have an equality of being and ways of knowing. That change of consciousness should be reflected in language. "A very small thing that [I do] whenever I'm writing – I say, 'The tree who, the river who...' I never say 'The river that, the tree that...' because they're *who's*. One of the things that we have to do is change discourse." If language reflects an actual belief in other-than-human sentience, then the natural corollary would be as human allies to ask other-than-humans what to do to be in solidarity with them. "What would the rivers themselves want?"[167] What do the salmon want? The redwood trees? The activist ally to the earth would ask, listen, and act accordingly.

This is theologian Marjorie Suchocki's view of solidarity that includes the other-than-human world, in *The Fall to Violence*:

> Our existence as part of an interdependent world, where relations to all others are internal to the constitution of the self, creates a solidarity with the human race, and possibly with all species in descending degrees of intensity. We are, then, no matter how personally in control of our violent tendencies, surrounded by and invaded by a vast amount of violence. We have relationally internalized these events, even

though the vast majority of them, if not all, are certainly far below the level of conscious experience.[168]

Suchocki's description of the deep and even unconscious influence of violence on our interconnectedness affirms the importance of bringing this impact into awareness.

The practices of asking, listening, and awareness on the part of privileged allies are part and parcel of deconstructing structural and cultural violence. According to Suchocki, privileged people rely on their "ability to achieve distance"[169] from suffering and violence in order to maintain the status quo and their material and psychological entitlements. Engaging in solidarity means doing ever-deeper levels of work to decrease the distance between privileged communities' awareness and practice of privilege, ideally among communities working together in struggle. Asking, listening, and awareness are *early-stage* requirements to begin to recognize how all beings are fundamentally interconnected, including the ways they are interconnected in a web of violence. An awareness of social location and the possibilities for reinforcing violence that dominant social location may impose indicates the potential for understanding and acting against the mechanisms of denial, reversal, and entitlement. Asking, listening, and awareness provide the possibility for valuing the lives of those within dominant culture that typically do not matter, undermining in practice the false portrayal and reversal of the privileged as having lives more valuable than others. Through asking, listening, and awareness of location, privileged allies practice giving up the assumption of superior status, superior knowledge, and control. These requirements for being an ally are not merely the acts of an individual. They are communal commitments within and across differences of social location. Particularly within privileged identity groups, deconstructing privilege through a practice of asking, listening, and awareness also serves the purpose of holding privileged persons accountable *within* their own communities for the dominant behaviors that are part and parcel of structural violence.

(Non)violence:
Not Imposing From a Position of Dominance

The same issues of power and privilege that plague social movements generally insinuate themselves in the conversations and practices of violence and (non)violence. As the analysis of previous chapters has shown, in light of the history of all forms of Christian violence, appeals to (non)violence from Christian voices within the dominant culture potentially sound like acts of domination. Recall Power said that, historically and theologically, Christianity is shot through with a sense of dominance mission. (Non)violent demands from Christians are perceived as a white, middle-class sensibility not to upset the dominant economic and political order. They smack of a reversed self-portrayal and false Christian morality and appear to maintain the benefits of structural and cultural violence. The dynamic of dominance asserts itself and reinforces structural and cultural violence when Christian identity groups come imposing (non)violence as normative belief and practice. From the perspective of most of the interviewees, Christian (non)violent activists continue to be largely unaware of the impact of their social location on their perception, if not the reality, of their dominance.

Churchill said he had never known any person engaged in armed struggle who expected that people who were not so engaged, should be so involved. He said, "I will support virtually anyone in a given moment, when we have confluence, when we have common ground." Ninety-five percent of his activist practice has been "within any reasonable set of definitional parameters" nonviolent. But since he won't take a pledge of (non)violence, he is considered unreasonable by pacifists. In his experience, that kind of stance is "a pervasive practice and attitude," among (non)violent activists, demonstrating that "…it's not a reciprocal relation."

Dear, one of the most clamorous advocates of (non)violence, spoke of his own marginalization by (non)violent allies as a result of working with all people in struggle. Before and after the second Gulf War began, he supported one of the largest and best organized anti-war groups in the country. ANSWER,[170] a communist pro-violence group, was accused of supporting terrorists and engaging in violent tactics in demonstrations and violent rhetoric during rallies and marches. Dear said of them,

> They were doing the most, best organizing.... A lot of my friends wouldn't have anything to do with them. They invited me to speak at their rally just before the war started.... I spoke to 300,000 people. People told me I was being violent by doing that but, I thought, well, they're the ones doing the work; I mean... the churches, what are they [doing]...?

As vehement a supporter of (non)violence as Dear is, he demonstrates that it is possible to remain committed to (non)violence without excluding support for groups who may employ other means to reach similar ends. Jensen said that being an ally "doesn't mean we have to agree. This is the same with pacifists. It doesn't mean we have to agree on everything. It doesn't mean we have to agree on very many things." For Jensen, being an ally means being willing to consider many things at one time, recognizing that all action is "context-based – it's all particular." Solidarity does not exclude the possibility of support and shared actions, even if differentiated, based on common goals.

If part of violence is imposing one's cultural viewpoint from a position within the dominant culture, then being a privileged ally for social change from within the dominant culture would include not imposing a (non)violent view. When allies grasp that (non)violence is much more than direct, physical violence, this reframing seeks to move (non)violent practitioners towards grasping underlying concepts of structural and cultural violence that may also be embedded in their speech and actions. Interviewees provided numerous examples of how they thought about this. Jensen said,

> Being an ally means that I try to put down the white man's burden. Because it's not my job to tell [people] how to resist. I was doing a talk at an Indigenous college one time and, before the talk, maybe ten or fifteen of us went to dinner. There was one white person, besides me, who was the other teacher and fourteen Indigenous students or so. One student was a little excited about my work, and he starts asking me questions, and

the teacher turns to me and says, "If you tell him it's okay to kill people, I will kill you." And she's kidding, but she's not kidding. We just sort of dropped it and made conversation. After dinner, he and I talked. One of the things I said to him is, "It is not the place of any white person, including me, including your teacher, to tell any Indigenous person how to resist. So you can do whatever you want. But that teacher has no right to tell you, as an Indigenous person, what is appropriate for you to do. Just as I have no right." So I think being an ally is also not being paternalistic, which is what we can get with "white man's disease" and "white man's burden."

This lesson can apply to any attempt to undo any position of dominance within structures of violence. Within the African-American community during the Civil Rights movement in the South, Umoja described that SNCC's internal shift away from a position based on (non)violence meant organizers, from a higher education and socio-economic class position, tried not to impose their views upon the local people:

After a point, SNCC kind of took this policy: "We can't really tell local people how to behave." This is the way they've been surviving and really kind of following from an orientation they got from Ella Baker,[171] who supported armed self-defense, too; we have to support the development of the Indigenous leadership. For Indigenous people, self-defense is how the majority of them are surviving down here. So I think that played a role in SNCC changing its orientation. That's what I mean by class orientation. How do you look to these people you're working with? Who might not speak the King's English? Who might not have a college degree? They might not have a high school degree. What's our relationship to them, even though we might have a college education? Are we here to serve these people, or are we here to tell them what to do? I think that changes over a period of time; first to respecting the folk but then actually learning from them, and then maybe applying some of the things that people are using in terms of survival there.

What (non)violent allyship from a dominant social location looks like is not telling people, whose identity and basic life experience you do not share or whose oppression results from your people's own violence, what to do or how to think. Kelly shared that when she and her organization (Voices for Creative Nonviolence) are in another country:

> It sounds like we are trying to proselytize. The more appropriate thing, when you are in somebody else's country and they are the ones whose blood is being shed in the process of a war, is to listen and to try to respectfully bring back from there what are the effects of U.S. war-making, but not to be telling them, "Would you like us to teach you how to be nonviolent?..." Yeah, that's a pretty repugnant idea.

Dear was in Nicaragua and El Salvador in the 1980s during the U.S. Contra-wars. The Jesuit priests with whom he stayed got into debates over the use of revolutionary violence. It was a different conversation among very poor people, "with the whole U.S. government bearing down upon them. There was no need to lecture them or say anything to them. I was there to learn and to listen to them."

Similarly, in the context of prisoner advocacy, Alice Lynd said, "We seldom would ever talk about nonviolence spelled out N-O-N and so forth." In the prison context, prisoners observe everything you do, "How you conduct yourself. They're very sensitive to things like that....Survival depends on being able to evaluate who's doing what and where and what their next move is likely to be, and why." Actions are what matters, not words or beliefs. From her experience as a prisoner, B♀ concurred:

> You have to build trust. That's one thing I think you learn from prison. Everybody's a number. Anybody can talk. Anybody can say all kinds of things. People spend all day lying. But what do they do when the shit hits the fan? People in prison see each other every day. They know what people do, and they know what people don't do.

The only way to build solidarity and trust, in B♀'s experience, is "by practice."

During the time of our interview, the Lynds were in relationship with prisoners in the Youngstown prison who were considering doing a hunger strike as a response to prison conditions.[172] While in sympathy with the prisoners, Staughton Lynd also shared,

> In this instance, if we had our druthers, they would not be bringing the hunger strike. But we are trying very hard not just to say but to mean and to do that *we're not telling somebody else what to do....* As to the particular tactic they're choosing, I have serious doubts about it.

The Lynds knew that a hunger strike could not last indefinitely. On a rolling basis, it might last a month or two. When the Lynds suggested a lawsuit as an alternative to the hunger strike, the prisoner response was, "That takes too long." The bottom line for Staughton Lynd was, "If that's the thing that they've decided is the way they can act out their resistance to oppression, it's good enough for me." The Lynds consistently confront the common perception among advocates for prisoners that prisoners in high-security prisons can't do anything to advocate for themselves. Staughton Lynd once responded to someone who expressed such a notion:

> "I don't believe it. I haven't been there myself. Don't know all of the things that people might think of, but there's no situation where human beings can't do something." ...It's not appropriate to call hunger-striking a mistaken strategy when it's almost the only form of self-activity that is left to people in that situation. That's what it represents to them. Taking control of their own lives.

Solidarity as (Non)violence

From Staughton Lynd's point of view, we might understand (non)violence itself as the practice of solidarity. He wrote that in movements of poor and working-class people, "Individual commitment to nonviolence as a matter of principle is rare."[173] Through analysis of working-class labor efforts and resistance movements in prison, Lynd further wrote:

> Solidarity can be built on the basis of practice, of action that is in the common interest, rather than on the basis of shared ideas. In the traditional culture of nonviolence, talk usually precedes action…. Practice follows principle, and practitioners of the traditional culture of nonviolence are careful to articulate why the action they undertake expresses concepts they have previously come to affirm. In the world of poor and working-class resistance, on the other hand, action often comes before talk… the experience of struggle gives rise to new understandings that may be put into words much later or never put into words at all.[174]

Lynd said, "People who are interested in nonviolence need to begin thinking about solidarity, recognizing solidarity as a form of nonviolence, and realizing the 1,801 different dilemmas involved in the nurturing of solidarity." These dilemmas have to do with the real differences in privilege and power among co-actors in social struggle. From the position of privileged social location, solidarity can be particularly sensitive and complicated. (Non)violence means not imposing beliefs and practice, not assuming knowledge, not replicating denial, not feeling entitled to lead. It means asking, listening, and awareness. This constellation of practices implies consciousness-raising and internal, dominant identity-group work that bears itself out in practice. These practices of solidarity will both 1) increase privileged communities' awareness of all forms of violence, and 2) reduce the distance between themselves and those who suffer most from multiple types of violence. Solidarity as (non)violence includes deepening the practices by which this awareness is increased, and the distance is breached.

I identified seven interrelated practices in the interviews that point toward an increasing commitment to reduce the distance between the privileged and oppressed.

1 – Showing Up

Despite separatist identity politics that emerged from the structures and betrayals of privileged and repressive violence, these veterans of the 1960s and 1970s social movements saw those times as also galvanizing identity-groups to work together across many kinds of difference. Huerta said that "a kind of revolutionary mindset… was the temper of the times." Within the problems and power of identity-politics, many different groups were trying to figure out what it meant to struggle together against a common oppressor by showing up for one another. Huerta indicated you rarely see that level of cross-group solidarity these days:

> Our movements are much more segregated now than they were in the sixties. People came together more around the peace movement. Now our peace movements seems to be very separate. Or the immigrant rights movement, for instance.… The new Civil Rights movement has got to be about incarceration and what's happening in our schools. But they seem very separate from each other. More segregated.

In very simple terms, when I asked the interviewees what solidarity meant in this era, all of them said it meant showing-up for social struggle in and beyond one's own community. Huerta described the days during the Farm Workers' movement when the Teamsters Union came to violently oppose the farm-workers' boycotting grape growers and organizing a union. Up to that time, Huerta explained, the farm-workers had not reached out to any other union. There was a tension between the need for local control and farm-worker self-determination and the concrete need for support. They reached out to the heavily white-dominated AFL-CIO, which sent members of local, action-oriented unions to California in cross-worker solidarity. Huerta recounted the presence of union Seafarers and United Auto Workers as critical to thwarting the Teamsters Union's attack, which was a huge victory in the course of the whole movement.

Many efforts of the George Jackson Brigade were also aimed at worker solidarity. Members of the GJB walked picket lines with striking city workers and stood with Black construction workers who were denied entrance to white unions. B♀ indicated this solidarity was based on simply showing up:

> When people are on strike, other people go and walk the picket line with them. You talk to them – they find out how you're doing, how they're doing. Do they need food? Do they need coffee? Once they get to trust you, they might just let you walk around while they take their kid to the doctor or something. That happened – a lot.

Due to the dominant behaviors of privileged groups in social movement, some separatist and nationalist movements rejected solidarity coming from dominant identity groups. Umoja no longer sees that as a predominant dynamic today. He said, "I know of few movements where people will say, 'Well, we don't need your help, thanks for the solidarity.'" While rejecting the imposition of Christian values and practices on oppressed communities, Umoja still believes a critical element of solidarity is "to step up and support one another." It is important for people not to just say they are conscious of an issue, but "to show up for other people, even if that's not my issue, to try to do something to show my support." Umoja added,

> People take risks, or are more likely to take risks if they believe they're going to be supported… that they're not just going to be out there by themselves…. and people are going to leave them. So that feeling of a collectivity and a connection is important, too.

Huerta said there was still "a lot of culturization that needs to happen," for white people to understand the experience of people of color. She understands that, on the one hand, it should not be the role of people of color to continually educate white people about their racism. At the same time, she sees her own role as both showing up across movements and consciousness-raising in the dominant culture. Huerta described several instances in which she tried to make such connections. When she is invited to speak at events for the environmental movement, the participants are mostly all white people. So she talks about toxic dump sites in communities of color, or immigration. "They're not working across issues. They're not reaching out."

> I don't need to talk to them on the environment, because they're there on the environment, right? They're probably there on gay issues also. I'm sure they are still sort of perplexed about the immigration issue. So I try to frame my talks depending on the audience. I spoke in Utah to a huge Mormon audience, and so my whole talk out there was about choice and gay marriage and immigration.

Most of the primarily white women's organizations with which she works today are "going out of their way to involve women of color." She said there are necessary spaces for self-determination, and there are necessary spaces for collaboration. The harsh lessons of dominance and the resulting exclusionary identity politics of former movements have caused current movements to isolate themselves. Huerta understands this problem but believes it works against unifying a progressive agenda for social change. Her commitment is to eldering and to "weaving movements together." With the lessons of the past in mind, it is critical to learn from the dominant patterns of the past, to have actors from across identity-groups recommit to a common struggle, and to consistently show up.

2 – Material Support

Huerta described how some militant Chicanos criticized the national Farm Workers' movement because there were too many outside religious white people involved in the movement. Many believed the religious community compromised the willingness of Farm Worker organizers to move beyond (non)violence. Huerta did not see it that way. She listed many names of priests who showed up as allies and walked alongside farm-workers in this struggle. In addition, churches provided critical material assistance to the movement as one of their most important forms of being allies:

> During the grape boycott we would stay at the seminaries and convents; these were the places that farmworkers went when

we went on a grape boycott. They gave us houses and shelter and places to stay and provided food, child care, and whatever. We had a very, very close connection.

Churchill recognized that there were potentially meaningful roles for Christian communities as allies. He said it would be pointless to

discard Christianity in the sense that it has nothing to offer. There are avenues within it which could serve to alleviate some of the worst of its own effects. Temper it. That goes to the tactical thing, slowing down.

It is important to "Always make common cause with a narrow ground." Churchill described an alliance in Denver, Colorado, to oppose the Columbus Day holiday and an annual parade which celebrates it. This protest draws a fair number of Christian allies, about whom he said, "If you want to come out and oppose it, it's the right thing to do. We can link arms – I'll sing one of your songs, and you sing one of mine, okay? But there's a lot beyond that."

Showing up matters, but Churchill thinks of concrete solidarity from a position of privilege as sacrificing something more:

What would I consider reasonable practitioners who will be in concrete solidarity or support rather than just mouthing it and announcing themselves to be in solidarity with armed struggle happening half a planet away? They will render support and assistance to those who need it, who are engaged in armed struggle. They do not fail to reciprocate... there would be a basic solidarity based upon opposition to a common oppressor. I will shelter you. I will feed you. I will incur risk on your behalf. I won't do what you do, but that doesn't mean that I'm entitled to a risk-free environment. And that's the comfort zone, which is the predominating thing; that, "No, I'm not obligated to incur any tangible risk or sacrifice in this process."

Churchill challenges privileged allies to extend the limits of what most dominant people think of as an ally role – expressions of solidarity, showing up to protest, and affirming militant struggle abroad but not at home. These practices mean little when they entail no risk, no actual threat to the privileges of dominant social location. They do nothing to actually reverse the reversals by, in any way, sacrificing entitlement. In particular, Christian individuals and institutions should not underestimate the material resources they have to offer social movements – money, buildings, access to political power, and moral authority (whether legitimate or not).

3 – Turning over Privilege

Effectively dismantling privileges means not only sacrificing money and material advantages but engaging in multiple practices that address the various levels of violence in a community. Jensen says that if privileged allies want to have integrity among oppressed communities, "We who are relatively privileged need to ask ourselves what we are willing to give up, what amount of security we are willing to sacrifice to change the status quo."[175] This is true for members of the dominant culture at whatever place of commitment, action, or inaction they find themselves. Social change requires getting out of a privileged comfort zone. Several practices take privileged persons out of their comfort zone:

- giving up material resources,
- gaining access for organizers,
- influencing structures of power, and
- applying educational privilege to raise consciousness.

Jensen said, "The point of being privileged is that it is my responsibility to use that privilege to undercut its basis." Jensen noted, "I never set out to be an ally to women. I never set out to be an ally to Indigenous people. I just told the truth as I understood it to be. That has sort of turned me into a de facto ally." When oppressed communities witness privileged people showing up, telling the truth, accepting the consequences and sacrifices of entitlement-denying practices, then privileged persons may be seen as allies.

Dear discussed how he has learned, over time, to turn over his privilege by continually sacrificing it:

I'm white, male, well-educated, a Catholic priest, Jesuit. If [Saint] Francis and Gandhi are right, everything is upside-down. I'm it. I'm the most awful oppressor on the planet. I should, before anybody else, be on a journey of downward mobility and should be in prison. I accept that. I'm trying to be on that journey. That's partly why I've come to New Mexico, and I'm not at Harvard or Berkeley or Georgetown. I'm trying to get out of the privilege. That's why I did not get a doctorate, although I would have loved to have. That's why I'm not teaching, although I would like to. I'm trying to be out there, an activist resister among the poor. I'm not doing a good job, but I'm trying. The layers of privilege are very, very deep. So I'm trying to use the gifts I have and turn that privilege over on behalf of the poor....

What primarily gives Dear credibility as an advocate of (non)violence among communities brutally violated by oppression is that he has taken the actions of which he speaks and has made significant sacrifices in the pursuit of peace. Everywhere he has traveled – from Central America to Palestine, the Philippines to Columbia – regarding the debate between violence and (non)violence, "They've been very respectful toward me because they know I have a prison record and they know that I'm not just talking about it." People from abroad can't fathom that a U.S. priest would voluntarily be in and out of jail. Dear described a time he visited Northern Ireland, where "there is a deep-seated hatred in the Catholic community and among some of the radicals that I was hanging out with" towards the Catholic Church. The vast majority of the priests in Northern Ireland didn't do anything for the struggle for independence. He described having dinner and dialogue for three hours with hard-core IRA, H-Block hunger strikers[176] who had survived their brutal protest. These veterans of struggle were interested in the tactic and tradition of militant (non)violence, for which they had little historical reference. Dear and the IRA members considered one another resisters. All of the interviewees have been considered reliable allies over time because of their practices and sacrifices, not because of their beliefs in the efficacy or justifiability of either violence or (non)violence. Until and unless oppressed communities witness these various practices and sacrifices over time, claims to solidarity by privileged people are held in question.

4 – Suffering Powerlessness With

The previously listed practices of solidarity may suggest that (non)violence is primarily a matter of giving something up from a position of privilege. This is certainly an aspect of understanding solidarity as a practice of (non)violence that address inequalities. But from a traditional liberationist view, solidarity is more than merely giving things up on behalf of others. Solidarity with the poor reflects God's own preference for the poor by becoming one with them. This was Dear's perspective:

> Nonviolence certainly means solidarity with the poorest of the poor. That's the question: How far do you want to be in solidarity with the poor? What does that mean? Simplifying your own life? Befriending actual poor people? Actually serving, not telling them what to do? Listening to them? Theologically I find God in the poor, and then I want to become one with the poor. Solidarity with the poor can take a billion different forms. But it does mean some kind of material poverty way beyond simple lifestyle. Active involvement with people who are materially poor, and advocating for justice for them so that they're no longer poor. Dorothy Day said, "I advocate poverty, and I condemn poverty." So solidarity is like that. But it means living your life with them, for them, in them, through them. For me, I go deep; I say, "that's where God is."

For Dear, this literally means putting yourself geographically with the poor. Speaking of his decision to live permanently in New Mexico,

> You want to be in solidarity with the poor; you have to go and be with them. Pack up and move to Mississippi. So for me, solidarity [is] just coming and living here. Not living in quite a rich place.... I was in India in very poor places, reflecting

about New Mexico. If you are going to be in solidarity with the people of Africa and India, it seems to me that you have to be among the poor of your own country. So I've always tried to be working with the homeless, and prisoners, and immigrants. Coming here was a movement, to my mind, an effort to stay closer to the poor. But it's a lifelong journey and struggle.

For Dear, (non)violence means giving up the material advantages of a privileged position in the dominant culture and aligning oneself with persons and communities who have been deprived of the same as a result of structural and cultural violence. As choices, such practices are still privileged ones. Yet, the motivation for these choices intends to understand and dismantle all forms of violence by engaging increasingly deeper ways of sharing the experience of the oppressed.

Power said she learned in prison that "suffering the powerlessness with" others, both materially and psychologically, is critical to identifying the ways in which any person might learn to act and to be in solidarity:

> Immerse yourself into the way that people in truly ground-down situations continue to live as humans and transform moments and have what I think of as graceful survival. This is not grim survival. This is not fighting-each-other survival. This is sharing-and-taking-care-of-each-other survival with lots of love and generosity in it.

Closely shared experience of suffering exposes that the resources for resisting violence are not merely about the privileged putting their resources at the disposal of the poor and oppressed, nor giving them up for the sake of not participating in the structures of material violence. Such experiences also reveal non-material resources and practices of resistance that are available for struggle and survival in a community where material resources are scarce.

5 – Do Your Work With Your Own People

For privileged allies, the work of solidarity is doubly located. On the one hand, there is the work of showing up, as well as suffering with communities who directly bear the burden of violence. But solidarity also means a willingness to work where one is. Staughton Lynd shared one of his favorite anecdotes:

> A Spanish anarchist leader was way back in a noontime lunch line when somebody said to him, "Comrade, your work is so important that, come with me; I'll help you get some lunch right away. After all, think of the revolution." To which the anarchist leader, without moving an inch, said, "This is the revolution."

Though the extreme circumstances which led her to prison proved to be her learning ground, Power said that the ability to learn how to act in solidarity does not necessarily require being in any kind of special circumstances. Power said that wherever one is, it is critical to analyze the precise place where one finds oneself for the ways in which action is required:

> One of the things that "be where you are and name what's where you are" does is, first of all, it expands the base of activism. Everybody is somewhere. Everybody is called to this. People write to me. This one guy says, "I'm an investment banker. I don't know why, but I'm really profoundly moved by your story. What should I do?" I said, "I think you should be an investment banker. I think that you should encounter the contradictions of that. I think that you should look at how you'd resolve those contradictions. Be that; do that." You know, withdraw and be pure? Well that's one possibility. But the real transformation is in… seeing that the contradictions in any system are the moments for change, for transformation.

As Power indicates, through a tangible, intentional encounter with our environment, transformation begins at the intersections of awareness of the contradictions between the various layers of privileged and oppressed identities and the active commitment to create a more just and (non)violent world. It is important to note, however, that encountering and resolving such contradictions must be engaged both individually and collectively, both inside and outside of one's own community.[177]

When Dear was in El Salvador at the age of twenty-one, Jesuits were running a refugee camp. Most of the refugees and the Jesuits were involved with the FMLN.[178] Regarding Dear's commitment to (non)violence:

> The Jesuit theologians, Ellacuría, who was killed, and Jon Sobrino, who is still alive...they totally dismissed me. All of the Jesuits still dismissed me. They knew me when I was a goofy kid, and I'm talking about Gandhi and King. They're smoking cigarettes and [saying], "Aw, gimme a break, kid." But I'm watching them and their lives, and they're getting ten death threats a day! We disagree. They do support just war for revolution. But their lives were by and large radically nonviolent. But I didn't get into it too much because they weren't going to listen to me. I mean, it wasn't my reality. The problem there started in the United States. They told me, "Well, if you really believe in that, get your government to stop sending money and weapons here that are killing our people.... Your work is in the States, not here." That was a transformative moment to hear them say that. They're right!

North American solidarity not only means being with and for the poor. It also means "resisting the forces of destruction that are killing the poor around the world"[179] – including those forces within United States power structures and in Christian culture more broadly. After this trip, Dear began resisting the wars in Central America within privileged populations in the United States. He "thought of, like, ten different things to do, and I did them": public speaking, recruiting speakers, showing films, and being arrested repeatedly in actions against aid to the Contras. Part and parcel of the practices and tactics suggested as effective and faithful in the previous chapter, (non)violent solidarity from a social location in culture means effectively raising consciousness within one's community in addition to acts of collective disruption.

Christians have a particular role to play – working with their own people within the structures of violence and power that are the Church. Through preaching and speaking on behalf of the gospel of nonviolence, Dear believes he is addressing the fundamental issue of violence where "Christians are the problem. So I'm writing and speaking to them and trying to convert Christians to the gospel of Jesus.[180] And myself. I'm not trying to convert poor people. I'm not trying to convert the people of El Salvador or Palestine." Dear said that he memorized one sentence in the Autobiography of Malcolm X that has instructed him where to direct his primary efforts to preach the gospel of nonviolence: "Let all sincere white people who care about nonviolence go and convert all other white people to practice nonviolence." In response to that sentence, Dear thought:

> "Okay, Malcolm, I'm trying to do that." I could have gone to live in El Salvador like I wanted to, but the problems in the world are the rich, white people in the world: in the United States – church people, Christians, Catholics. They're the ones; we're the ones who need to be converted. So I'm trying to live that and to teach that.

For privileged allies, practicing (non)violence means doing so among the communities who are most responsible for violence – in one's own context.

6 – Accompanying as Reciprocal Relationship

The preferential option for the poor serves as a necessary corrective to the unfortunate history of the behaviors of "allies" who control knowledge and action in poor and oppressed communities. But Lynd critiques this essential insight of Latin American liberation theology as limited. He said,

> The idea implicitly assumed that he or she who exercised that option was a middle-class religious personage or intellectual responding to the needs of the less fortunate. But if accompanier and accompanied are conceptualized, not as one person assisting another person in need, but as two experts,

the intellectual universe is transformed. No longer do we have one kind of person helping a person of another kind. Instead we have two persons exploring the way forward together.[181]

Staughton Lynd said what it means to be a privileged person working within dominant culture power differences is to emphasize in practice the imperative to learn to work together on a more reciprocal basis. This aspect of solidarity includes all of the practices previously shared throughout this chapter but has a fundamentally different orientation. The Lynds explained how a mutually shared commitment to change has worked on a very practical level in their activism, beginning with Alice's counseling draft resisters during the Vietnam War. Stanton began,

> What nonviolent revolution consists of is persons who have something to offer: some kind of training, some kind of expertise, going to live with or in the presence of oppressed people, and each kind of person putting his or her form of expertise on the table. This is something Alice came to as a draft counselor. In draft counseling, there were two experts.[182] There was the person like Alice who knew the laws and the regulations and the practice of Selective Service boards. Then there were people who were struggling with this momentous life decision. When we became lawyers... here were two upper-middle-class persons who had no particular reason to pal around with Eastern European steel workers in Youngstown, Ohio, let alone the worst of the worst, prisoners sentenced to death. But because we had this skill, or this expertise, I can't begin to tell you how quickly all of that evaporated. We became very close comrades and friends of an unending series of rank-and-file workers and prisoners.

Alice added, "And really loving and respectful and appreciative, trusting relationships." These relationships are more than just privileged allies helping oppressed people. Alice Lynd described the most meaningful of her work as "touching the life of an individual at a very deep level" and "the taking on of life together." Learning to work on a reciprocal basis is the cornerstone for (non)violent revolution itself.

If oppressors truly cannot share in the knowledge and experience of those in the position of being oppressed, can they truly be held accountable for failing to honor the oppressed community's perspectives?[183] The liberationist commitment to the poor and oppressed continues to push the privileged to recognize that there is no neutral ground in their own commitments – the work of solidarity means concretely practicing the belief that God stands on the side of the oppressed over against oppression and its agents. Therefore, justice-seeking persons are called to stand on the side of the "victims of history." Such persons seek to know and act on the basis of an oppressed community's experience, knowledge, and assessment of what is needed for their liberation. However, this does not mean that the oppressors' identity, knowledge, experience, and even privilege are of no value whatsoever.

Harding and the Lynds embrace the language of accompaniment coming out of Latin American liberation struggles as the most helpful model for what it means to work in solidarity. Staughton Lynd credits El Salvadoran Archbishop Oscar Romero as the first person to use this term, "pastoral de acompañamiento (pastoral work of accompanying)."[184] Throughout Romero's speeches, sermons and letters, there are constant references to the Latin American liberation theology concept of "the preferential option of the poor." But Lynd says that Romero moved from a concept whereby the "option" to be with and among the poor is "something different, more equal, more in the nature of a joint undertaking" than "a choice made by Church personnel and middle-class intellectuals who are not poor [taking] up a new way of life in the midst of the poverty surrounding them."[185]

In the accompanying model, the privileged person not only brings a message but receives a message, listens more than talks, and gives way to an "ultimate vision of the poor themselves taking responsibility for their own liberation."[186] Particularly for the church, this final element of ceding the vision of justice to the poor serves the purpose of "unmasking the root of false paternalism."[187] It is a serious difficulty and a crucial challenge for privileged allies to share in movements while unlearning their patterns of dominance, putting their entitlements at the service of social struggles, and learning to struggle across differences in a truly reciprocal relationship.

In the context of the interviews, even my own question about allies elicited a criticism of the concept of being an ally altogether, suggesting that ally language may reinforce the differences of power and inequality between persons and groups. During our interview, when I asked Harding, "What has been your own experience in the struggle of a meaningful, helpful role for allies?" he responded,

> I think we are at a stage where white allies are not what we most need... that the essence of this is a struggle that *belongs* to x, y, z and here come the allies along to help out. My feeling is that we are now at a point where we have got to claim the whole business as *our* struggle. We might have allies in Mexico, or Cuba, or Canada. But within America, I think it is absolutely crucial to try to start thinking more and more of the struggle being *all* of our struggles. The ally formulation may be too much of a twentieth-century formulation. That might mean that we must all be figuring out how to lay claim to all of it. Because, in the GLBT situation, I don't want to be saying, "You guys go ahead, and you take care; you work on this as best you can, because this is your struggle, and I want to be your ally as best I can." That's not inclusive enough for me.

My own language in the interview guide betrayed that I believe an ally has a "role" to play in social struggle – a cause in which "to be involved." The idea of a role stands in contrast to having a mutual relationship with persons and communities in struggle. Ally language and practice may reinforce a dominant position, thereby reinforcing unjust socio-economic and political hierarchies that are the basis of all forms of violence. Nonetheless, activists must realize there are existing inequalities of material and psychological power among movement participants. Solidarity means recognizing the power dynamics inherent in structural and cultural violence, resisting and acting against dominant behaviors brought into movements from privileged social locations, while remaining committed to shared struggle across differences.

As Schulman noted, there are issues of sexism in the queer liberation struggle. But a main difference is there is a "community of gay men and women who work together to win rights for each other and so your friends and your partners are in the same movement that you're in." To Schulman, being a straight ally demands a tremendous commitment. It means taking up the struggle for gay and lesbian liberation as a shared struggle. She gave examples within a family:

> If a gay person is not allowed to babysit a same-sex niece or nephew, then the straight people in the family should refuse to do so as well. The deprivation of resources will force the homophobes, in most cases, to reassess their behavior or be alienated.... If... homophobic Uncle Arthur organizes Christmas dinner around the schedules of the heterosexual couples in the family and the homosexual partner's schedule is not considered, then no one should participate in Christmas dinner. Since the originating Arthur may decide that something is better than nothing, the social consensus created by the other straight family members will force the homosexual partner's needs to be fully and equally considered. Of course, for this to be organized currently depends on the gay members actively agitating for supportive action on the part of straights. But if there were a broad cultural agreement that heterosexual non-participation was the expected mode of behavior, the burden would be off the individual gay people in the family.[188]

Schulman's examples make the risks inherent in practices of solidarity and turning over privilege in the struggle for justice evident. Schulman decries a false discourse of tolerance that suggests communities that have historically been violated and excluded can be "painlessly included without anyone else's position having to be adjusted."[189] Once again, a mutually shared struggle requires privileged actors within dominant culture to give up their material and psychological advantages.

The basic idea of accompanying is walking alongside in the context of differences. Additionally, in the context of shared action in social struggle, Lynd defines accompanying as an umbrella term "that includes a family of related practices: equality, listening, seeking consensus, and exemplary action" in coalition among parties that experience different levels of impact.

> The equality of participants is foundational…. An altogether different atmosphere comes into being if there is mutual recognition that no one has all the answers and that it is accordingly necessary to search together so that (in the Quaker phrase) "way may open." Listening then becomes intense and may be prolonged. The desired place of arrival will be consensus. However, should consensus not emerge, instead of maneuvering to win a vote the next step is likely to be a time in which individuals or small groups act out perceived images of the road ahead. The process will be understood in the manner of sowing. We ourselves are the seed that is thrown onto various kinds of soil. Whether or not something grows and flourishes is not so much a test of our abilities as an experiment, the results of which, whether good or ill, will contribute to the common store of understanding.[190]

In Lynd's experience, getting "thrown out of the history profession made it possible for me to get to know workers and then prisoners as a lawyer in a way that I never, never could have done as an Ivy League historian."

> So the big news is, the headline is, to all the other [people like us], gotta get out of Cambridge, Massachusetts; Berkeley, California. It cannot be done just as a projection of the university campus or academic life. You want the United States to become one big Tea Party. You want our society to lurch toward fascism. Continue your present lifestyle. You want to do something about it; leave those enclaves of liberalism and find a way to take up life in the rest of the United States, that portion that extends from the Sierra Nevada mountains to the Appalachians where most of America lives. There has, in the past, been an American radicalism that flourished in those parts – a life like that of

Eugene Debs, an event like the so-called Green Corn rebellion in Oklahoma during the first World War. I mean there's nothing about radicalism that is incomprehensible or essentially alien to the spirit of middle America. But nothing is going to happen until people with radical ideas take up residence in those places. It really is as simple as that.

"Taking up residence" will require academics on the left in the United States abandoning their "preoccupation with a novel vocabulary, or a new organization," but instead to "venture forth into relationships of companionship with ordinary people in places where there may be few fellow radicals."[191] Jensen noted that radical consciousness among common people is "incendiary" when paired with the action of privileged persons with access to power and constitutes a great threat to structures of violence.

7 – Mutual Accountability Practices

Huerta and the Lynds both believe the primary obstacles to successful social movements are internal accountability and interpersonal solidarity. In her own organization, Huerta said that one of the worst problems internal to organizing was *chisme* – gossip, in Spanish. Her foundation spends a tremendous amount of time on intra-organization training in communication, conflict resolution, and accountability processes. Similarly, the Lynds said that in their experience, they saw movements crushed by a lack of direct speaking, an unwillingness to engage problems and issues openly instead of engaging in power struggles behind the backs of comrades in social change.[192] Based on the Lynds' experience of watching good social movements and their organizations destroy themselves, Staughton Lynd writes,

> We need to proceed in a way that builds community. There must be certain ground rules. We should practice direct speaking: if something bothers you about another person, go speak to him or her and do not gossip to a third person. No one should be permitted to present themselves in caucuses that define a fixed position beforehand and are impervious to the exchange of experiences. We must allow spontaneity and

experiment without fear of humiliation and disgrace. Not only our organizing but our conduct toward one another must be paradigmatic in engendering a sense of truly being brothers and sisters.[193]

Communities need articulated rules about behavior, not articulated rules for belief.

Four interviewees spoke about the need to establish rules for community that relate to solidarity. One of B♀'s primary commitments is to All Of Us Or None, an organization formed by former political prisoners. This group had to articulate very concrete rules that worked directly to hold in check different dimensions of dominance within the group.

> I'm on this committee; that's the mediation committee. There's about ten of us now. We have to have rules. You can't bring your pistol to the fucking meeting. You can't come loaded. You have to be respectful. You can't be a sexist pig. You can't be a racist pig. You can't be a queer-hater, all that shit. We have to lay all that out in language that everybody can understand. What happens if people do that? How do we handle that? We have to police ourselves, for lack of a better word. So we've been working on that. That's how we get to know each other. It's by working together. And talking together and eating together and joking together.

Other interviewees proposed other rules. Jensen suggested that communities of resistance take on and enforce a code of defense, something like the United Nations' Responsibility to Protect (R2P). "Part of what being an ally means is we have an R2P; we have a responsibility to protect." Concretely this might mean "if some man rapes a woman in some certain community, there have to be consequences." The man might be kicked out of the community or face other consequences based on the context and community decision-making structures and lines of accountability.

Schulman spoke regarding setting out clear guidelines about when defensive intervention from outside the community is appropriate. She also writes, "There is one case in which third-party intervention is the moral imperative" on behalf of gay people: "when the shunned, scapegoated, and oppressed person asks you to intervene."[194] Defensive intervention, on behalf of a violated person or community who asks, creates several potentially positive outcomes:

1) builds integrity for the intervener, even if the intervention is not successful;

2) shows the victimized person that someone cares;

3) gives perpetrators the knowledge that their behavior is offensive;

4) increases possibilities for accountability and consequences for the perpetrator; and

5) creates a zeitgeist in which other persons might be protected from suffering in the same way in the future.[195]

Schulman writes that intervention "reposition[s] one's self towards the acknowledgment that other people are real, even if they have less status and are more endangered."[196] Schulman's language here recalls that (non)violent practices of solidarity are meant to concretely address and embody the necessary shifts in reversal and entitlement that are a part of the rationalizing of violence.

All people in social struggle must be willing to be accountable for their behaviors. In particular, persons from privileged social locations should be open and humble in accepting responsibility for replicating dominance in social movements and remain committed to changing those behaviors collectively.[197]

Yet both Jensen and Lynd said that solidarity and accountability to oppressed communities do not necessarily amount to doing or believing whatever oppressed groups tell you. Jensen said that solidarity "means listening. It doesn't mean that you have to put up with shit…. It doesn't mean that all of us [privileged people] have to do" everything and meet every demand and request of individuals simply because of their oppressed social location. Occasionally criticized that his theory of solidarity "defers to whatever poor people are demanding at the moment," Staughton Lynd writes that "accompaniment is not deference."[198] He cites Archbishop Oscar Romero who said the church's aim in solidarity with the poor is to support them in their claims for justice, but equally to denounce all injustice among the poor and oppressed, and to hold them accountable for wrong behaviors.[199]

Practical Theology and Social Change: Self-Critical Solidarity

In his writing and work, Staughton Lynd records that the most dramatic instances of solidarity across racial difference that he has seen have been in the labor movement, during wartime, and in prisons.[200] Extreme circumstances of struggle against inhumane conditions in the Attica and Lucasville[201] prison uprisings suggest a theory for social change today:

> The key at Attica and Lucasville was for members of each race first to organize separately, with whatever music, dress, and symbolism spoke to each group's particular culture, and then unite and fight. Separation in the first stages of group activity was a necessary tactic.... But the strategy was racial solidarity on behalf of common goals. In Vietnam and in American prisons, these bonds of "black and white together" formed under the hammer of common danger and oppression. It remains to be seen whether the same process can bring together African-Americans, Caucasians, and Hispanics when they are in civilian life rather than in a war zone, or on the street instead of behind bars. I believe that whether we succeed in creating a new, interracial movement of poor and working people depends on first recognizing the need for this two-step process. The formation of identity groups of African-Americans, or Aryans, or women, or gays, or any other identifiable minority, is a stage and a tactic that must be followed by the creation of a united movement. Sub-groups should feel free to gather by themselves as needed, but the purpose of forming a new, united Movement must be recognized as paramount by all.[202]

Lynd's delineation of a "two-step process" of separation and solidarity is helpful. This may not be a linear process, but a cycle of separation and collaboration among groups with differences of identity, tactics, and beliefs. Lynd's previously shared metaphor of sowing seeds of actions, which may not be agreed to by everyone in struggle, is useful. When consensus cannot be achieved, it should be possible for individuals and small groups to act and strategize separately. An ideology of unity should not preclude self-determined activity in social struggle.

If separation of identity groups is necessary and desired, it is clear that persons from primarily privileged identity groups have a primary task to nurture solidarity by intentionally dismantling their dominance within movements. A particularly helpful term is individual and community "self-critical solidarity."[203] Self-critical solidarity implies first and foremost critical, structural analysis of any given context of action. As the previous chapters have displayed, this analysis is useful to determine effective practices of social transformation. A second goal, for solidarity within an intentional stage of separate identity group formation and action, is the analysis of the operative structures of violence present and replicating themselves within movement participants. Self-critical analysis includes thoughtful reflection by advocates of (non)violence on the various forms of violence in which activists are likely to be implicated, many of which may remain unknown or unidentified. Violence that is difficult to recognize includes the imposition of knowledge, the imperialism of cultural superiority (racism, sexism, homophobia, etc.), and the acceptance of state violence to maintain order as justified. An analysis of the impact of social locations within a movement is intended to turn into practices of nurturing (non)violent solidarity, both internal and external. Many practices of solidarity have been suggested throughout this chapter: asking, listening, awareness, intervention, and accountability. From a practical perspective, this would mean the development of conscious models of self-reflexive solidarity. These may include the formal articulation of guidelines, which are subject to evaluation by different interests within the movement.[204]

It is critical for Christians engaged in social struggle to examine the particular role of Christianity in the violence, domination, and liberation of the movement's trajectory. Heitink notes that this self-critical reflexivity of Christians should not focus abstractly on "the church," but instead on concrete people and moments within the church/es or other groups under consideration. Clearly, the notion of self-criticism should not be limited by individualism.[205]

This chapter on solidarity shows that privileged allies need to, internally and actively, deconstruct their social location in the midst of their own community. Solidarity as (non)violence includes commitments to individual and community self-examination and the development of group rules around asking, listening, and awareness across the boundaries of various differences. These practices seek to concretely dismantle and sacrifice material privileges and a sense of psychological entitlement to know and to lead. Persons who benefit from the structures of violence must establish accountability practices that concretely address the denial, reversal, and entitlement endemic to all forms of violence. Doing this collective, self-critical, historical-analytical work from a Christian social location with a concrete situation of social struggle is a practice of "true discipleship."[206]

That the idea of solidarity as (non)violence intends an increasingly reciprocal relationship undermines the notion that poor and oppressed people can be the only source of knowledge and the sole agents to determine the future directions for liberation. Individual and group identity is such a complicated mix that separating privileged from marginalized experiences is extremely complicated. Additionally, if privileged allies have no helpful resources, knowledge, or ability to really understand the situation of violence, it means that real solidarity and mutually shared vision and action for a just world are impossible. Nonetheless, it is possible to accompany one another toward social change, through multiple practices of solidarity for the complicated and challenging work of undoing dominance in movements.

CONCLUSION

A Critical, Practical, Theological Model of Social Change

The foregoing chapters have evaluated (non)violence in light of conversation with twelve diverse interviewees about the means of social change and the relationship of these means to social location, including Christian social location. In view of this evaluation, there are two tasks for this conclusion:

1) summarizing elements of a Christian model for social change implied by the analysis of the interviews, and

2) questioning the adequacy of Christian perspective as a centering frame for this project.

I offer some reflections on a practical theological method along with the model for thinking about (non)violent social change from a critical, Christian perspective.

1 – Critical – Structural Analysis and Transformative Historiography

Critical historiography is one of the unique processes of a theological method that centers practices in the real world. Chapters Two and Three demonstrated that any evaluation of the transformative effect of a Christian theology or practice of social change must

1) be set within an analysis of the historical and current contexts of struggle and violence;

2) seek to understand the complex nature of violence in its direct, structural, and cultural forms: and

3) remain committed to examining all three forms of violence – direct, structural, and cultural – in which Christian

individuals, institutions, and theology participate and play a role.

This analysis intends to identify how Christian (non)violence serves as an ideology that reinforces the dominant culture's rationalization of violence through denial, reversal, and entitlement.

But as José Míguez Bonino points out, "The identification of the ideology implicit in any given historical praxis does not as such disqualify it."[207] De-ideologizing Christian (non)violence sees analysis as an expanded practice of (non)violence itself. The identification of an ideological function implicit in Christian (non)violence proposes to self-implicate Christians in their own violence for the express purpose of meeting the goal of (non)violence – confronting and dismantling violence. Ignoring the complexity of violence is where the (non)violent thought and practice represented by white, liberal Christians has fallen short. A critical, practical theology of social change must pass through an analysis and awareness of violence at the intersections of history, the context of struggle, and any given individual or community's social location. Without such broad-ranging critical analysis, the practice of (non)violence is incomplete. Critical analysis, as a (non)violent practice, develops insights into the realities of history through which we seek new and renewed collective practices of transformation towards the creation of a new world.[208]

Critical analysis informs Christian (non)violence in a number of fruitful ways. An accurate portrayal of U.S. history displays the pervasive involvement of Christians and their theological and cultural traditions in the perpetration of all forms of violence in this country. Since all social change practices take place within the context of an ongoing legacy and context of violence, activists committed to Christian (non)violence have no credibility with oppressed communities without an awareness of this history. This awareness includes the ways in which, historically, practices of (non)violence may have:

- limited their effectiveness,
- played a role in pacification instead of liberation,

- supported the structurally violent status quo and its material and psychological benefits by failing to demand or force significant changes, and
- worked in tension or tandem with organized violence.

Additionally, this knowledge would indicate when and how (non)violence has been effectively deployed and what particular factors made it effective in context. To understand how violence and (non)violence have been effective for liberation, and how they have not, is to remove them from theological abstraction and refuse to place either of them on a false, moral high ground. A critical analysis that seeks to work for structural transformation must reject strictly dichotomizing violence and (non)violence in historical and current practices.

Analysis within the context of actual struggle will seek to have a realistic grasp of the conditions of structural violence and make every effort to determine who or what the opponent in social struggle is. Since the agents of violence are often obscured in structural violence, contextual analysis within social struggle means identifying concrete individual and collective, organizational, and institutional targets of change. When such agents are identified, they are, with rare exceptions, members of dominant cultural groups and rarely held accountable for their actions and oversight of pervasive acts and conditions of violence within their personal relationships, their organizations, or the public at large. Therefore, investigation is crucial to determine the next steps of deciding how these agents will be held accountable. Structural analysis also takes seriously that everyone in the United States is implicated in violence. Therefore, analysis and awareness of one's own social location in the context of struggle is also essential. For effective social change, it is essential to both name and distinguish the perpetration of violence and its benefits to the dominant culture and then to hold people responsible at the various, appropriate levels of accountability.

A critical analysis and understanding of violence and (non)violence must seek to undermine individualism at every turn. Systematic analysis seeks to expand the common conception of violence from only direct violence to structural and cultural violence. Individuals who do not engage in violent, interpersonal acts do not often see themselves as violent. This reinforcement of the commonsense understanding of violence as primarily individual, physical behavior absolves individuals from further self-examination of their role in violence. Individualism contributes to the practice of denial and supports the entitlements born of unacknowledged structures of violence. As an active practice, Christian (non)violence should promote these broader understandings of structural and cultural violence as violence within the dominant society. In terms of effective action, the promotion of a broader understanding of violence expands the common conception of (non)violence typically implied by traditional Christian practice beyond the practice of physical, non-resistant non-retaliation.

Critical analysis should not be a mere intellectual enterprise. If a privileged individual or community is committed to struggling against injustice, this analysis should be taking place in the context of action in and with the communities who are most impacted by the structures of violence.

> If the oppressed are silent while theologians or other intellectuals speak, no empowerment occurs.... The test of the seriousness of our commitment is whether we welcome having those who were previously silent wrest our theory from us, altering and transforming it through their unique appropriation.[209]

In social action, critical analysis relates to solidarity.

Critique

A critique of the practical theological method, including this project, arises here. Practical theology aspires to create social transformation. Yet like all academic disciplines, it primarily belongs to academic elites within the church. Outside of a purely participatory action research method,[210] I do not know how to overcome this problem. How do the privileged practical theologian and the Christian community deal with their distance from daily violence and oppression?

— Conclusion —

Throughout the interviews and the preparation required for them, I gave myself my own U.S. history lesson about the conditions of oppression and genocide that have periodically created the conditions for resistance and social transformation in this country. I began the critical analysis that this model proposes as a (non)violent practice. The most highly educated people mostly do not know about the fundamentally violent history of our country. This reflects the deep problem of denial and mystification as functions that support structures of violence. We do not know for reasons of race and class privilege, and this is part of the problem of violence. Primarily privileged people have little idea what most people go through, struggle through, survive through, live through, and die through that motivates them to take serious and remarkable action for change, be it violent or (non)violent.

At a certain point during the interviews, I began to feel the difference between my experience as a person of relative privilege, a relative lack of bodily experience of oppression and repression, and the interviewees' experiences, which were very real. How was I possibly to understand the depth of the nature of these issues? I experienced this distance despite my involvement in social justice activism and the education this research has given me. Even though this project was more collaborative and engaged with some level of activist reality, it was still primarily an individual, intellectual endeavor. What impact this research effort has on a larger community remains to be seen.

I bring this self-criticism to broaden the criticism of practitioners in the field of practical theology whose critical tools are perhaps irreconcilably distant from, while intimately related to, the conditions, experiences, and knowledge of oppressed people themselves. How does this distance not replicate structural and cultural violence? Is this type of work really only relevant to the church and academy? How do scholars reckon with these problems in light of a stated commitment of practical theology to social transformation in the real world? Despite the interviewees being social change agents of relative privilege, this project strove to connect with real differences in diverse communities in the real world. Given the focus of typical practical theological projects on fairly homogeneous Christian ministry settings, I cannot help but think that by-and-large, this field primarily fails to rise to its own declaration of socially transformational intent.

2 – Practical –
Contextual Experimentation
with Diverse Modes of Action

Again and again, during the interviews and throughout the course of the interview analysis, I was struck by the way in which these very experienced and knowledgeable scholars and activists spoke about the deep ambiguity and possibility for social transformation in the context of the United States in these times. Are we entering into a period of impending barbarism and fascism, or are the possibilities of true democracy only beginning to be revealed? Are we in a reactionary, conservative phase of U.S. history or a pre-revolutionary phase? Will the structures of violence destroy the earth and its inhabitants, or will an impending crisis finally awaken humans to take radical action to avoid environmental and economic collapse?

Harding said that we

> …have a great capacity that we are not knowing at this stage how to nurture, how to encourage, and I think it is both in terms of dreaming the possibilities of America and imagining the varying kinds of ways in which we could bring healing oil to the society.

Others expressed that the time for believing in America has come to an end. Yet the current variety of socio-economic and environmental breakdowns all provide opportunities for previously unimagined resistance. Lynd wrote that his structural analysis had led him to the simple conclusion that "crises of capitalism will continue"; such uncertainties mean that "Opportunities will endlessly present themselves to try to change things for the better."[211]

Similarly, Schulman writes,

> It's a moment filled with opportunity for people who can think for themselves. There are holes in the cultural fabric, and

no one seems to be in tight control. Even the horrifying lack of jobs means that the yuppie road that some were blindly, socially obliged to follow is no longer a realistic option for many who were once invited. This means having to piece together "a living" through an eclectic combination of one's abilities, dreams, relationships, visions, will and skill. Not a great set-up for most, but very enriching for all if enough people can take advantage of the moment to create new paths.[212]

Whenever it looks like "there's no way forward here, this is blinding, this is destructive, this is stupid, this is not the truth," Power said she asks herself questions that seek newness:

What else is there? What else can I encounter? What can I allow to come into being? What can I see from there? What's available to me from there? What actions might I take right now to change the dynamic? How do we continue to be activists? How do we come up against this entrenched power with all that we know about the suffering that it's causing?

Power said such questions beg for new and renewed practices and not the same old set of practices, attitudes, and limited frameworks that continue to replicate the "dominance modes' definition of who we are and what the world is." The interviewees suggested that as currently practiced in the U.S., (non)violence offers little that is new to recent struggles, nor has it influenced substantial reform or revolutionary change. There is a failure of imagination, a failure to strategize, and a failure to risk bodies and entitlements. For those desirous of claiming faithful (non)violence there is plenty more creative room. The difficult nature of the current period, Power said, "…is kind of a command to expand rather than to contract in what we're considering and where we're looking for possibilities."

The ambiguity of the historical moment in the United States suggests that it is a time ripe for experimentation of all kinds. Here we should recall that Mahatma Gandhi referred to (non)violence primarily as "experiments with truth." (Non)violence advocates should focus on developing their own creative means and work towards shared effectiveness across difference instead of condemning violence as unfaithful, immoral, or ineffective. Jensen said that the exclusionary thought-pattern of (non)violence, by itself, is "a framework that truncates actions that could otherwise be effective."[213] Non-exclusionary, non-dogmatic thinking opens up space for creative thinking and action. The challenges which advocates of all means of social change charge to (non)violence should inspire advocates of (non)violence to reach beyond those limits. All types of action can be taken up by liberal-to-radical individuals and communities. The key for Jensen is for all activists – be they assassins, lawyers, healers, therapists, writers, publishers, doctors, teachers, ministers – "to think like members of a resistance." B♀ said a comprehensive, effective "movement with teeth" included all kinds of community discussion and action. She said that the nature of struggle is "not one thing. It's a multi-faceted struggle, because it's a multi-faceted enemy." The key to struggle, she said, is "never giving up."

As the first element of this model suggests, analysis is one of the first practices necessary to create social change. But analysis should move to strategizing, asking questions like: Who are we? What are our skills? What is our context? Who is the enemy? What do we want? What is our vision? How do we get there effectively? Who else do we need to join us in this struggle? The four practices suggested by Chapter Five – consciousness-raising, organizing, creating alternative communities, and sustained, disruptive action – are a constellation of practices that must be strategized. When they are practiced simultaneously and collectively (though perhaps with different emphases at different times), they increasingly work toward effective social transformation.

Within these four generalized tactics, it is important, from the start, not to dichotomize violence and (non)violence. There is a way of affirming that the goals we seek to achieve are a just, (non)violent world without imposing that vision in a morally normative way. Collective, practical experimentation intentionally seeks to live within the awareness and realities of the contradictions of violence and (non)violence at every level. An attitude of openness to a diversity of actors, beliefs, and tactics encourages the tensions within the so-called liberal-to-radical divide. A "diversity of tactics" approach to action supports the need for different people to work in different arenas in different ways. Nonetheless, this model encourages action that always pushes towards the radical, collective, disruptive edge. This includes maintaining an open mind towards the use of property destruction. This collective, multi-faceted tactical model affirms a diversity of actors and actions when there is no consensus. I affirm Staughton Lynd's insight that communities that are differently socially located may need to engage in multiple stages of separation and collaboration while working towards shared ends of social transformation. The development of clear accountability structures and practices, including rules of interpersonal engagement, seems wise both within and across identity groups.

Why push the radical, collective, disruptive edge of practice? There are a few primary responses to this question that have recurred throughout this project:

1) Since the nature of all forms of violence is to individualize, individualist solutions to violence address none of the structural and cultural understandings of violence.

2) While a variety of practices and tactics are necessary to create the conditions by which social transformation might occur, structures and cultures of violence will ultimately not be changed without collective disruption.

3) Privileged persons in primarily comfortable circumstances have proven themselves consistently co-opted by their own normative vision of a pacifistic, idealistic, bourgeois existence.

The pairing of Christian tradition with democracy under capitalism has resulted in notorious compromises and "third ways."[214] These bargains regularly concede radical demands to the order of the status quo, invariably keep the privileged in a material comfort zone, and result in sacrificing justice for unity and peace. Consistently pushing the edges of disruptive practice for social change is the best means by which (non)violent actors push themselves to disrupt their own comfort zones. Privileged actors who affirm social change activism must directly confront systems of domination and consistently resist their own temptations not to resist.

There are many other practices for privileged actors in social change meant to address both reversal and entitlement that constitute expanded practices of (non)violence. Practicing (non)violence means not only affirming the need to dismantle inequalities and false portrayals of the oppressed as violent but actually dismantling the reversals through practicing non-dominant behaviors. This is going to require privileged persons in all of the myriad intersections of identity to consider, collectively, what they are going to do, what they can concretely bring to struggle, and what they are going to give up. In very tangible terms, economically privileged persons can bring their material resources to bear on movement organizing without imposing control. As disruption requires research, training, legal and medical work, and all manner of organization and administration, privileged persons with certain kinds of skills in these areas should offer them.

Those who understand their privilege will attempt not to impose but to undo their sense of entitlement and practices of dominance within one's own immediate community and in the context of movement solidarity. As the previous chapter explained, these practices actively address inequalities by intentionally seeking to bridge material and cultural differences and reversing the cultural, structural hierarchies by

- asking,
- listening,
- awareness of one's (community's) social location,
- not imposing one's (community's) beliefs,
- showing up,
- material support,
- turning over privilege,
- suffering powerlessness with,
- doing your work with your own people,
- accompanying as a reciprocal relationship, and
- mutual accountability practices.

These practices intend to tangibly decrease, if not reverse, the actual distance between one's privileged self and the ones most impacted by oppression in the context of actual struggle. Collective, disruptive action-taking often demands the practice of actively turning over privilege through making material sacrifices. Privileged people engaging in transformative practice will increasingly seek to dismantle their material and psychological entitlements by an increased willingness and practice that disrupts concrete systems and institutions of power and to accept the consequences of such action. The goal of solidarity is developing genuinely reciprocal relationships in the context of mutually shared struggle.

Critique

The emphasis of the practical theological approach is ostensibly on practice. A practical theological Christian (non)violence asserts the need for effective practices determined in context over against any claims to (non)violence through appeals to theological abstractions such as love or faithfulness. Throughout this work, I consistently struggled with the problem of correlating diverse thought and practice with Christian categories of meaning. I often felt the analysis was bound by the categories of Christian analysis themselves – love, faithfulness, concepts of God and Jesus, theological anthropology, and sin. In this boundedness, I wondered how truly relevant a particularly Christian practice of (non)violence is to social transformation in this diverse world. Many times I wished the interviewee data would simply speak on its own, so I would not have to interact with these notions. I wondered if the categories of Christian analysis might be better left aside. Yet as a Christian theological project, it seemed to demand that I impose these categories on the data. This was particularly true of the tactics chapter and the concept of "faithful, not effective." As I deconstructed this phrase, the totality of the diverse interviewee data on effective practice made the idea of faithfulness seem altogether irrelevant. Yet my own Christian social location and commitment to (non)violence struggled against rejecting the idea of faithfulness as meaningful to social change. I had no remedy for this problem. As the previous chapter on solidarity demonstrates, the act of imposition from a position of dominance is an act of violence. I did not intend to do violence to the perspectives of my diverse interviewees. Yet the interpretation of the depth and nuance of what they shared could not help but be limited by the imposition of Christian theological analysis, particularly when it came to interpreting practices.

Certainly, the interviewee data opened up a meaningful critique and a renewal of some ways of thinking about and practicing (non)violence from a privileged, Christian social location. Both the critiques of and expansions on thought and practice are helpful for my people – white, middle-to-upper-middle-class, U.S. Christians invested in progressive or revolutionary social change. Beyond this community, these critiques are useful in understanding the practice of (non)violence in general terms. In this way, I reaffirm the minority trend within practical theology, which seeks to reckon with how an engagement with differences of social location, experience with, opinions about, and practices of social transformation might affect Christian practice and theology. Yet a very real problem remains in the practice of practical theology. Given the legacy of Christian supremacist violence across history and real differences in practice and thought on the ground, this project fundamentally challenges the usefulness of Christian categories and the legitimacy of Christian theological projects supportive of (non)violence.

3 – Theology –
Disrupting a Unified Christian Discourse

If practical theology is truly committed to engaging differences in the real world, then the main task of practical theology would seek to disrupt the violence of a unified, Christian theological discourse. When practical theology undermines the imposition of Christian norms and beliefs as dominant cultural practices of violence, it becomes a practice of (non)violence. For example, while affirming the theological abstraction fundamental to Christian (non)violence that we are all "one," interconnectedness as a practice betrays this abstraction as a lie. Interconnectedness understood in purely theological or existential terms should not obscure the very real differences of power that are at the heart of all forms of violence. These differences in power destroy interconnectedness and function to objectify the powerless, exploited, and oppressed humans and other-than-human beings. The abstract appeal of a divine connectedness to reconnect all forms of life may serve as a theological background against which the reality of inequality and fundamental disconnectedness may be truthfully displayed. True differences in and between all forms of life should not be denigrated through a false claim to connection. Particularly when doing analysis beyond the Christian community, practical theology's commitment to examining practices must resist reliance upon certain religious essences as a basis of common human experience. In as far as it represents a privileged perspective of the dominant culture, if Christian practical theology seeks to transform the world, it must also seek to be transformed by the world by privileging data outside of the Christian tradition.

For example, in the case of human supremacism, the qualitative data has something very important to tell the normative, dominant Christian tradition about the nature of violence. This is the harsh realization that human supremacism in the Christian tradition may be the foundation of all forms of violence within its sphere of influence. How does this impact the practice of the dominant tradition of Christian (non)violence? What would it mean for the dominant culture's Christian tradition to take this critique, this actual difference of experience and understanding, into the center of the tradition and allow it to be transformed? In order for Christian (non)violence to have credibility in practice, it must allow for real differences to transform specific theological claims and practices at the heart of its tradition.

Therefore, (non)violent theologizing for social change must commit itself to (non)violent theological practices. Among these practices is the breaking down of transcendent dualisms such as the human and other-than-human, which is at the heart of traditional Christian theology and is an underlying mechanism of the dominant culture's violence. From a practical standpoint internal to the Christian tradition, (non)violence would entail a practice of eradicating these theological hierarchies from all worship and liturgy, rituals, scriptures, and even local church business practices. The transformation of these practices internal to Christian tradition themselves might be usefully considered as (non)violent "sites of struggle."[215]

Furthermore, a transformed Christian theology for social change would reject any singular vision of a uniquely Christian salvation and recognize proselytizing as inherently violent theology and practice. Christian theology would also reject notions of salvation history as linear, human-divine progress. Christian theology would no longer align itself with institutions of structural violence, such as the military and the police. Its primary directives for ministry would be directed towards the most oppressed in society. Theological claims would work towards the dismantling of individual and collective privileges. Their primary aim would be prophetic. Theological claims would serve as a foundation for Christian practices that disrupt the violent status quo and end structural violence, including within Christian institutions and theology themselves.

If justice is defined as the end of violence and the liberation of the oppressed, then social change is change for the sake of achieving a new order. Establishing a just order will require a disruption of any current illusion of peace through collective practice, only, and will also require a disruption of theologies of pacification and subordination. Christian (non)violence brings to light the history of Christian individuals, institutions, and theologies that have perpetrated all forms of violence in this country and in the world. Therefore, Christian practical theologizing for social change can no longer claim a unique, moral high ground in the struggle for social transformation. Christian (non)violence would not be conceived of as a fixed, theological, or ideological point or practice but, to use Staughton Lynd's words, "a contested terrain of action."

4 – Social Change – Communities of Creative, Counter-Cultural Resistance

Practices of social change must be collective. Christian communities already provide this as a built-in feature of their existence. I have expressed skepticism that Christian communities within the dominant culture will take on the constellation of practices that seek to dismantle all forms of violence. Such communities, should they exist, are likely to locate themselves outside of traditional Christian institutions. Yet I remain a Christian and am left to state and affirm that any attempts at social transformation without such alternative communities of resistance and solidarity are doomed.

If Christian (non)violence is a vision for a renewed world without violence, then that vision must not amount to the reproduction of middle-class, U.S. Christian values that support the socio-political and economic orders. As the descriptions of direct, structural, and cultural violence suggested, today, violence of every kind and at every level appears related to capitalism. Therefore, the practice of Christian (non)violence must embody a counter-cultural rejection of capitalism's culture and structures.[216] This rejection affirms the interconnectedness of all of life. This vision directs Christian practitioners of (non)violence to a thorough self-examination of the entitlements implied by U.S. economic domination internal to churches, the country, in the world, and of the earth. This practice implies the creation of alternative, radical models of economic living. This practice implies creative forms of collective disruption. This practice implies solidarity across differences among communities of difference who share these counter-cultural values and willingness to confront and disrupt power by any means.

There is meaningful language within Christian traditions and practices that can serve as resources to resistance, dissent, and disruption of this vast culture of violence and its structures. In particular, the Christian tradition provides "counter-disciplines,"[217] – language, if not practices, that encourage least four ways to a new community:

1) the loss of material entitlements;
2) the work of reversing structural inequalities and cultural hierarchies;
3) the banishing of fear and the taking up of courage; and

4) the spiritual and practical, tactical preparation of individuals and communities for the strength necessary to make the voluntary sacrifices required by disruptive practice.

If privileged, Christian (non)violent activists want to continue to claim their Christian communal identity as essential to a decidedly Christian social change practice, then we have our internal work cut out for us. We must think in terms of creative, courageous, counter-cultural resistance. We must move beyond the common limits of Christian (non)violence as it is traditionally, currently conceived. Dismantling behaviors of Christian domination in the context of social struggle in solidarity with those persons most impacted by the structures of violence is an essential part of this Christian (non)violent practice. Recognizing the practices and temptations which inevitably reappear to replicate dominance and the violent status quo, Christian communities that claim a (non)violent tradition will resist the claims to being "exemplary human communities."[218] Recognizing that our ways of knowing and acting have been and are limited and that we have participated in and perpetuated violence, we will understand ourselves as only one of many and diverse communities that imperfectly seek social transformation and justice.

Appendix – Interviewees

The following list of those I interviewed is in order of the interviews.

Kathy Kelly is a peace activist associated with Voices for Creative Nonviolence (VCNV) based in Chicago. Kelly travels with teams into active war zones: Central America during the 1980s and throughout the Middle East (Palestine, Lebanon, Afghanistan, Iraq, and Pakistan). She has been arrested dozens of times. She was a passenger on the Audacity of Hope, the U.S. ship in the Freedom Flotillas, attempting to break the blockade on the Gaza Strip in Palestine. She has served a number of prison sentences, through which experience she makes the connection between U.S. domestic and international violence. She has been a tax refuser since 1980. She is white of Irish descent, Roman Catholic, cis-gender, heterosexual, and lives in voluntary poverty. Her autobiography is *Other Lands Have Dreams: From Baghdad to Pekin Prison* (Petrolia, CA: Counterpunch, 2005). I interviewed Kelly on June 9, 2010, at the Maryhouse Catholic Worker House in New York City.

Sarah Schulman has been associated with a number of social movements: gay liberation and feminist movements, abortion rights, tenants' rights, and Palestinian self-determination. Schulman is the author of fiction and non-fiction works and numerous plays whose characters and themes are oriented towards gay and lesbian life and politics. She is well-known for her journalism, documenting the AIDS epidemic in New York City in local publications during the 1980s from her perspective as an active leader in the AIDS Coalition to Unleash Power (ACT UP). She is Distinguished Professor of the Humanities at City University of New York (CUNY) at Staten Island and co-director of the ACT UP Oral History Project. Schulman is a cisgender, Jewish woman, lesbian, and middle-class. Her most recent works are *Gentrification of the Mind: Witness to a Lost Imagination* (Berkeley, CA:

University of California Press, 2012) and *Conflict is Not Abuse: Overstating Harm, Community Responsibility, and the Duty of Repair* (Arsenal Pulp Press, 2016). I interviewed Schulman on June 23, 2010, in her apartment in New York City.

Katherine Power was a student activist who joined a small revolutionary action group in the Boston area in the 1970s, which advocated the use of violence to oppose U.S. imperialism (in particular, the war in Vietnam) and support Black Nationalism. After the murder of Boston Police Officer Walter Schroeder by a member of her group during the course of a bank robbery, Power lived as a fugitive for twenty-three years. She turned herself in and served six years in prison. She is an AIDS activist in Boston, Massachusetts. She is a cisgender, white woman, raised Roman Catholic with no current religious affiliation, middle-class, married to a woman. She is the subject of a book about her life: *Looking for Revolution, Finding Murder: The Crimes and Transformation of Katherine Ann Power* (Paragon House, 2019). I interviewed her on July 2, 2010, at the Lexington (MA) United Methodist Church.

John Dear was a Jesuit priest, primarily associated with anti-war and nuclear disarmament movements. He has authored and edited over two dozen books on peace and nonviolence, as well as an autobiography: *A Persistent Peace: One Man's Struggle for a Nonviolent World* (Maryknoll, NY: Loyola Press, 2008). He has lived and worked in Central America and lectures throughout the world full-time. He has been arrested dozens of times and has served time in federal prison for his involvement in a Plowshares action trespassing on a military base and attempting to destroy a weapon of mass destruction. He makes his residence in Cerrillos, New Mexico. He is a white, cisgender man. As a former Jesuit priest, he took a vow of poverty, chastity, and obedience. I interviewed John Dear on August 3, 2010, at Ghost Ranch Education and Retreat Center in Abiquiu, New Mexico.

Ward Churchill is an activist scholar, teacher, and writer. He has authored or edited more than twenty books and published well over a hundred book chapters and journal articles. A member of the early Rainbow Coalition in Chicago, he was associated with the Black Panther Party, Students for a Democratic Society (Weatherman faction), Vietnam Veterans Against the War, and the American Indian Movement. A self-described "mongrel," his heritage includes German, Scotch-Irish, Cherokee, and Creek. He identified a Methodist upbringing. Although his background is decidedly working-class, he described his class station as middle-class. Among his many books, *Pacifism as Pathology: Reflections on the Role of Armed Struggle* (Oakland, CA: AK Press, 2007) was most relevant to my research. I interviewed Churchill on September 1, 2010, in his home in Boulder, Colorado

Vincent Harding (deceased) was Professor Emeritus of Religion and Social Transformation at the Iliff School of Theology in Denver, CO. He was president of the Veterans of Hope Project, an educational initiative at the intersections of religion, culture, and participatory democracy. He was an author of over fifty books, essays, and articles. He was well-known as an advocate of nonviolence in the southern movement for freedom and penned the first draft of Martin Luther King, Jr.'s famous speech, "A Time to Break Silence."[219] An African-American, cisgender, heterosexual man, he identified a Christian background but claimed no formal religious affiliation. His most well-known full-length book is *There is a River: The Black Struggle for Freedom in America* (New York: Harcourt Brace, 1981). I interviewed Harding on October 19, 2010, at the Veterans of Hope office in Denver, CO.

Akinyele Umoja is Professor of African-American Studies at Georgia State University. His area of scholarly expertise is Black resistance, particularly the Civil Rights and Black Power movements. He has written dozens of articles and is the author of *We Will Shoot Back: Armed Resistance in the Mississippi Freedom Struggle* (New York: NYU Press, 2013). He was associated with Black Nationalist movements in the

1970s; specifically, two successor organizations to the Revolutionary Action Movement: the Afrikan People's Party and the House of Umoja. He identifies as a New Afrikan. He is cisgender, heterosexual, and middle-class. He identified a conservative Christian upbringing, has no current formal religious affiliation, but connects with traditional African religions and their offspring in the Diaspora. He is one of the founders of the New Afrikan People's Organization, out of which he and others also founded the Malcolm X Grassroots Movement. I interviewed Umoja on November 2, 2010, in his office at Georgia State University.

Dolores Huerta is known primarily for her role as a founder and organizer of the United Farm Workers (UFW) union in California in the 1960s and 1970s. She has been organizing farm workers in California for her entire life. Currently, she is associated with the immigrant rights and feminist liberation movements. She is the President of the Dolores Huerta Foundation. She is Mexican-American, Roman Catholic, in her 80s, cisgender, and heterosexual. I interviewed Dolores Huerta on November 26, 2010, at her home in Bakersfield, California.

Rita Bo Brown (B♀) was a member of a radical, anti-imperialist/ anti-authoritarian, anti-racist group in the Pacific Northwest called the George Jackson Brigade during the 1970s. She was a political prisoner for eight years as a result of her involvement in the bombings and bank robberies of the Brigade. She resides in Oakland, where she was a long-time highway worker for the California Highway Department. Her other vocation is as a volunteer with the Prison Activist Resource Center in Oakland, California, and the national organization All of Us or None. She was an editor of *Out of Time*, a newsletter sponsored by Out of Control: Lesbian Committee to Support Women Political Prisoners, and later incorporated into LAGAI's (Lesbians and Gays Against Interventions) online publication *Ultra Violet*. She had an unaffiliated Christian upbringing and currently has no religious affiliation. She identifies as a queer, white, working-class, butch dyke. Her activist work with the George Jackson Brigade is the subject of the film *The Gentleman*

Bank Robber: The Story of Butch Lesbian Freedom Fighter rita bo brown. I interviewed Brown on December 1, 2010, at the Prison Activist Resource Center in Oakland, California. Brown requested that she be referred to as B♀ in writing.

Derrick Jensen lives and works in Crescent City, California. He is a writer of fiction and non-fiction dealing with the destruction of the environment and the end of civilization. He has authored and co-authored over twenty books. He is cisgender, middle-class, heterosexual. He was raised in the Seventh Day Adventist tradition. His largest volumes most directly related to the matter of violence and (non)violence in human and ecological transformation are *Endgame: The Problem of Civilization, Volumes 1 & 2* (New York: Seven Stories Press, 2006). All of his written and recorded work is available at his website, derrickjensen.org. Though he rejects a personal label, he said his spiritual perspective might be considered animist. I interviewed Jensen on December 6, 2010, at the United Methodist Church in Crescent City, California.

Staughton Lynd and **Alice Lynd** were interviewed together in their home in Niles, Ohio, on December 28, 2010.

Staughton Lynd is a historian and lawyer. He was the director of the Mississippi Summer Freedom Schools in 1964. He is also generally associated with the early anti-Vietnam war movement. His antiwar activity caused him to be blacklisted as an academic historian. After that, he went to law school and associated himself with the labor movement and prisoner advocacy as a lawyer. He was raised in the tradition of ethical humanism and is a Quaker.

Alice Lynd was a draft counselor during the Vietnam War. She served for years as a lawyer for workers and retirees and currently for prisoners in supermaximum security and on death row. She has authored and co-authored with Staughton a number of oral histories on draft resisters and rank-and-file workers. She was raised in the Quaker tradition. They are married, white, cisgender, and heterosexual.

Their shared memoir is *Stepping Stones: Memoir of a Life Together* (Lanham, Maryland: Lexington Books, 2009). They are also the co-editors of *Nonviolence in America: A Documentary History*, rev. ed. (Maryknoll: New York: Orbis Books, 1995).

Endnotes

1 John Dear, interview with author, August 3, 2010, Ghost Ranch Education and Retreat Center, Abiquiú, New Mexico. As all of the twelve interviewees are quoted at length from their interviews throughout the book, I will only cite each participant's interview the first time I make reference to it. Throughout the book I will make clear the distinction between quotations from the interviews and other sources, uniquely citing references to interviewee materials from sources other than the interviews.

2 Dolores Huerta, interview with author, November 26, 2010, in Huerta's home, Bakersfield, California.

3 Rita "Bo" Brown, interview with the author, December 1, 2010, Prison Activist Resource Center, Oakland, CA. Bo Brown requested that throughout the dissertation she be referred to as B♀.

4 Ward Churchill, interview with author, September 1, 2010, in Churchill's home, Boulder, Colorado.

5 "By any means necessary" is a phrase popularized by Malcolm X implying that all means – violent and nonviolent – may be justified for the purposes of social transformation. Malcolm X employed this phrase in many of his public speeches. Among many sources, see *Malcolm X, The Final Speeches: February 1965* (New York: Pathfinder Press, 1992).

6 The first place I read Walter Wink's thesis was in *Engaging the Powers: Discernment and Resistance in a World of Domination.* (Minneapolis: Fortress Press, 1992). I wrote a full critique of Wink's interpretation of the Matthew 5 text in "Engaging the Powers of Nonviolence: A Critique of Walter Wink," in the *Journal of Religion, Conflict, and Peace* 2(1), Fall 2008, http://religionconflictpeace.org/node/41.

7 Cain Hope Felder, *Stony the Road We Trod: African Americans and Biblical Interpretation* (Minneapolis: Augsburg Fortress Publishers, 1991): 61.

8 Paul Ricouer, "The Historical Presence of Nonviolence," *Cross Currents* 14:1, Winter (1964): 16.

9 Johan Galtung, "Violence, Peace and Peace Research," *Journal of Peace Research* 6, no. 3 (1969): 168.

10 I only use the parenthetical formulation when I am using my own words, not when I am quoting interviews or other texts.

11 Wildung Harrison, *Making the Connections: Essays in Feminist Social Ethics*, Carol S. Robb, ed. (Boston: Beacon Press, 1985): 257.

12 Churchill uses this term in *Pacifism as Pathology: Reflections on the Role of Armed Struggle in North America*, 2nd ed. (Oakland, CA: AK Press, 2007).

13 Martin Luther King, Jr., "A Time to Break Silence," *A Testament of Hope: The Essential Writings of Martin Luther King, Jr.*, edited by James M. Washington (San Francisco: Harper Collins, 1986): 233.

---

[14] Information about the interviewees is found on page 221.

[15] This idea is commonly referred to as "intersectionality." This concept was developed by women of color to describe their experience with "interlocking" forms of oppression: race, class, gender, sexual orientation. For example, see: Combahee River Collective, "A Black Feminist Statement," in *This Bridge Called My Back: Writings by Radical Women of Color*, ed. by Gloria Anzaldúa and Cherríe Moraga, 210–218 (Boston: Kitchen Table Press, 1982). The term intersectionality was later coined by scholar-activists Kimberlé Crenshaw and Patricia Hill Collins.

[16] Robert McAfee Brown, *Religion and Violence* (Philadelphia: Westminster Press, 1987): 6.

[17] Johan Galtung, "Violence, Peace and Peace Research," *Journal of Peace Research*, Vol. 6, No. 3 (1969): 170.

[18] Galtung, "Violence, Peace and Peace Research," 173.

[19] As quoted in McAfee Brown, *Religion and Violence*, 44–45, from the document "Latin America: A Continent of Violence," in *Between Honesty and Hope: Documents from and about the Church in Latin America*. Issued at Lima by the Peruvian Bishop's *Commission for Social Action. John Drury, trans.(Maryknoll, NY: Maryknoll Publications, 1970): 81–84.*

[20] Celine-Marie Pascale, *Making Sense of Race, Class and Gender: Commonsense, Power, and Privilege in the United States* (New York: Routledge, 2007): 4.

[21] Throughout the book, there is language that reflects physical ableism. For example, "where you stand determines what you see," and numerous references to blindness. I have left this language intact, since it is true to the exact language of the interviewees. While I regret its usage, I intend that this recognition of the use of ableist language will raise awareness.

[22] Sarah Schulman, *The Gentrification of the Mind: Witness to a Lost Imagination*, (Berkeley, CA: University of California Press, 2012): 34.

[23] While Jensen writes about this in a number of texts, he uses this experience of abuse as a touchstone to understanding the devastation of the earth in *A Language Older than Words* (White River Junction, VT: Chelsea Green Publishing, 2000).

[24] Kathy Kelly, *Other Lands Have Dreams: From Baghdad to Pekin Prison*, (Petrolia, CA: CounterPunch, 2005): 36. Here Kelly refers in particular to the comments of former U.S. Secretary of State Madeline Albright, who, "when she was asked about the fact that more children had died in Iraq than in Hiroshima and Nagasaki combined," responded, "It's a difficult choice to make, but we think the price is worth it."

[25] Johan Galtung. "Cultural Violence," *Journal of Peace Research*, vol. 27, no. 3, 1990: 291.

[26] Galtung, "Cultural Violence," 294.

[27] Galtung, "Cultural Violence," 291.

— Endnotes —

28 Vincent Harding, *There is a River: The Black Struggle for Freedom in America* (New York: Harcourt Brace, 1981). See also Harding's earlier volume *The Other American Revolution* (Los Angeles: University of California Center for Afro-American Studies, 1980).

29 Harding, *There is a River*, 26.

30 Harding, *There is a River*, 27.

31 Harding, *There is a River*, 28.

32 Harding, *There is a River*, 29.

33 Throughout the book, I sometimes use American Indian to describe Indigenous peoples of the United States. While considered politically incorrect, I continue to use American Indian for a couple of reasons. First, I am using it consistent with its use by Ward Churchill. Secondly, at the time of writing my dissertation, I was influenced by persons in the American Indian Movement in Colorado, who used this collective term in addition to personal identification with sovereign nations.

34 Ward Churchill, "Genocide in the Americas: Landmarks from 'Latin' America Since 1492," in *Since Predator Came: Notes from the Struggle for American Indian Liberation*, (Oakland, CA: AK Press, 1995): 41.

35 Ward Churchill, "Encountering the American Holocaust: The Politics of Affirmation and Denial," in *A Little Matter of Genocide: Holocaust and Denial in the Americas 1492 to the Present*, (San Francisco: City Lights Books, 1997): 1.

36 Churchill explains the United Nations' definition of genocide, in which mass killing is only one of five ways in which genocide occurs. See "Defining the Unthinkable: Towards a Viable Understanding of Genocide," in *A Little Matter of Genocide: Holocaust and Denial in the Americas 1492 to the Present*, (San Francisco: City Lights Books, 1997): 399–437.

37 Schulman describes this gentrification process in much more detail and its relationship to AIDS in *Gentrification of the Mind*, particularly in Chapter One, "The Dynamics of Death and Replacement."

38 Derrick Jensen, *Endgame Volume 1: The Problem of Civilization*. (New York: Seven Stories Press, 2006): ix.

39 Jensen, *Endgame I*, 92.

40 Goodman quoting hooks in Diane J. Goodman, *Promoting Diversity and Social Justice: Educating People from Privileged Groups*, (Thousand Oaks, CA: Sage Publications, 2001): 19.

41 Schulman, *Gentrification of the Mind*, 47.

42 Sarah Schulman, *The Ties that Bind: Familial Homophobia and Its Consequences* (New York: New Press, 2009): 2.

43 Schulman, *The Ties that Bind*, 32.

44 Schulman, *The Ties that Bind*, 49–50.

45 The full description of the spiral of violence is found in Hélder Câmara's *Spiral of Violence* (London: Sheed and Ward, 1971): 29–34.

46 Max Weber, "Politics as Vocation," in From *Max Weber: Essays in Sociology*, H.H. Gerth and C. Wright Mills, eds. (New York: Oxford University Press, 1946): 78.

47 Câmara, *Spiral of Violence*, 22.

48 McAfee Brown, *Religion and Violence*, 56–57. In this chapter, McAfee Brown is arguing that principles of just war be applied to the possibility of just revolution.

49 SNCC is the Student Nonviolent Coordinating Committee, in which Stokely Carmichael (a.k.a. Kwame Ture) was a key leader and organizer.

50 CORE is the Congress On Racial Equality.

51 Umoja describes the combination of economic boycott and paramilitary organization as a strategy for social transformation in Natchez, Mississippi, in *We Will Shoot Back: Armed Resistance in the Mississippi Freedom Movement* (NYU Press, 2013).

52 For example, see Christopher B. Strain, *Pure Fire: Self-Defense as Activism in the Civil Rights Era*, (Athens, GA: University of Georgia Press, 2005).

53 Strain, *Pure Fire*, 6–7.

54 Ward Churchill, "I am Indigenist: Notes on the Ideology of the Fourth World," in *ZNet*, February 27, 2009, https://revolutionarystrategicstudies.wordpress.com/2011/05/01/i-am-indigenist-notes-on-the-ideology-of-the-fourth-world-by-ward-churchill/

55 Galtung, "Cultural Violence," 296–297.

56 Galtung, "Cultural Violence," 298.

57 These characteristics of "hard" religions were compiled from four Galtung articles: Galtung (1990); Galtung, "Religions, Hard and Soft," *Cross Currents*; Winter 97/98, Vol. 47 Issue 4, p 437–451; "Religion as a Factor," paper, Wissenschaftskollegzu Berlin, Germany. February 1983;"Religion and Peace: Some Reflections," paper, Center of International Studies, Princeton, New Jersey: Princeton University, December 1986.

58 Information about ACT UP's "Stop the Church" action at St. Patrick's Cathedral in New York City is available at http://www.actupny.org/YELL/stopchurch99.html. For one participant's perception of violence at that action, see Patrick Moore interview at http://www.actuporalhistory.org/interviews/interviews_01.html#moore.

59 Jensen, Language *Older Than Words*, 86.

60 Robert Williams Jr.'s *The American Indian in Western Legal Thought: The Discourses of Conquest*, (New York: Oxford University Press, 1990) traces the foundations of official U.S. law, both federal American Indian policy and all U.S. property law, directly to the Christian tradition and its theological justifications for colonial conquest beginning in 1246 C.E.. *Terra nullius* argues that Indigenous lands were not properly "used," empty, and therefore subject to conquest.

232

61 Known as the "3/5 Compromise," Article 1, Section 2, Paragraph 3 of the U.S. Constitution determined how representation and taxes would be determined in the republic based on the number of free persons. In this compromise, American Indians were also not counted unless they were taxed on property, also effectively excluding them.

62 The concept of the ordering of the earthly and heavenly cities is found in Augustine, *City of God*, (New York: Penguin Classics, 2003).

63 José Míguez Bonino, *Toward a Christian Political Ethics*, (Philadelphia: Fortress Press, 1983): 83.

64 Míguez Bonino, *Toward a Christian Political Ethics*, 86.

65 Míguez Bonino, *Toward a Christian Political Ethics*, 86.

66 Jensen deals with these ideas about the impact of the great religions of the world arising from civilization to enforce pacification by spiritualizing a relationship to the land throughout *Endgame I*, see for example pages 285–6, 295, 301.

67 Galtung, "Cultural Violence," 301.

68 Johan Galtung, "Western Deep Culture and Western Historical Thinking," in *Western Historical Thinking: An Intercultural Debate*, Jörn Rüsen, ed. (New York: Berghahn Books, 2002): 85–100.

69 Galtung, "Cultural Violence," 292.

70 Galtung deals briefly and unsatisfactorily with this central problem he calls "God-above-man-above-nature" in "Religion and Peace: Some Reflections," paper, Center of International Studies, Princeton, New Jersey: Princeton University, December 1986): 4, https://www.transcend.org/galtung/papers/Religion%20and%20Peace-Some%20Reflections.pdf.

71 Interview with Ward Churchill in *Listening to the Land: Conversations About Nature, Culture, Eros*, (White River Junction, Vermont: Chelsea Green Publishing, 2002): 163.

72 Read Genesis 1:28, *King James Version* of the Bible.

73 Jensen, *Endgame I*, 283.

74 Here Churchill is referring to John Trudell. Trudell was the spokesperson for All Tribes Occupation of Alcatraz Island and was present with the American Indian Movement during the occupation of Pine Ridge, South Dakota, in 1973, which Churchill refers to here. For more information on Pine Ridge, see Churchill and Vander Wall's "Why Pine Ridge?" and "The Pine Ridge Battleground," Chapters 4 and 5 in *Agents of Repression*.

75 Jensen, *Endgame I*, 31.

76 Jensen, *Endgame I*, 37.

77 Galtung, "Social Structure, Religious Structure, and the Fight for Peace," 362.

78 Galtung, "Social Structure, Religious Structure, and the Fight for Peace," 362.

79 Author interview with George "Tink" Tinker, March 25, 2010, at the Penrose Library, University of Denver, Colorado. This interview fell outside of the scope of the formal interviews for this dissertation. See Dr. Tinker's description of this "American Indians, Conquest, the Christian Story, and Invasive Nation-building," *Wading Through Many Voices: Toward A Theology of Public Conversation*, Harold Recinos, ed.. (New York: Rowman and Littlefield, 2011): 271–274.

80 Jensen, *Endgame I*, 32.

81 Jensen, *Endgame I*, 288.

82 Jensen, *Endgame I*, 286.

83 Míguez Bonino, *Toward a Christian Political Ethics*, 42–43.

84 José Míguez Bonino, *Doing Theology in a Revolutionary Situation*, (Philadelphia: Fortress Press, 1975): 126–127.

85 The entire relevant section from Jesus' Sermon on the Mount is Matthew 5:38–48; see below.

86 A parallel version is found in the gospel of Luke 6:27–36.

87 Yoder, John Howard, *The Politics of Jesus: Behold the Lamb! Our Victorious Lamb* (2nd rev. ed.). (Grand Rapids, MI: William B. Eerdmans Publishing, 1994): 38–39.

88 Yoder, *Politics of Jesus*, 171–172.

89 Yoder, *Politics of Jesus*, 177.

90 Yoder, *Politics of Jesus*, 187. Although the Constantinian co-optation of Christianity into the empire would turn the potential for agency into further reinforcement of the hierarchical structures of patriarchy and slavery, Yoder maintains that revolutionary potential remains in the text and in Christian communities. Neither then nor now is the ethic of revolutionary subordination intended for imposition on the world, but remains within the confines of the church so that it might serve as a witness to a non-dominant way (Yoder, *Politics of Jesus*, 149–153,185).

91 Walter Wink, *Engaging the Powers: Discernment and Resistance in a World of Domination* (Minneapolis: Fortress Press, 1992): 176.

92 Wink, *Engaging the Powers*, 179.

93 Jensen, *Endgame I*, 146.

94 Vine DeLoria, Jr. "Non-violence in American Society," *Katallagete* 5 (Winter 1974): 5. Gene Sharp notes that two of the nine most common misconceptions of nonviolent action are that nonviolence depends upon the idea that people are fundamentally good and that they therefore can be morally persuaded by nonviolent words, actions, and attitudes (Sharp, *The Politics of Nonviolent Action, Part I*, 70–71).

95 James Cone, *A Black Theology of Liberation* (20th anniv. ed.) (Maryknoll, NY: Orbis Books, 1990): 20.

96 James Cone, *Martin & Malcolm & America: A Dream or a Nightmare?* (Maryknoll, NY: Orbis Books, 1991).

97 Cone, *Martin & Malcolm & America*, 151.

98 Johan Galtung, *Nonviolence and Israel/Palestine* (Honolulu: University of Hawaii Institute for Peace, 1989): 25.

99 Richard A. Horsley, "Ethics and Exegesis: "Love Your Enemies" and the Doctrine of Non-Violence," *Journal of the American Academy of Religion* 54, no. 1 (Spring 1986): 13–14; and Richard A. Horsley, "Response to Walter Wink: 'Neither Passivity nor Violence: Jesus' Third Way,'" in *The Love of Enemy and Nonretaliation in the New Testament*, edited by Willard M. Swartley (Louisville: Westminster/John Knox, 1992): 72–132.

100 Schulman, *Gentrification of the Mind*, 51–52.

101 Schulman, *Gentrification of the Mind*, 156.

102 Schulman, *Gentrification of the Mind*, 129.

103 Wink, *Engaging the Powers*, 176.

104 Wink, *Engaging the Powers*, 127.

105 Wink, *Engaging the Powers*, 55.

106 Wink, *Engaging the Powers*, 195.

107 Wink, *Engaging the Powers*, 189.

108 Wink, *Engaging the Powers*, 237–238.

109 Wink first published this Matthean exegesis in *Violence and Nonviolence in South Africa*. In that volume he offered a more nuanced presentation of violence. Writing within the historical context of apartheid South Africa, blacks justifiably rejected nonviolence as a "white" gospel of submission (5). Whites "must not raise a single finger in judgment of those who have despaired of nonviolent change and have turned to violence as a last resort" (28). In context, Wink refrained from equating all forms of violence as evil (66). In the preface to *Engaging the Powers*, Wink tells the reader that *Violence and Nonviolence* is really the first volume in the "Powers" trilogy, and "the book on South Africa provides what this one lacks: a practical case study of the relevance of nonviolent direct action applied to a concrete situation." (Wink, *Engaging the Powers*, xiii.) *Engaging the Powers* is far more widely read and referenced, while *Violence and Nonviolence in South Africa* is virtually unknown.

110 Lynd, *Wobblies and Zapatistas*, 92. Lynd writes that there are very few instances in history of revolutionary groups "taking state power" who do not "lose their way."

111 Gene Sharp also wrote that psychological identification with and emotional dependence on dominant classes is a reason for obedience to oppressive rule (*Politics of Nonviolent Action, Part I*, 23).

112 Schulman, *Gentrification of the Mind*, 2–3.

113 Derrick Jensen, "Forget Shorter Showers: Why Personal Change Does Not Equal Political Change," *CommonDreams.org*, July 8, 2009, https://www.commondreams.org/views/2009/07/08/forget-shorter-showers-why-personal-change-does-not-equal-political-change.

114 Ward Churchill, *Pacifism as Pathology: Reflections on the Role of Armed Struggle in North America* (Oakland, CA: AK Press, 2007): 89.

115 Churchill, *Pacifism as Pathology*, 97–98.

116 Churchill, *Pacifism as Pathology*, 99.

117 Gustavo Gutiérrez: first identified theological reflection is always the "second step" after practice in *A Theology of Liberation* (Maryknoll, NY: Orbis Press, 1988): 9

118 Juan Luis Segundo, *The Liberation of Theology* (Maryknoll, NY: Orbis Press, 1982): 155.

119 Segundo, *The Liberation of Theology*, 166.

120 Deming was a feminist, lesbian, (non)violent activist and writer who confronted a number of social issues from racism to anti-war and anti-nuke throughout the 1960s to the 1980s. For more information on the life, work and writings of Barbara Deming, see *We Are All Part of One Another: A Barbara Deming Reader*, Jane Meyerding, ed. (Philadelphia: New Society Publishers, 1984). The Lynds cite Deming's idea of the "two hands" in their introduction to *Nonviolence in America, xxxiii–xxxiv*.

121 Churchill, *Pacifism as Pathology*, 103–104.

122 For example, Míguez-Bonino critiques Reinhold Niebuhr's Christian political realism for being so pragmatic as to serve the status quo. Niebuhr's understanding of human nature and the nature of groups to be such that there is a certain amount of injustice to be expected, leaving out room for human agency and the ability of persons to imagine a new reality. See Míguez-Bonino's understanding of utopianism in Chapter 7 on "Hope and Power" in *Toward a Christian Political Ethics*.

123 Dear attributed his thought here to author and activist Arundahti Roy.

124 See interview with Derrick Jensen on DemocracyNow!, November 26, 2010, http://www.democracynow.org/2010/11/26/author_and_activist_derrick_jensen_the.

125 Lynd, Wobblies and Zapatistas, 99.

126 Churchill, *Pacifism as Pathology*, 55.

127 Manfred B. Steger describes Gandhi's complex relationship with and contradictory incarnations of the principle and practice of (non)violence in *Gandhi's Dilemma: Nonviolent Principles and Nationalist Power* (New York: St. Martin's Press, 2000).

128 Jensen, *Language Older Than Words*, 322–324.

129 *Zeitgeist* is a German word, which generally means "the spirit of the times."

130 Schulman, *Gentrification of the Mind*, 164.

— Endnotes —

131 Gene Sharp wrote at length about the concept of nonviolent coercion and the factors influencing effective coercion (versus persuasion) for social change in Part III of *The Politics of Nonviolent Action: The Dynamics of Nonviolent Action*, 741–755.

132 Churchill, *Pacifism as Pathology*, 93.

133 Lynd, *Wobblies and Zapatistas*, 95.

134 Lynd, *Wobblies and Zapatistas*, 96–97.

135 Schulman, *Gentrification of the Mind*, 161.

136 Jensen, *Language Older Than Words*, 288.

137 Schulman noted that many queer persons coming from different class positions, have a similar lack of consciousness about the nature of queer oppression and heteronormativity. Multiple conditions of consciousness and intersecting identities all have an impact on the ability to imagine "a more humane, truthful, open way of life...." *Gentrification of the Mind*, 11.

138 Umoja echoes Gene Sharp's theory of nonviolent revolution where the tyrannized eventually refuse to cooperate with rulers on a mass level (*Politics of Nonviolent Action, Part I*, 47).

139 Schulman, *Gentrification of the Mind*, 12.

140 Lynd expands on this idea in *Here to There*, 16, 215.

141 Saul Alinsky is generally considered to be the founder of the contemporary, post-Civil Rights community organizing tradition in the United States. Lynd was one of the original faculty in Alinsky's training school.

142 Lynd, *From Here to There*, 94.

143 Lynd, *Accompanying: Pathways to Social Change* (Oakland, CA: PM Press, 2012): 2.

144 Lynd, *Accompanying*, 21, 25.

145 The vow of nonviolence was developed for use by the organization Pax Christi. See http://paxchristiusa.org/resources/vow-of-nonviolence/. Dear lamented that it was not taken with the seriousness of commitment which he intended.

146 "Pre-figurative relations" is a term and practice popularly used within anarchist communities where a new society is built "within the shell of the old" (Lynd, *Wobblies & Zapatistas*, 49) by creating relationships, actions and community practices that reject hierarchy and affirm participatory democracy.

147 Lynd, *Wobblies & Zapatistas*, 68-69. Lynd writes that he sees the most hope for the longevity of such communities in models coming out of Latin America, such as the Zapatistas.

148 Lynd, *Here to There*, 90; another reference addressing "bread and land" is on 291.

149 Lynd, *Accompanying*, 75–76.

150 Schulman refers to King's laying out this strategy in "Letter from Birmingham City Jail;" see Washington, *A Testament of Hope*, 290.

151 Lynd writes about this at length in Chapter 24 of *From Here to There*, "Someday They'll Have a War and Nobody Will Come," 265–278. He also writes about it in *Accompanying*, 81–85.

152 The notion of repressive tolerance is described in Marcuse's book *A Critique of Pure Tolerance* (Boston: Beacon Press, 1969).

153 Lynd discusses this in *Accompanying*, 42–43 and *From Here to There*, 190.

154 Lynd, *From Here to There*, 190.

155 Jensen, *Endgame I*, 80–81.

156 Jensen, *Endgame I*, 196.

157 The New York City St. Patrick's Day parade has historically excluded gay people from marching in it.

158 Schulman, *Gentrification of the Mind*, 6.

159 Jensen, *Endgame I*, 80–81.

160 Schulman, *Gentrification of the Mind*, 71.

161 Jensen, *Endgame I*, 265. Jensen's perspective echoes Gene Sharp's in that the base fear of participating in disruptive action is the fear of physical sanctions (state violence) as much as economic or social losses. The threat of such sanctions may be as powerful as the sanctions themselves. *The Politics of Nonviolent Action, Part I Power and Struggle*, 19–20.

162 Jensen, *Endgame I*, 202.

163 Jensen, McBay and Keith, *Deep Green Resistance*, 102.

164 Kelly Rae Kraemer, "Solidarity in Action: Exploring the Work of Allies in Social Movements," in *Peace & Change* Vol. 32 (1), January 2007: 20.

165 Schulman, *Gentrification of the Mind*, 157–158.

166 Schulman, *Gentrification of the Mind*, 158.

167 Jensen, *Endgame I*, 13.

168 Suchocki, Marjorie Hewitt. *The Fall to Violence: Original Sin in Relational Theology*. (New York: Continuum Publishing, 1994): 109.

169 Suchocki. *The Fall to Violence*, 102.

170 Act Now to Stop War and End Racism, also known as the ANSWER coalition, an umbrella group for various anti-war organizations.

171 Ella Baker was a leader in the Black Freedom struggle in the South and in New York City. She was employed by the Southern Christian Leadership Council during the time of Martin Luther King, Jr., helped to organize the Mississippi Freedom Democratic Party, and was primarily responsible for the formation of SNCC, and mentoring its youth leaders. See her biography by Barbara Ransby, *Ella Baker and the Black Freedom Movement: A Radical Democratic Vision* (University of North Carolina Press, 2005).

172 Three men sentenced to death for murders that occurred during the Lucasville Riot were held in solitary confinement instead of on death row, which meant they had fewer privileges than death row inmates. Their strike took place for approximately twelve days in January 2011 and won the inmates certain privileges they desired. Inspired by the tactics and successes of the Ohio State Penitentiary hunger strike, inmates at the Pelican Bay Security Housing Unit (California) successfully used a hunger strike to win a number of demands, many of which compelled prisons to follow already mandated federal regulations on prisoner rights. Lynd details these events in *Accompanying*, pages 144–154.

173 Lynd, "Nonviolence as Solidarity," *From Here to There*, 188.

174 Lynd, "Nonviolence as Solidarity," 193.

175 Jensen, *Language Older Than Words*, 206.

176 Dear is referring to a 1981 hunger strike by Irish Republican Army political prisoners in which ten hunger strikers died. Among many sources, see http://bobbysandstrust .com/hungerstrikers/history and David Beresford, *Ten Men Dead: The Story of the 1981 Irish Hunger Strike* (New York: Atlantic Monthly Press, 1987).

177 Power echoes Beverly Harrison, but Harrison emphasizes the necessity to do this work collectively. "Awareness of contradictions is never the result of individual striving. It comes from a process of concrete engagement, an entering into struggle against oppressive conditions that also involved being drawn into collective effort to overcome these conditions. Such consciousness takes hold only in concrete engagement; it's through the struggle that we acquire more profound awareness of the range of social oppression and its interconnectedness. Each of us must learn to extend a critical analysis of the contradictions of our lives in an ever-widening circle, until it inclusively incorporates those whose situations differ from our own. This involves naming structures that create the social privilege we possess as well as understanding how we have been victims" (Harrison, *Making the Connections*, 236).

178 The FMLN is the Frente Farabundo Martí para la Liberación Nacional, a coalition of guerrilla groups resisting political and economic oppression in El Salvador in the 1980s. It is now a legal, left-wing political party in the country.

179 John Dear, *The God of Peace: Toward a Theology of Nonviolence,* (Maryknoll, NY: Orbis Books, 1994), 151.

180 Dear echoes the sentiment of liberationist theologian Robert McAfee Brown, who wrote that if white North American Christians want to impose (non)violence on someone, they should impose it on themselves. McAfee Brown wrote, "To be as direct as possible, I see no less exacting task for white churches than that of seeking, at whatever cost, to embody revolutionary nonviolent love. Anything else is no longer worth the bother and can be done quite adequately by other groups in our society. If we are going to talk about a special role for the Church – a role that might make a difference to the human family – then nothing short of the stance of revolutionary nonviolent love will do." (McAfee Brown, *Religion and Violence*, 99). Galtung also makes a similar point: If (non)violence is going to destroy oppressive structures, it should be conducted by those who are the primary beneficiaries of violence (Galtung, *Nonviolence and Israel/Palestine*, 20).

181 Lynd, *Accompanying*, 6.

182 "The counselee was an expert on his own life experience, on the predictable response of parents and significant others, and on how much risk the counselee was prepared to confront." Staughton Lynd, *Accompanying: Pathways to Social Change*. The "two experts" model is also described by Alice and Staughton Lynd in *Stepping Stones, 84–87.*

183 I am grateful to my colleague in the doctoral program, now Dr. David Scott, for asking me this question.

184 Lynd, *Accompanying*, 91, 128.

185 Lynd, *Accompanying*, 133.

186 Lynd, *Accompanying*, 133–134.

187 Lynd, *Accompanying*, 135.

188 Schulman, *Ties that Bind*, 49–50.

189 Schulman, *Ties that Bind*, 51.

190 Lynd, *Accompanying*, 155.

191 Lynd, *Accompanying*, 175.

192 Staughton Lynd writes about the dimensions of "the apparently limitless capacity of the Left for self-destruction and fratricide," *From Here to There*, 215.

193 Lynd, *Wobblies and Zapatistas*, 114–115. Lynd writes about the need for community rules in social solidarity and movement work in *From Here to There* on pages 94 and 104.

194 Schulman, *The Ties That Bind*, 98.

195 Schulman, *The Ties That Bind*, 98-99.

196 Schulman, *Gentrification of the Mind*, 72.

---

197 Since I finished my dissertation in 2012, the Transformative Justice (TJ) movement has emerged as a response to dominant modes of addressing violence through practices of deep interpersonal, structural, and cultural transformation.

"Transformative Justice (TJ) is a political framework and approach for responding to violence, harm, and abuse. At its most basic, it seeks to respond to violence without creating more violence and/or engaging in harm reduction to lessen the violence. TJ can be thought of as a way of 'making things right,' getting in 'right relation,' or creating justice together. Transformative Justice responses and interventions 1) do not rely on the state (e.g. police, prisons, the criminal legal system, I.C.E., foster care system, though some TJ responses do rely on or incorporate social services like counseling); 2) do not reinforce or perpetuate violence such as oppressive norms or vigilantism; and, most importantly, 3) actively cultivate the things we know prevent violence such as healing, accountability, resilience, and safety for all involved." For a further description of TJ, see https://transformharm.org/transformative-justice-a-brief-description/. The Transform Harm website contains myriad resources to connect with more information on the TJ approach to addressing violence in all its forms.

198 Lynd, *Wobblies and Zapatistas*, 174.

199 Lynd, *Wobblies and Zapatistas*, 176.

200 See Lynd, "Overcoming Racism," in *From Here to There*, 198–204.

201 See Staughton Lynd, *Lucasville: The Untold Story of a Prison Uprising* (Philadelphia: Temple University Press, 2004).

202 Lynd, Accompanying, 75.

203 This phrase comes from Matthew Lamb in *Solidarity with Victims: Toward a Theology of Social Transformation* (New York: Crossroad Publishing, 1982).

204 McCann and Strain write that Christian communities must invent and construct practical theologies that are "models of reality and for action" (*Polity and Praxis*, 204), which are "subject to evaluation" by a relevant, overlapping community of inquirers (34–35).

205 Heitink, *Practical Theology: History, Theory, Action Domains* (Grand Rapids, MI: William B. Eerdmans Publishing, 1999). Referring to the work of Henning Luther, Heitink notes that "the church" as an abstract point of analysis is "a subject without subjects" (264).

206 Míguez Bonino, *Doing Theology in a Revolutionary Situation*, xxvi.

207 Míguez Bonino, *Doing Theology in a Revolutionary Situation*, 94.

208 Feminist and womanist Christian liberationist theologians and ethicists have named this kind of critical historical and structural analysis as a part of a process of concrete liberation in various ways. In *Mining the Motherlode: Methods in Womanist Ethics* (Cleveland: Pilgrim Press, 2006) Stacey Floyd-Thomas traces the lineage of what she terms "emancipatory historiography"(153) from Beverly Harrison through Katie Cannon (82–90, 154–165).

209 Beverly Wildung Harrison, *Making the Connections*, 243-244.

[210] Swinton and Mowat describe that, at heart, participatory research "assumes that the best people to research a given topic are those who have the most experience of it" as both the subjects of study and co-researchers (*Practical Theology and Qualitative Research*, 227–228)..

[211] Lynd, *From Here to There*, 285.

[212] Schulman, *Gentrification of the Mind*, 19.

[213] Jensen, et. al., *Deep Green Resistance*, 103.

[214] Recall that Walter Wink refers to (non)violence as "Jesus' Third Way." Liberationist Juan Luis Segundo has a critique of the ideological function of "third ways" in *The Liberation of Theology*, 90–95.

[215] Gloria Albrecht, *The Character of Our Communities: Toward an Ethic of Liberation for the Church* (Nashville: Abingdon Press, 1995): 152–155. See also Jack Nelson-Pallmeyer and Bret Hesla, *Worship in the Spirit of Jesus: Theology, Liturgy, and Songs Without Violence* (Cleveland, OH: Pilgrim Press, 2005).

[216] In line with the analysis of (non)violence as an ideological discourse that conceals and reveals, the rejection of capitalism as a center-point of revolutionary (non)violence is often downplayed or ignored in the histories of some of the most well-known figures of (non)violence, including Gandhi and King. Harding wrote that there is a "profound sense of national amnesia that has distorted so much of America's approach to Martin Luther King" (Harding, *Martin Luther King: The Inconvenient Hero*, Maryknoll, NY: Orbis Books, 1996: vii). This is particularly true in relation to the last years of his life, where King focused on the interconnections between "the triple American evils of racism, militarism and materialism" (ix).

[217] The language of "counter-disciplines" comes from Daniel Bell in Chapter Four of *Liberation Theology After the End of History: The Refusal to Cease Suffering* (New York: Routledge, 2001). I like this concept and language. However, Bell's main counter-discipline to capitalism is the divine gift and therapy of forgiveness that he believes will interrupt cycles of violence and re-structure the rational logic of economics, which is far from adequate and still fails to rise to the level of a full analysis and confrontation of violence.

[218] Bell uses the language of Christians as "exemplary human communities" in the face of capitalism in *Liberation Theology After the End of History*, 86; 144. Sharon Welch rejects such cohesive communities as possible sites for resistance, as "the moral critique of structural forms of injustice emerges, rather, from the material interaction of different communities" (*A Feminist Ethic of Risk*, 124).

[219] Martin Luther King, Jr., "A Time to Break Silence," *A Testament of Hope: The Essential Writings of Martin Luther King, Jr.*, James M. Washington, ed., (San Francisco: Harper Collins, 1986): 231–243.

Bibliography

Abron, JoNina M. "'Serving the People': The Survival Programs of the Black Panther Party." *The Black Panther Party [Reconsidered]*. Charles E Jones, ed., 177–192. Baltimore: Black Classic Press, 1998.

Adams, Maurianne, Warren J. Blumenfeld, Carmelita Castañeda, Heather W. Hackman, Madeline L. Peters, and Ximena Zúñiga, eds. *Readings for Diversity and Social Justice* (2nd ed.). New York: Routledge, 2010.

Ahlman, Jeffrey S. "The Algerian Question in Nkrumah's Ghana, 1958-1960: "Debating 'Violence' and 'Nonviolence' in African Decolonization." *Africa TODAY* 57:2 (Winter 2010): 67-84.

Al-Amin, Jamil Abdullah. *Die Nigger, Die! A Political Autobiography of Jamil Abdullah al-Amin*. Lawrence Hill Books, 2002.

Alexander, Michelle. *The New Jim Crow: Mass Incarceration in the Age of Colorblindness*. New York: New Press, 2010.

Albrecht, Gloria. *The Character of Our Communities: Toward an Ethic of Liberation for the Church*. Nashville: Abingdon Press, 1995.

Alfred, Taiaiake. Wasáse: *Indigenous Pathways of Action and Freedom*. Toronto: University of Toronto Press, 2009.

Allen, Theodore W. *The Invention of the White Race, Volume One: Racial Oppression and Social Control*. London: Verso, 1994.

Amster, Randall. "Perspectives on Ecoterrorism: Catalysts, Conflations, and Casualties." *Contemporary Justice Review* Vol. 9, No. 3 (September 2006): 287–301.

Arendt, Hannah. *On Violence*. New York: Harcourt Brace and Company, 1970.

Ash, Timothy Garton. "A Century of Civil Resistance: Some Lessons and Questions." In *Civil Resistance and Power Politics: The Experience of Non-violent Action from Gandhi to Present*. Adam Roberts and Timothy Garton Ash, eds., 371–392. New York: Oxford University Press, 2009.

Augustine of Hippo. *City of God*. New York: Penguin Classics, 2003.

Austin, Curtis J. Up *Against the Wall: Violence in the Making and Unmaking of the Black Panther Party*. Fayetteville, AR: University of Arkansas Press, 2006.

Ayers, Bill. *Fugitive Days: A Memoir*. Boston: Beacon Press, 2001.

Baldwin, Bridgette. "In the Shadow of the Gun: The Black Panther Party, the Ninth Amendment, and Discourses of Self-Defense." In *In Search of the Black Panther Party: New Perspectives on a Revolutionary Movement*. Jama Lazerow and Yohuru Williams, eds., 67-93. Durham, NC: Duke University Press, 2006.

Bass, Dorothy C. and Craig Dykstra, eds. *For Life Abundant: Practical Theology, Theological Education, and Christian Ministry*. Grand Rapids, MI: William B. Eerdmans Publishing, 2008.

Bell, Daniel M., Jr. *Liberation Theology After the End of History: The Refusal to Cease Suffering*. New York: Routledge, 2001.

Bell, Inge Powell. *CORE and the Strategy of Non-Violence*. New York: Random House, 1968.

Benderman, Kevin. *Letters from Fort Lewis Brig: A Matter of Conscience*. Guilford, CT: Lyons Press, 2007.

Beresford, David. *Ten Men Dead: The Story of the 1981 Irish Hunger Strike*. New York: Atlantic Monthly Press, 1989.

Bermanzohn, Sally Avery. *Through Survivor's Eyes: From the Sixties to the Greensboro Massacre*. Nashville: Vanderbilt University Press, 2003.

Biko, Steve. *I Write What I Like: Selected Writings*. Chicago: University of Chicago Press, 2002.

Bondurant, Joan V. *Conquest of Violence: The Gandhian Philosophy of Conflict*. Princeton: Princeton Univ. Press, 1988.

Brock, Rita Nakashima and Rebecca Ann Parker. *Proverbs of Ashes: Violence, Redemptive Suffering, and the Search for What Saves Us*. Boston: Beacon Press, 2001.

Brown, Judith M. "Gandhi and Civil Resistance in India, 1917-1947: Key Issues." In *Civil Resistance and Power Politics: The Experience of Non-violent Action from Gandhi to the Present*. Adam Roberts and Timothy Garton Ash, eds., 43–57. New York: Oxford University Press, 2009.

Brown, Rita Bo. "Biography," and "White North American Political Prisoners." In *Imprisoned Intellectuals: America's Political Prisoners Write on Life, Liberation and Rebellion.* Joy James, ed., 216–226. Lanham, MD: Rowman and Littlefield Publishers, 2003.

Browning, Don. *A Fundamental Practical Theology: Descriptive and Strategic Proposals.* Minneapolis, MN: Fortress Press, 1991.

Burton-Rose, Daniel. *Guerrilla USA: The George Jackson Brigade and the Anticapitalist Underground of the 1970s.* Berkeley: University of California Press, 2010.

Burton-Rose, Daniel, ed. *Creating a Movement with Teeth: A Documentary History of the George Jackson Brigade.* Oakland, CA: PM Press, 2010.

Cahalan, Kathleen A. and James R. Nieman. "Mapping the Field of Practical Theology." In *For Life Abundant: Practical Theology, Theological Education, and Christian Ministry.* Dorothy C. Bass and Craig Dykstra, eds., 62–85. Grand Rapids, MI: William B. Eerdmans Publishing, 2008.

Cámara, Hélder. *Spiral of Violence.* London: Sheed and Ward, 1971.

Campbell, David. "Why Fight? Humanitarianism, Principles, and Poststructuralism." In *Ethics and International Relations.* Hakan Seckinelgin and Hideaki Shinoda, eds., 132–160. New York: Palgrave, 2001.

Carter, April. *Direct Action and Democracy Today.* Malden, MA: Polity Press, 2005.

Carter Jackson, Kellie. "Force and Freedom: Black Abolitionists and the Politics of Violence, 1850–1861." New York: Columbia University, Ph.D. dissertation, 2010.

Casey-Rutland, Ransom Eugene. "An Examination of the Issue of Violence in the Writings of Selected Latin American Liberation Theologians." Emory University, Ph.D. dissertation, 1991.

Cavanaugh, William T. *The Myth of Religious Violence: Secular Ideology and the Roots of Modern Conflict.* New York: Oxford University Press, 2009.

Chopp, Rebecca S. *The Praxis of Suffering: An Interpretation of Liberation and Political Theologies.* Maryknoll, NY: Orbis Books, 1986.

---. "Practical Theology and Liberation." In *Formation and Reflection: The Promise of Practical Theology.* Lewis S. Mudge and James N. Poling, eds., 120-138. Philadelphia: Fortress Press, 1987.

Churchill, Ward. *A Little Matter of Genocide: Holocaust and Denial in the Americas 1492 to the Present.* San Francisco: City Lights Books, 1997.

---. "To Disrupt, Discredit and Destroy: The FBI's Secret War Against the Black Panther Party." In *Liberation, Imagination, and the Black Panther Party: A New Look at the Panthers and Their Legacy.* Kathleen Cleaver and George Katsiaficas, eds., 78–117. New York: Routledge, 2001.

---. "Interview with Ward Churchill." In *Listening to the Land: Conversations About Nature, Culture, Eros.* Derrick Jensen, ed., 155–157. White River Junction, Vermont: Chelsea Green Publishing, 2002.

---. *On the Justice of Roosting Chickens: Reflections on the Consequence of U.S. Imperial Arrogance and Criminality.* Oakland, CA: AK Press, 2003.

---. *Kill the Indian, Save the Man: The Genocidal Impact of American Indian Residential Schools.* San Francisco: City Lights, 2004.

---. *Since Predator Came: Notes from the Struggle for American Indian Liberation.* Oakland, CA: AK Press, 2005.

---. *Pacifism as Pathology: Reflections on the Role of Armed Struggle in North America.* Oakland, CA: AK Press, 2007.

---. "I am Indigenist: Notes on the Ideology of the Fourth World," in *ZNet* February 27, 2009. Accessed 10/13/2009, https://revolutionarystrategicstudies.wordpress.com/2011/05/01/i-am-indigenist-notes-on-the-ideology-of-the-fourth-world-by-ward-churchill/.

Churchill, Ward and Jim Vander Wall. *Agents of Repression: The FBI's Secret War Against the Black Panther Party and the American Indian Movement.* Boston: South End Press, 1988.

Combahee River Collective. "A Black Feminist Statement." In *This Bridge Called My Back: Writings by Radical Women of Color.* Gloria

Anzaldúa and Cherrie Moraga, eds., 210–218. Boston: Kitchen Table Press, 1982.

Confortini, Catia C. "Galling, Violence and Gender: The Case for a Peace Studies/Feminism Alliance." *Peace and Change,* Vol. 31 (3), July 2006.

Conde-Frazier, Elizabeth. "Participatory Action Research." In *The Wiley-Blackwell Companion to Practical Theology.* Bonnie J. Miller-McLemore, ed., 234-243. Malden, MA: Blackwell Publishing, 2012.

Cone, James H. *Martin & Malcolm & America: A Dream or a Nightmare.* Maryknoll, NY: Orbis Books, 1991.

---. *A Black Theology of Liberation* (20th anniv. ed.). Maryknoll, NY: Orbis Books, 1990.

---. *The Cross and the Lynching Tree.* Maryknoll, NY: Orbis Books, 2011.

Cordaro, Tom. "Nonviolent Direct Action for Personal and Social Transformation." http://www.cpt.org/resources/writings/cordaro.

Cornell, Andrew. *Oppose and Propose! Lessons from Movement for a New Society.* Oakland, CA: AK Press, 2011.

Cross, Theodore. *The Black Power Imperative: Racial Inequality and the Politics of Nonviolence.* New York: Faulkner Books, 1987.

Culleton Colwell, Mary Anna. "Do Peace Movement Groups Condone Violence in the Pursuit of Justice?" *Polity.* Vol. 28, No. 4 (Summer, 1996): 541–557.

Daloz, Laurent A. Parks, et.al. *Common Fire: Leading Lives of Commitment in a Complex World.* Boston: Beacon Press, 1997.

Danielson, Leilah C. "'In My Extremity I Turned to Gandhi': American Pacifists, Christianity, and Gandhian Nonviolence, 1915–1941." *Church History,* 72:2 (June 2003): 361–388.

---. "The 'Two-Ness' of the Movement: James Farmer, Nonviolence, and Black Nationalism." *Peace & Change,* Vol. 29, No. 3&4 (July 2004): 431–452.

Davies, J.G. *Christians, Politics and Violent Revolution.* Maryknoll, NY: Orbis Books, 1976.

Dear, John. *Disarming the Heart: Toward a Vow of Nonviolence.* Scottdale, PA: Herald Press, 1993.

---. *The God of Peace: Toward a Theology of Nonviolence.* Maryknoll, NY: Orbis Books, 1994.

---. *A Persistent Peace: One Man's Struggle for a Nonviolent World.* Chicago: Loyola Press, 2008.

---. *Lazarus, Come Forth! How Jesus Confronts the Culture of Death and Invites Us into the New Life of Peace.* Maryknoll: Orbis Press, 2011.

DeLoria, Vine, Jr. "Non-violence in American Society." *Katallagete* 5 (Winter 1974).

---. *Behind the Trail of Broken Treaties: An Indian Declaration of Independence.* Austin: University of Texas Press, 1985.

---. *God is Red: A Native View of Religion* (2nd edition). Boulder, CO: North American Press, 1992.

Deming, Barbara. *Revolution and Equilibrium.* New York: Grossman Publishers, 1971.

---. *We Are All Part of One Another: A Barbara Deming Reader.* Jane Meyerding, ed. Philadelphia: New Society Publishers, 1984.

Denzin, Norman K. "Emancipatory Discourses and the Ethics and Politics of Interpretation." In *Collecting and Interpreting Qualitative Materials*, Norman K. Denzin and Yvonna S. Lincoln, eds., 435-471. Los Angeles, CA: Sage Publications, 2008.

DeVault, Marjorie L. "Personal Writing in Social Science: Issues of Production and Interpretation." In *Reflexivity and Voice.* Rosanna Hertz, ed., 216-228. Thousand Oaks, CA: Sage Publications, 1997.

Diamond, Stanley. *In Search of the Primitive: A Critique of Civilization.* Somerset, NJ: Transaction Publishers, 1993.

Dohrn, Bernardine, et. al., eds. *Sing a Battle Song: The Revolutionary Poetry, Statements and Communiques of the Weather Underground 1970-1974.* New York: Seven Stories Press, 2006.

Dominick, Brian. "Pacifism and 'Diversity of Tactics': A Compromise Proposal." *ZNet.* Accessed November 12, 2011, https://zcomm.org/znetarticle/pacifism-and-diversity-of-tactics-a-compromise-proposal-by-brian-dominick/.

Douglass, James W. *The Non-violent Coming of God.* Maryknoll, NY: Orbis Press, 1991.

Durnbaugh, Donald, ed. *On Earth Peace : Discussions on War/Peace Issues Between Friends, Mennonites, Brethren, and European Churches, 1935-75.* Elgin, IL: Brethren Press, 1978.

EarthFirst! Direct Action Manual. Eugene, OR: DAM Collective, 1997. https://earthfirstjournal.org.

Fanon, Frantz. *The Wretched of the Earth.* New York, NY: Grove Press, 1963.

Felder, Cain. *Hope. Stony the Road We Trod: African Americans and Biblical Interpretation.* Minneapolis: Augsburg Fortress Publishers, 1991.

Findlay, James F., Jr. *Church People in the Struggle: The National Council of Churches and the Black Freedom Movement, 1950–1970.* New York: Oxford University Press, 1993.

Fine, Michelle, et. al. "For Whom? Qualitative Research, Representations, and Social Responsibilities." In *The Landscape of Qualitative Research: Theories and Issues* (2nd ed.), Norman K. Denzin and Yvonna S. Lincoln, eds., 167–207. Thousand Oaks, CA: Sage Publications, 2003.

Fleming, Cynthia Griggs. *Soon We Will Not Cry: The Liberation of Ruby Doris Smith Robinson.* New York: Rowman and Littlefield, 2000.

Floyd-Thomas, Stacey. *Mining the Motherlode: Methods in Womanist Ethics.* Cleveland: Pilgrim Press, 2006.

Foner, Philip S., ed. *The Black Panthers Speak.* New York: DA Capo Press, 1995.

Forrester, Duncan B. *Truthful Action: Explorations in Practical Theology.* Edinburgh, Scotland: T & T Clark, 2000.

Foreman, Dave and Bill Haywood, eds. *Ecodefense: A Field Guide to Monkeywrenching.* Tucson, AZ: Ned Ludd Books, 1988.

Francis, Diana. From *Pacification to Peacebuilding: A Call to Global Transformation.* New York: Pluto Press, 2010.

Franks, Lucinda. "Return of the Fugitive." *The New Yorker* (June 13, 1994): 40–59.

Freire, Paulo. *Pedagogy of the Oppressed.* New York: Continuum Press, 1970.

Galtung, Johan. "Violence, Peace and Peace Research." *Journal of Peace Research* 6, no. 3 (1969): 167–191.

---. *Essays in Peace Research, Volume I.* Copenhagen: Christian Ejlers, 1975.

---. "Religion as a Factor." Paper, *Wissenschaftskollegzu.* Berlin, Germany. February 1983. https://www.transcend.org/galtung/papers/Religion%20As%20a%20Factor.pdf

---. "Religion and Peace: Some Reflections." Paper. Center of International Studies. Princeton, New Jersey: Princeton University, December 1986. https://www.transcend.org/galtung/papers/Religion%20and%20Peace-Some%20Reflections.pdf.

---. *Nonviolence and Israel/Palestine.* Honolulu: University of Hawaii Institute for Peace, 1989.

---. "Cultural Violence." *Journal of Peace Research* vol. 27, no. 3 (August 1990): 291–305.

---. "Religions, Hard and Soft." In *Cross Currents.* Winter 97/98, Vol. 47 Issue 4, p 437–451.

---. "Western Deep Culture and Western Historical Thinking." In *Western Historical Thinking: An Intercultural Debate*, Jörn Rüsen, ed., 85–100. New York: Berghahn Books, 2002.

Garrow, David J. *Bearing the Cross: Martin Luther King, Jr., and the Southern Christian Leadership Conference.* New York: Vintage Books, 1986.

Gelderloos, Peter. *How Nonviolence Protects the State.* Cambridge, MA: South End Press, 2007.

Girard, René. *Violence and the Sacred.* Baltimore: Johns Hopkins University Press, 1977.

---. *The Scapegoat.* Baltimore: Johns Hopkins University Press, 1986.

---. *Things Hidden Since the Foundation of the World.* Stephen Bann and Michael Metteer, trans. Stanford: Stanford University Press, 1987.

Goodman, Diane J. *Promoting Diversity and Social Justice: Educating People from Privileged Groups.* Thousand Oaks, CA: Sage Publications, 2001.

Graeber, David. *Direct Action: An Ethnography.* Oakland, CA: AK Press, 2009.

Greider, Kathleen. "Religious Pluralism and Christian-Centrism." In *The Wiley-Blackwell Companion to Practical Theology.* Bonnie J. Miller-McLemore, ed. Malden, MA: Blackwell Publishing, 2012: 452–462.

Graham, Elaine L. *Transforming Practice: Pastoral Theology in an Age of Uncertainty.* London: Mowbray, 1996.

Grundy, Kenneth W. and Michael A. Weinstein. *The Ideologies of Violence.* Columbus, OH: Chase Merrill Publishing, 1974.

Gutiérrez, Gustavo. *A Theology of Liberation* (15th anniversary ed.). Maryknoll, NY: Orbis Press, 1988.

Guggenheim, David. *Waiting for Superman.* DVD. Hollywood, CA: Paramount Pictures, 2010.

Harding, Rachel. *Dolores Huerta: Labor Organizer and Co-Founder, United Farmworkers Union.* DVD. Denver, CO: Veterans of Hope Project, 2000.

Harding, Vincent. *The Other American Revolution.* Los Angeles: University of California Center for Afro-American Studies, 1980.

---. *There is a River: The Black Struggle for Freedom in America.* New York: Harcourt Brace, 1981.

---. *Martin Luther King: The Inconvenient Hero.* Maryknoll, NY: Orbis Books, 1996.

Harrison, Beverly Wildung. *Making the Connections: Essays in Feminist Social Ethics.* Carol S. Robb, ed. Boston: Beacon Press, 1985.

Hauerwas, Stanley. *The Peaceable Kingdom: A Primer in Christian Ethics.* Minneapolis: Fortress Press, 1983.

---. *The Hauerwas Reader.* John Berkman and Michael Cartwright, eds. Durham, NC: Duke University Press, 2001.

Harvey, Jennifer. *Whiteness and Morality: Pursuing Racial Justice through Reparations and Sovereignty.* New York: Palgrave Macmillan, 2007.

Heitink, Gerben. *Practical Theology: History, Theory, Action Domains: Manual for Practical Theology.* Grand Rapids, MI: William B. Eerdmans Publishing Company, 1999.

Hill, Lance. *The Deacons for Defense: Armed Resistance and the Civil Rights Movement.* Chapel Hill: University of North Carolina Press, 2006.

Honderich, Ted. *Terrorism for Humanity Inquiries in Political Philosophy.* London: Pluto Press, 2003.

Horsley, Richard A. "Ethics and Exegesis: 'Love Your Enemies' and the Doctrine of Non-Violence." *Journal of the American Academy of Religion* 54, no. 1 (Spring 1986): 3–31.

---. "Response to Walter Wink, 'Neither Passivity nor Violence: Jesus' Third Way.'" In *The Love of Enemy and Nonretaliation in the New Testament.* Willard M. Swartley, ed., 126–132. Louisville: Westminster/John Knox Press, 1992.

Hough, Joseph C., Jr. *Black Power and White Protestants: A Christian Response to the New Negro Pluralism.* New York: Oxford University Press, 1968.

Howes, Dustin Ells. *Toward a Credible Pacifism: Violence and the Possibilities of Politics.* Albany: State University of New York Press, 2009.

Iadicola, Peter and Anson Shupe. *Violence, Inequality, and Human Freedom* (2nd ed). New York: Rowman and Littlefield Publisher, Inc., 2003.

Ignatiev, Noel. *How the Irish Became White.* New York: Routledge, 1996.

INCITE! Women of Color Against Violence. *The Revolution Will Not Be Funded: Beyond the Non-Profit Industrial Complex.* Boston: South End Press, 2007.

Jensen, Derrick. *A Language Older than Words.* White River Junction, VT: Chelsea Green Publishing, 2000.

---. *The Culture of Make Believe.* White River Junction, Vermont: Chelsea Green Publishing Company, 2002.

---. *Endgame, Volume 1: The Problem of Civilization.* New York: Seven Stories Press, 2006.

---. "Forget Shorter Showers: Why Personal Change Does Not Equal Political Change." *CommonDreams.org* July 8, 2009. https://www.commondreams.org/views/2009/07/08/forget-shorter-showers-why-personal-change-does-not-equal-political-change.

Jensen, Derrick, et. al. *Deep Green Resistance: Strategy to Save the Planet.* New York: Seven Stories Press, 2011.

Johnson, Allan G. *Privilege, Power, and Difference* (2nd ed.). Boston: McGraw-Hill, 2006.

Kairos Document. *Challenge to the Church, A Theological Comment on the Political Crisis in South Africa* (Revised 2nd ed.). Grand Rapids, MI: William Eerdmans Publishing, 1987.

Kaunda, Kenneth. *The Riddle of Violence.* San Francisco: Harper and Row, 1980.

Kelly, Kathy. *Other Lands Have Dreams: From Baghdad to Pekin Prison.* Petrolia, CA: CounterPunch, 2005.

Kendall, Frances E. *Understanding White Privilege: Creating Pathways to Authentic Relationships Across Race.* New York: Routledge, 2006.

Kincheloe, Joe L. and Peter L. McLaren. "Rethinking Critical Theory and Qualitative Research." In *The Landscape of Qualitative Research: Theories and Issues* (2nd ed.), Norman K. Denzin and Yvonna S. Lincoln, eds., 433–488. Thousand Oaks, CA: Sage Publications, 2003.

King, Martin Luther, Jr. *Strength to Love.* Philadelphia: Fortress Press, 1988.

---. *A Testament of Hope: The Essential Writings of Martin Luther King, Jr.,* James M. Washington, ed. San Francisco: Harper Collins, 1986.

Kirk-Duggan, Cheryl. *Misbegotten Anguish: A Theology and Ethics of Violence.* St. Louis: Chalice Press, 2001.

Kosek, Joseph Kip. *Acts of Conscience: Christian Nonviolence and Modern American Democracy.* New York: Columbia University Press, 2011.

Kraemer, Kelly Rae. "Solidarity in Action: Exploring the Work of Allies in Social Movements." *Peace & Change* Vol. 32 (1), January 2007: 20–38.

Kurlansky, Mark. *Nonviolence: The History of a Dangerous Idea.* New York: Modern Library, 2009.

Laffin, Arthur J. *Swords into Plowshares: A Chronology of Plowshares Disarmament Actions 1980-2003.* New York: Rose Hill Books, 2003.

Lakey, George. "Diversity of Tactics and Democracy." Originally published in *Clamor Magazine* (March-April 2012). Accessed at the University of Denver on February 25, 2012.

Lamb, Matthew. *Solidarity with Victims: Toward a Theology of Social Transformation*. New York: Crossroad Publishing, 1982.

Leonard, Gary. *The Moment of Truth: The Kairos Documents*. Scottsville, South Africa: Ujamaa Center for Biblical and Theological Community Development and Research, University of KwaZulu-Natal, 2010.

Lewis, Jerry M. and Thomas R. Hensley. "The May 4 Shootings at Kent State University: The Search for Historical Accuracy." https://www.kent.edu/may-4-historical-accuracy.

Lincoln, Yvonna S. and Egon G. Guba. *Naturalistic Inquiry*. Thousand Oaks, CA: Sage Publications, 1985.

---. "Paradigmatic Controversies, Contradictions, and Emerging Confluences." In *The Landscape of Qualitative Research: Theories and Issues* (2nd ed.), Norman K. Denzin and Yvonna S. Lincoln, eds., 253–291. Thousand Oaks, CA: Sage Publications, 2003.

Loewen, James W. *Lies My Teacher Told Me: Everything Your American History Textbook Got Wrong*. New York: New Press, 2008.

Long, Michael G., ed. *Christian Peace and Nonviolence: A Documentary History*. Maryknoll, NY: Orbis Books, 2011.

Lynd, Alice, ed. *We Won't Go: Personal Accounts of War Objectors*. Boston: Beacon Press, 1968.

Lynd, Alice and Staughton. *Stepping Stones: Memoir of a Life Together*. Lanham, MD: Lexington Books, 2009.

Lynd, Alice and Staughton, eds. *Rank and File: Personal Histories by Working-Class Organizers*. Princeton, NJ: Princeton University Press, 1981.

---. eds. *Nonviolence in America: A Documentary History* (rev. ed.). Maryknoll, NY: Orbis Books, 1995.

---. eds. *The New Rank and File*. Ithaca, NY: ILR Press, 2000.

Lynd, Staughton. *Lucasville: The Untold Story of a Prison Uprising*. Philadelphia: Temple University Press, 2004.

---. *From Here to There: The Staughton Lynd Reader*. Andrej Grubacic, ed. Oakland, CA: PM Press, 2010.

---. *Accompanying: Pathways to Social Change*. Oakland, CA: PM Press 2012.

Lynd, Staughton and Andrej Grubacic, *Wobblies and Zapatistas: Conversations on Anarchism, Marxism, and Radical History*. Oakland, CA: PM Press, 2008.

Malcolm X. *The Final Speeches: February 1965*. New York: Pathfinder Press, 1992.

Marcuse, Herbert. *A Critique of Pure Tolerance*. Boston: Beacon Press, 1969.

Martin, Brian. *Nonviolence Versus Capitalism*. London: War Resisters' International, 2001.

Macgregor, G.H.C. "The Relevance of an Impossible Ideal." In *Peace is the Way: Writings on Nonviolence from the Fellowship of Reconciliation*. Walter Wink, ed., 17–29. Maryknoll, NY: Orbis Books, 2000.

McAfee Brown, Robert. *Religion and Violence* (2nd ed.). Philadelphia: Westminster Press, 1987.

McAllister, Pam. *You Can't Kill the Spirit*. Philadelphia: New Society Publishers, 1988.

---. *This River of Courage: Generations of Women's Resistance and Action*. Philadelphia: New Society Publishers, 1991.

McAllister, Pam, ed. *Reweaving the Web of Life: Feminism and Nonviolence*. Philadelphia: New Society Publishers, 1982.

McCann, Dennis P. and Charles R. Strain. *Polity and Praxis: A Program for American Practical Theology*. Minneapolis: Winston Press, 1985.

McKivigan, John R. and Stanley Harrold, eds. *Antislavery Violence: Sectional, Racial, and Cultural Conflict in Antebellum America*. Knoxville: University of Tennessee Press, 1999.

McGuire, Danielle L. *At The Dark End of the Street: Black Women, Rape and Resistance – A New History of the Civil Rights Movement from Rosa Parks to the Rise of Black Power*. New York: Alfred Knopf, 2010.

Mejía, Camilo. *Road from Ar Ramadi: The Private Rebellion of Staff Sergeant Camilo Mejía*. New York: New Press, 2007.

Míguez Bonino, José. *Doing Theology in a Revolutionary Situation*. Philadelphia: Fortress Press, 1975.

---. *Toward a Christian Political Ethics*. Philadelphia: Fortress Press, 1983.

---. "Challenge to the Church: A Comment on the Kairos Documents." *Challenge to the Church: A Theological Comment on the Political Crisis in South Africa, The Kairos Document and Commentaries*. Geneva: Commission on the Programme to Combat Racism, World Council of Churches, 1985.

Miller, Tina, Maxine Birch, Melanie Mauthner, and Julie Jessop, eds. *Ethics in Qualitative Research*. Thousand Oaks, CA: Sage Publications, 2002.

Miller-McLemore, Bonnie J., ed. *The Wiley-Blackwell Companion to Practical Theology*. Malden, MA: Blackwell Publishing, 2012.

Mirra, Carl. *The Admirable Radical: Staughton Lynd and Cold War Dissent, 1945–1970*. Kent, OH: Kent State University Press, 2010.

Mollin, Marian. *Radical Pacifism in Modern America: Egalitarianism and Protest*. Philadelphia: University of Pennsylvania Press, 2006.

Mott, Stephen Charles. *Biblical Ethics and Social Change*. New York: Oxford University Press, 1982.

Mudge, Lewis S. and James N. Poling, eds. *Formation and Reflection: The Promise of Practical Theology*. Philadelphia: Fortress Press, 1987.

Nelson-Pallmeyer, Jack. *War Against the Poor: Low-Intensity Conflict and Christian Faith*. Maryknoll, NY: Orbis Press, 1989.

Nelson-Pallmeyer, Jack and Bret Hesla. *Worship in the Spirit of Jesus: Theology, Liturgy, and Songs Without Violence*. Cleveland, OH: Pilgrim Press, 2005.

Newton, Huey P. *The Huey P. Newton Reader*. David Hilliard and Donald Wise, eds. New York: Seven Stories Press, 2002.

Niebuhr, Reinhold. *Moral Man and Immoral Society*. New York: Charles Scribner's Sons, 1932.

---. *The Irony of American History*. New York: Charles Scribner Books, 1952.

Pahl, Jon. *Empire of Sacrifice: The Religious Origins of American Violence*. New York: New York University Press, 2010.

Pandey, Gyanendra. *Routine Violence: Nations, Fragments, Histories.* Stanford, CA: Stanford University Press, 2006.

Pascale, Celine-Marie. *Making Sense of Race, Class and Gender: Commonsense, Power, and Privilege in the United States.* New York: Routledge, 2007.

Patton, Michael Quinn. "Enhancing the Quality and Credibility of Qualitative Analysis." In *Health Services Research* 34, no. 5 (1999): 1189–1208.

---. *Qualitative Evaluation and Research Methods* (3rd ed.). Beverly Hills, CA: Sage Publications, 2002.

Pérez Esquivel, Adolfo. *Christ in a Poncho: Witnesses to the Nonviolent Struggles in Latin America.* Maryknoll, NY: Orbis Press, 1983.

Peruvian Bishops' Commission for Social Action. *Between Honesty and Hope: Documents from and about the Church in Latin America.* Issued at Lima by the Peruvian Bishops' Commission for Social Action. John Drury, trans. Maryknoll, NY: Maryknoll Publications, 1970.

Presbey, Gail M. "Evaluating the Legacy of Nonviolence in South Africa." *Peace & Change,* Vol. 31, No. 2 (April 2006): 141–174.

Ramsay, Nancy J. "Emancipatory Theory and Method." In *The Wiley-Blackwell Companion to Practical Theology.* Bonnie J. Miller-McLemore, ed., 183-192. Malden, MA: Blackwell Publishing, 2012.

Ransby, Barbara. *Ella Baker and the Black Freedom Movement: A Radical Democratic Vision.* University of North Carolina Press, 2005.

Reynolds, David S. *John Brown Abolitionist: The Man Who Killed Slavery, Sparked the Civil War, and Seeded Civil Rights.* New York: Alfred A. Knopf, 2005.

Ricoeur, Paul. "The Historical Presence of Nonviolence." *Cross Currents* 14:1 (Winter 1964).

Roberts, Adam and Timothy Garton Ash, eds. *Civil Resistance and Power Politics: The Experience of Non-violent Action from Gandhi to the Present.* New York: Oxford University Press, 2009.

Roedel, John Charles. "Love is Not a Strategy: Reconsidering Principled Nonviolence." Berkeley, CA: Graduate Theological Union, Ph.D. dissertation, 2011. Roediger, David R. *The Wages of Whiteness: Race and the Making of the American Working Class.* London: Verso, 1991.

Ruether, Rosemary Radford. *Sexism and God-Talk: Toward a Feminist Theology*. Boston: Beacon Press, 1983.

---. *New Woman, New Earth: Sexist Ideologies and Human Liberation*. Boston: Beacon Press, 1995.

---. *America, Amerikkka: Elect Nation and Imperial Violence*. London: Equinox Publishing, 2007.

Rynne, Terrence J. *Gandhi and Jesus: The Saving Power of Nonviolence*. Maryknoll, NY: Orbis Books, 2008.

Saldaña, Johnny. *The Coding Manual for Qualitative Researchers*. Thousand Oaks, CA: Sage Publications, 2009.

Schofield Clark, Lynn. "Critical Theory and Constructivism: Theory and Methods for the Teens and New Media @ Home Project." https://www.ihrcs.ch/?p=92.

Schubeck, Thomas L. *Liberation Ethics: Sources, Models, and Norms*. Minneapolis: Augsburg Fortress Press, 1993.

Schulman, Sarah. *My American History: Lesbian and Gay Life During the Reagan/Bush Years*. New York: Routledge, 1994.

---. *The Ties that Bind: Familial Homophobia and Its Consequences*. New York: New Press, 2009.

---. *The Gentrification of the Mind: Witness to a Lost Imagination*. Berkeley, CA: University of California Press, 2012.

Scruggs, Sarah. "Understandings of Nonviolence and Violence: Joint Palestinian and International Nonviolent Resistance." M.A. Thesis. Washington, D.C." American University, 2009.

Second General Conference of Latin American Bishops. *The Church in the Present-Day Transformation of Latin America in Light of the Council*. Washington, DC: Secretariat for Latin American National Conference of Catholic Bishops: 1979.

Segundo, Juan Luis. *The Liberation of Theology*. Maryknoll, NY: Orbis Books, 1982.

---. *Faith and Ideologies*. Maryknoll, NY: Orbis Books, 1984.

Sharp, Gene. *The Politics of Nonviolent Action* (3 vols.). Boston: Porter Sargent Publishers, 1973.

---. *Social Power and Political Freedom*. Boston: Porter Sargent Publishers, 1980.

---. *Civilian-Based Defense: A Post-Military Weapons System*. Princeton, NJ: Princeton University Press, 1990.

---. *Waging Nonviolent Struggle: 20th Century Practice and 21st Century Potential*. Boston: Porter Sargent Publishers, 2005.

Shiva, Vandana. *Stolen Harvest: The Hijacking of the Global Food Supply*. Boston: South End Press, 2000.

Sobrino, Jon. *Spirituality of Liberation: Toward Political Holiness*. Maryknoll, NY: Orbis Books, 1985.

Starr, Amory. "'…(Excepting Barricades Erected to Prevent Us from Peacefully Assembling)': So-called 'Violence' in the Global North Alterglobalization Movement." *Social Movement Studies* Vol. 5, No. 1 (May 2006): 61–81.

Stassen, Glen, ed. *Just Peacemaking: Ten Practices for Abolishing War*. Cleveland, OH: Pilgrim Press, 1998.

Stassen, Glen. *Kingdom Ethics: Following Jesus in Contemporary Context*. Downer's Grove, IL: Intervarsity Press, 2003.

Steger, Manfred B. *Gandhi's Dilemma: Nonviolent Principles and Nationalist Power*. New York: St. Martin's Press, 2000.

Strain, Christopher B. *Pure Fire: Self-Defense as Activism in the Civil Rights Era*. Athens, GA: University of Georgia Press, 2005.

Suchocki, Marjorie Hewitt. *The Fall to Violence: Original Sin in Relational Theology*. New York: Continuum Publishing, 1994.

Sutherland, Bill and Matt Meyer. *Guns and Gandhi in Africa: Pan African Insights on Nonviolence, Armed Struggle and Liberation in Africa*. Trenton, NJ: African World Press, 2000.

Swinton, John and Harriet Mowat. *Practical Theology and Qualitative Research*. London: SCM Press, 2006.

Swomley, John. "A Post-Liberal Pacifism." In *Peace is the Way: Writings on Nonviolence from the Fellowship of Reconciliation*. Walter Wink, ed., 37–40. Maryknoll, NY: Orbis Books, 2000.

Takaki, Ronald. *A Different Mirror: A History of Multicultural America* (2nd ed). Boston: Back Bay Books, 2008.

Telles, Ray and Rick Tejada Flores. *The Fight in the Fields: Cesar Chavez and the Farmworkers' Struggle*. DVD. New York: Cinema Guild, 2003.

Thandeka. *Learning to be White: Money, Race, and God in America*. New York: Continuum, 1999.

Tinker, George E. "Tink". *Missionary Conquest: The Gospel and Native American Cultural Genocide*. Minneapolis: Fortress Press, 1993.

---. "American Indians, Conquest, the Christian Story, and Invasive Nation-building," *Wading Through Many Voices: Toward A Theology of Public Conversation*, Harold Recinos, ed. New York: Rowman and Littlefield, 2011.

Todd, Julie. "Engaging the Powers of Nonviolence: A Critique of Walter Wink." *Journal of Religion, Conflict and Peace* 2(1), Fall 2008. http://www.religionconflictpeace.org/node/41.

---. "Confessions of a Christian Supremacist." *Reflections: Narratives of Professional Helping*. Vol. 16 (1), Fall 2010: 140–146.

Townes, Emilie. *Womanist Justice, Womanist Hope*. Atlanta: American Academy of Religion Scholars Press, 1993.

Tracy, David. *The Analogical Imagination: Christian Theology and the Culture of Pluralism*. New York: Crossroad, 1986.

---. "Practical Theology in the Situation of Global Pluralism." In *Formation and Reflection: The Promise of Practical Theology*. Lewis S. Mudge and James N. Poling, eds.,139–154. Philadelphia: Fortress Press, 1987.

Ture, Kwame and Charles V. Hamilton. *Black Power: The Politics of Liberation* (2nd ed.). New York: Vintage Books, 1992.

Umoja, Akinyele. *We Will Shoot Back: Armed Resistance in the Mississippi Freedom Movement*. New York: NYU Press, 2013.

---. "Set Our Warriors Free: The Legacy of the Black Panthers and Political Prisoners." *The Black Panther Party [Reconsidered]*. Charles E Jones, ed., 417–441. Baltimore: Black Classic Press, 1998.

---. "The Ballot and the Bullet: A Comparative Analysis of Armed Resistance in the Civil Rights Movement." *Journal of Black Studies*, Vol. 29, No. 4 (March 1999): 558–578.

---. "Repression Breeds Resistance: The Black Liberation Army and the Radical Legacy of the Black Panther Party." *New Political Science* Volume 21, Number 2 (1999): 131–155.

---. "'We Will Shoot Back': The Natchez Model and Paramilitary Organization in the Mississippi Freedom Movement." *Journal of Black Studies* Vol. 32, No. 3 (January 2002): 271–294.

---. "1964: The Beginning of the End of Nonviolence in the Mississippi Freedom Movement." *Radical History Review* Issue 85 (Winter 2003): 201–226.

Vanderheiden, Steve. "Radical Environmentalism in an Age of Antiterrorism." *Environmental Politics* 17:2 (2008): 299–318

Wallace, Mary S. "Confronting Wrongs, Affirming Difference: The Limits of Violence, the Power of Nonviolence, and the Case of Nonviolent Intervention in Sri Lanka." Brown University, Ph.D. dissertation, 2010.

Waller, Signe. *Love and Revolution: A Political Memoir; People's History of the Greensboro Massacre, Its Setting and Aftermath.* New York: Rowman and Littlefield, 2002.

Wasserfall, Rahel R. "Reflexivity, Feminism, and Difference." In *Reflexivity and Voice*, Rosanna Hertz, ed., 150–168. Thousand Oaks, CA: Sage Publications, 1997.

Weber, Max. "Politics as Vocation." In *From Max Weber: Essays in Sociology*. H.H. Gerth and C. Wright Mills, eds. New York: Oxford University Press, 1946: 77–128.

Weber, Thomas. "Nonviolence is Who? Gene Sharp and Gandhi." *Peace and Change*, Vol. 28, No. 2 (April 2003): 250–270.

Weigert, Kathleen Maas. "Structural Violence." In *Encyclopedia of Violence, Peace and Conflict*, Lester Kurtz, ed., 431–439. San Diego: Academic Press, 1999.

Welch, Sharon D. *A Feminist Ethic of Risk* (2nd ed.). Minneapolis: Fortress Press, 2000.

Williams, Chancellor. *Destruction of Black Civilization: Great Issues of a Race from 4500 B.C. to 2000 A.D.* Chicago: Third World Press, 1987.

Williams, Robert F. *Negroes With Guns.* Detroit, MI: Wayne State University Press, 1998.

Williams, Jr., Robert. *The American Indian in Western Legal Thought: The Discourses of Conquest.* New York: Oxford University Press, 1990.

Wink, Walter. *Violence and Nonviolence in South Africa: Jesus' Third Way.* Philadelphia, PA: New Society Publishers, 1987.

---. *Engaging the Powers: Discernment and Resistance in a World of Domination.* Minneapolis: Fortress Press, 1992.

---. *Jesus and Nonviolence: A Third Way.* Minneapolis: Fortress Press, 2003.

Wink, Walter, ed. *Peace is the Way: Writings on Nonviolence from the Fellowship of Reconciliation.* Maryknoll, NY: Orbis Books, 2000.

Wiredu, Kwasi. "The Akan Worldview." Colloquium paper for the Program on History, Culture, and Society presented at the Woodrow Wilson International Center for Scholars, May 19, 1985.

---. "The Question of Violence in Contemporary African Political Thought." *Praxis International,* Issue 3 (1986): 373–381.

Woodward, James and Stephen Pattison. *The Blackwell Reader in Pastoral and Practical Theology.* Malden, MA: Blackwell Publishing, 2000.

World Council of Churches. *The Ecumenical Review.* Vol. XXV, No. 4 (October 1973).

Yoder, John Howard. *The Original Revolution: Essays on Christian Pacifism.* Scottdale, PA: Herald Press, 1972.

---. *The Politics of Jesus: Behold the Lamb! Our Victorious Lamb* (2nd rev. ed.). Grand Rapids, MI: William B. Eerdmans Publishing, 1994.

---. "The 'Power' of 'Non-violence.'" Unpublished paper. Presented at the American Academy of Religion Section on Religion, Peace and War in Philadelphia, PA. November 18, 1995.

Young, Iris Marion. *Justice and the Politics of Difference.* Princeton, NJ: Princeton University Press, 1990.

Zinn, Howard. *A People's History of the United States: 1492 to Present.* New York: Perennial Classics, 2003.

Author Information

Julie Marie Todd is a scholar-activist living in Lawrence, Massachusetts. She is the John Wesley Iliff Senior Lecturer in Justice & Peace Studies at the Iliff School of Theology, teaching all of her courses in online and hybrid formats. Her scholarship focuses on social change theory and praxis, violence and (non)violence, ecology and earth activism, and matters of privilege, oppression, and solidarity across axes of difference.

A published essayist and poet on matters of justice-seeking and the spiritual life, Julie is the author of *50: thorns & blossoms* and *Nothing About Us Without Us: LGBTQ Liberation and the United Methodist Church*.

As a trained herbalist and aromatherapist, she is the owner of JustJulie, which provides products supportive of living an abundant, just, simple, and natural life.

Julie's contact information as well as links to her other publications can be found at this website: https://JustJulie.me.